Nuclear Terrorism

Threat Perception and Response in South Asia

NUCLEAR TERRORISM
THREAT PERCEPTION AND RESPONSE IN SOUTH ASIA

Col. Puneet Raina (Retd.)

GAURAV BOOK CENTRE PVT LTD
DELHI

Publisher
GAURAV BOOK CENTRE PVT LTD
4832/24,Prahlad Lane,S-207 Ansari
Road, Daryaganj, Delhi-110002
Ph.: 43570976, 23278261
Email: gauravbookcentre@gmail.com

Edition: 2015

ISBN: 978-93-83316-12-0

Laser Typesetting
JEE-VEE Graphics, Delhi

Price: 1195/-

Printed
Vikas Computers, Delhi

Contents

Preface

Nuclear terrorism denotes the detonation of a yield-producing nuclear bomb containing fissile material by terrorists. Some definitions of nuclear terrorism include the sabotage of a nuclear facility and/or the detonation of a radiological device, colloquially termed a dirty bomb, but consensus is lacking.

Nuclear power plants, civilian research reactors, certain naval fuel facilities, uranium enrichment plants, and fuel fabrication plants, are vulnerable to attacks which could lead to widespread radioactive contamination. The attack threat is of several general types: commando-like ground-based attacks on equipment which if disabled could lead to a reactor core meltdown or widespread dispersal of radioactivity; and external attacks such as an aircraft crash into a reactor complex, or cyber attacks.

Nuclear weapons materials on the black market are a global concern, and there is concern about the possible detonation of a small, crude nuclear weapon by a terrorist group, in a major U.S. city, with significant loss of life and property. The Obama administration says they will focus on reducing the risk of such nuclear threats and aims to strengthen homeland nuclear security.".

Since terrorism is not restricted to any one jurisdiction, it mandates a global response. Repercussions are felt everywhere, and at some point, counterterrorism must require more than the ability of one state to combat terrorism. Extradition and deportation schemes have been the traditional global counterterrorism tools. Extradition is the surrender by one state to another of an individual accused or convicted of an offence outside its own territory and within the territorial jurisdiction of the other, which, being competent to try and punish him, demands the surrender.

This book is a modest attempt to discuss all these issues.

—Editor

1

Nuclear Security and Terrorist Attacks

Nuclear power plants, civilian research reactors, certain naval fuel facilities, uranium enrichment plants, and fuel fabrication plants, are vulnerable to attacks which could lead to widespread radioactive contamination. The attack threat is of several general types: commando-like ground-based attacks on equipment which if disabled could lead to a reactor core meltdown or widespread dispersal of radioactivity; and external attacks such as an aircraft crash into a reactor complex, or cyber attacks. The United States 9/11 Commission has said that nuclear power plants were potential targets originally considered for theSeptember 11, 2001 attacks. If terrorist groups could sufficiently damage safety systems to cause a core meltdown at a nuclear power plant, and/or sufficiently damage spent fuel pools, such an attack could lead to widespread radioactive contamination. The Federation of American Scientists have said that if nuclear power use is to expand significantly, nuclear facilities will have to be made extremely safe from attacks that could release massive quantities of radioactivity into the community. New reactor designs have features of passive safety, which may help. In the United States, the NRC carries out "Force on Force" (FOF) exercises at all Nuclear Power Plant (NPP) sites at least once every three years.

Nuclear reactors become preferred targets during military conflict and, over the past three decades, have been repeatedly attacked during military air strikes, occupations, invasions and campaigns. Various acts of civil disobedience since 1980 by the peace group Plowshares have shown how nuclear weapons facilities can be penetrated, and the groups actions represent extraordinary breaches of security at nuclear weapons plants in the United States. The National Nuclear Security Administration has acknowledged the seriousness of the 2012 Plowshares action. Non-proliferation policy experts have questioned "the use of private contractors to provide security at facilities that manufacture and store the government's most dangerous military material". Nuclear weapons materials on the black market are a global concern, and there is concern about the possible detonation of a small, crude nuclear weapon by a militant group in a major city, with significant loss of life and property. *Stuxnet* is a computer worm discovered in June 2010 that is believed to have been created by the United States and Israel to attack Iran's nuclear facilities.

FUSION POWER

Fusion power is a developing technology still under research. It relies on fusing rather than fissioning (splitting) atomic nuclei, using very different processes compared to current nuclear power plants. Commercial plants and prototype generators are not anticipated before 2030-2050. Nuclear fusion uses only tiny amounts of fuel at any time, and requires precisely controlled conditions to generate any net energy.

Fusion reaction processes are so delicate that this level of safety is inherent; no elaborate failsafe mechanism is required. The fuel itself is extremely safe at any temperature outside that of a working fusion reactor and only tiny amounts are used. If the reactor were damaged or control impaired, or the fuel supply stops, reactions and heat generation would cease almost immediately.

For the same reason, there is also no risk of a thermal runaway or nuclear meltdown, since any significant change will render the reactions unable to produce excess heat. In comparison, a fission reactor is typically loaded with enough fuel for one or several years, enough fuel in a sufficiently small space will always produce thermal runaway or "meltdown", and no additional fuel is necessary to keep the reaction going. In the event of fire, calculations suggest that the total amount of radioactive gases from a typical fusion plant would be so small, about 1 kg, that they would have diluted to legally acceptable limits by the time they blew as far as the plant's perimeter fence.

In general terms, fusion reactors also create less radioactive material than a fission reactor, the material it would create is less damaging biologically, and the radioactivity "falls off" within a time period that is within existing engineering capabilities. The main byproduct is a small amount of helium, which is harmless to life. Of more concern is tritium, which, like other isotopes of hydrogen, is a very light gas, and difficult to retain completely. Although volatile and biologically active, the health risk is lower than most other radioactive contaminants, due to tritium's short half-life (12 years), very low decay energy (~14.95 keV), and the fact that it does not bioaccumulate (instead being cycled out of the body as water, with a biological half-life of 7 to 14 days). However the effect of widespread fusion power may require attention in this area.

Unlike fission reactors, whose used fuel rods and other waste remains highly radioactive for thousands of years, most of the radioactive material in a fusion reactor would be the reactor core itself, which would be dangerous for about 50 years, and low-level waste another 100. Fusion reactors can more easily be designed using "low activation" materials that do not easily become radioactive, such as vanadium or carbon fiber. Although the core of a decommissioned reactor will be considerably more radioactive during those 50 years than fission waste, the relatively short time period makes waste management fairly straightforward. By 300 years it would have the same radioactivity as coal ash.

More Stringent Safety Standards

Matthew Bunn, the former US Office of Science and Technology Policy adviser, and Heinonen, the former Deputy Director General of the IAEA, have said that there is a need for more stringent nuclear safety standards, and propose six major areas for improvement:

- operators must plan for events beyond design bases;
- more stringent standards for protecting nuclear facilities against terrorist sabotage;
- a stronger international emergency response;
- international reviews of security and safety;
- binding international standards on safety and security; and
- international co-operation to ensure regulatory effectiveness.

Coastal nuclear sites must also be further protected against rising sea levels, storm surges, flooding, and possible eventual "nuclear site islanding".

SECURITY, DEVELOPMENT AND PERSPECTIVE

Security, an essential public good, is widely seen as a central issue for Afghanistan's reconstruction and development. Security impacts on the whole range of development issues faced by Afghanistan, ranging from state building and capacity development to revenue collection, service delivery, and encouraging private sector-led growth. For the purpose of Afghanistan's National Development Strategy (ANDS), currently under preparation, the Government has added a Millennium Development Goal (MDG) on enhancing security to the internationally agreed list of MDGs. This demonstrates the importance assigned by the Government to security and rule of law as a critical development issue. Afghanistan's external partners (including the World Bank) have consistently highlighted the importance of security as a key enabling factor for Afghanistan's reconstruction and development And most important, the Afghan people themselves emphasize the importance of security and the protection of property rights in their daily lives and for building their livelihoods and communities.

More specifically:

- Security and rule of law as public goods have been grossly underprovided in Afghanistan during the past quarter-century, with state functions in this regard usurped by factions, regional and local powerbrokers, and external actors. Remedying this situation is an urgent, high-priority task.

- Improving security is also a core component of the state-building agenda, seen by most Afghans as an essential function of an effective, accountable government.
- Moreover, an adequate level of security is a critical prerequisite for effective delivery of other public services.
- Politically, security improvements have been and will continue to be essential for the success of Afghanistan's transition toward political normalcy.
- Economically, security and law and order, along with the protection of property rights, are required for robust private sector development, which will be the only way to achieve sustained rapid economic growth over the medium term.
- Insecurity and narcotics are closely linked-insecurity is the environment in which Afghanistan's opium economy thrives, and the drug industry is a major source of instability and insecurity.
- And finally, from the individual, household, and community standpoints, security and rule of law are extremely important components and enabling factors in the quality of life, as is almost universally recognized by Afghans.

In addition to its importance as a central development issue for Afghanistan, the security sector accounts for a very high proportion of the country's total public expenditures as well as external assistance and raises major public expenditure management issues including risks to fiscal sustainability and possible crowding out of spending on other basic services. Therefore the security sector is also very important from a public finance management perspective. In view of these considerations, the Government of Afghanistan requested that the security sector be included in the World Bank's Public Finance Management (PFM) Review, and this volume is the result. There are in addition a number of specific rationales for the World Bank's engagement in analytical work on Afghanistan's security sector as part of the PFM

Review and from a development perspective. First, as indicated above, security is of central importance for Afghanistan's development prospects, including in particular the state-building agenda. This means it has to be incorporated in the country's development strategy and planning (which the Government is doing), and that development partners need to be engaged in areas of their competence.

Second, given the great importance of security spending in the national budget (accounting for around 40% of total Core and External Budget expenditures), the security sector must be incorporated in the analysis of expenditure composition, budget prioritization and trade-offs, downstream expenditure implications of decisions and investments, fiscal sustainability, etc. These issues lie at the heart of the PFM Review.

Third, a weak PFM system in the security sector (and particularly if the security sector gets left behind while improvements in the PFM system are occurring elsewhere) would adversely affect the overall progress of PFM reform and institutional strengthening, distort choices made by the Government, reduce the effectiveness and efficiency of public spending, and increase vulnerability to corruption. All of these areas are of concern to the Bank.

And fourth, security sector expenditures are largely donor-financed, raising important issues of aid management, aid harmonization, and aid effectiveness, as well as capacity development and effectiveness of technical assistance. These issues comprise an important part of the overall PFM agenda and hence need in the context of the security sector to be included in the PFM Review.

The main objectives of this review of security sector expenditures in the context of the PFM Review and taking a development perspective are as follows:

- To gain as complete an understanding as possible of the current level and structure of security related expenditures, recent trends, and likely future expenditure requirements based on current plans.

- To assess the extent to which coherent strategies, for the security sector and the major parts of the security sector, guide public expenditure allocations.
- To review the processes for determining funding levels, expenditure allocations, budget execution, and post-execution functions, with a view to assessing the extent to which they follow sound PFM principles.
- To describe the institutional framework for the security sector and ascertain the extent to which it embeds or is conducive to sound public financial management.
- To assess the strategic coherence and consistency and the fiscal sustainability of security sector expenditures.

This chapter sets forth the conceptual framework for analysis of security sector expenditures from a development and public finance management perspective. It first provides a working definition of the security sector. The chapter goes on to outline key linkages between security and development (based on recent international thinking on this subject). It then discusses key public finance management principles and their application to the security sector.

Some background on the historical legacy from the long period of conflict in Afghanistan, and summarizes the progress made in building the security sector since 2001. It then overviews Afghanistan's security sector at present-its legal basis, size, institutions, salient characteristics, and coordination-and at the end outlines the key security issues faced by Afghanistan from a development perspective. PFM principles and their application to the security sector, the implications for Afghanistan including gaps and constraints, and the Afghan budget process for the security sector.

The crucial issue of the fiscal sustainability of security sector decisions and investments, which is an important driver of the fiscal sustainability of Afghanistan's public finances as a whole.

Building on the analysis of fiscal sustainability, At strategic prioritization and sequencing issues in the security sector and how these can be managed in particular through the national budget process. The budget execution for effective and efficient use of funds provided to the security sector.

Meaning of the Security Sector

The security "system" is defined broadly in OECD (2005b) as including the following main components: core security actors, security management and oversight bodies, justice and law enforcement institutions, and non-statutory security bodies. A broad definition of the security sector along these lines makes the most sense from a development and PFM perspective, as all different parts of the security sector have significant development implications as well as varying budgetary implications (for both expenditures and revenues). However, some components clearly do not apply to Afghanistan (e.g. coast guards), while other institutions like Parliaments have not been functioning and hence are not relevant for analysis of recent developments and the current situation (although the role of the legislature will be important starting in the very near future).

Moreover, non-statutory security bodies, although they have been major actors in Afghanistan (and mirror the breakdown of the formal security system during the protracted conflict), for the most part do not have direct budgetary implications and would require a very different mode of analysis. Therefore they are not looked at closely in this volume except in terms of their immediate budgetary implications-notably the Disarmament, Demobilization, and Reintegration (DDR) program-although their development implications and impact on the formal security sector will be kept in mind. In sum, consistent with the overall objectives and approach of the PFM Review and in line with the increasingly recognized development implications of the security sector, this volume uses a broad definition of the security sector but focuses on those components which are of major importance from a PFM perspective. In terms of budget categories and programs, those that form part of the security sector and which are analyzed in the PFM Review include: defence, police and other internal security services, intelligence, counter-narcotics, the judiciary and penal system, mine clearance, and the DDR program.

The main security institutions in Afghanistan which will be looked at in the PFM Review include the following: (i) *government security management and oversight bodies:* National Security Council and National Security Advisor, Ministry of Defence, Ministry of Interior, Ministry of Counter Narcotics, Ministry of Border and Tribal Affairs, Ministry of Justice, Ministry of Finance, and the Auditor General's Office; (ii) *security services:* Afghan National Army (ANA), Afghan National Police (ANP), National Border Guards, Counter-Narcotics forces, National Directorate of Security (NDS-responsible for intelligence), Customs General Directorate under MoF, remnants of earlier military and police forces (the former subjected to DDR); and (iii) *justice and legal institutions:* Supreme Court, Judiciary, Attorney General's Office and prosecutorial offices *(saranwal).*

Excluded from detailed analysis in this volume are the non-statutory security bodies, including remaining unofficial militias and armed factional groups, private body-guards, and security companies. Foreign and international armed forces operating in Afghanistan also will not be analyzed in detail, except to some extent the Provincial Reconstruction Team (PRTs) which are intended to help strengthen governance and carry out reconstruction activities. However, the overall size and cost of these forces will be considered and their impact on the fiscal and PFM aspects of the formal security system will be taken into account. The absence of a Parliament means that its oversight role with respect to security can be incorporated in terms of future options and recommendations, but not in relation to the analysis of recent developments and the current situation. Independent and civil society institutions which play a monitoring and advocacy role with respect to security, such as the Afghanistan Independent Human Rights Commission (AIHRC) are extremely important but are not analysed in detail in this volume.

SECURITY AND GROWTH

Costs of insecurity and conflict. The close linkages between security, an essential public good, and development have become increasingly recognized and closely studied in recent years, although knowledge gaps remain. The crucial enabling role of security in virtually all dimensions of development tends to be invisible in countries where there is a reasonable level of security. As noted more broadly in Chalmers (2005, p. 7), "The relationships between socio-economic governance, conflict, and growth are multi-directional, with poor governance and conflict reinforcing each other, and both phenomena undermining the possibilities for economic development."

In particular, it is where security is absent-most notably in countries in conflict-that its role in development becomes glaringly obvious. Insecurity, and in particular conflict, carry major costs from an economic and social development perspective:

Cost of resources devoted to conflict and/or combating insecurity, which otherwise could have been used for other, more developmentally productive purposes. Moreover, these resources impose a double loss, since they inflict damage during conflict as enumerated below.

Human costs, including deaths, wounds, displacement, and flight, as well as loss of private property and psychological damage. In addition, disruption of public services like education and health due to conflict or insecurity results in lower levels of human capital (due to disruption of education) and higher rates of mortality and morbidity (aggravated by the direct adverse impact of conflict-related phenomena like displacement on health). Moreover, it should be emphasized that modern warfare, and especially internal conflicts like civil wars and insurgencies, tend to generate high casualties and other costs among the civilian population.

Social costs, including weakening of national, community, and family links, shorter time horizons, and weaker constraints on criminal and opportunistic behaviour.

Loss of physical assets, directly by destruction during conflict, and indirectly due to lack of maintenance, falling into disuse, etc.

Loss of financial assets, through capital flight, can be a major cost of conflict or generalized insecurity.

Costs to government, including government revenues lost/foregone due to conflict, and destruction or erosion of the state and state assets as it becomes weakened and contested by different factions during conflict.

Costs to the private sector, including disruption of trade and markets, theft of business property by armed groups, "protection costs" frequently imposed, shifting incentives away from formal-sector activity in favour of the informal sector, and the like.

Unfortunately, the adverse implications of conflict/insecurity for development continue, and in some respects may increase, after the end of outright conflict. So-called "legacy" costs of conflict, based on cross-country analysis reported in World Bank, include in particular (i) higher residual military expenditure; (ii) capital flight (which tends to continue or even increase after conflict); (iii) loss of social capital-which can take a long time to rebuild after conflict; (iv) government policies, which on average are negatively affected after conflict; (v) deterioration of political institutions which takes time to reverse; and (vi) destruction of the revenue apparatus and loss of revenue culture, which tends to persist after conflict.

Insecurity in a conflict or post-conflict situation also can be part of a set of mutually reinforcing tendencies that promote perpetuation of insecurity and associated development costs, including in particular state weakness. For example in the case of Afghanistan, World Bank (2005) emphasizes that lack of rule of law and continuing existence of non-state powers (warlords and commanders and their forces) can lead to a vicious circle whereby insecurity, low revenues, and a weak, ineffective state are perpetuated.

Another important aspect is the costs to national development of criminality, which as noted above is fostered by conflict but can be a major problem even in the absence of conflict and in a post-conflict situation where social norms and law enforcement have been eroded. When pervasive, crime may also fuel wider conflict. Although the direct damage caused by crime is far less than that of major conflict, it can have major adverse effects on development, especially if a high level of criminality becomes the norm. More specifically:

Crime erodes social and human capital: Loss of trust in communities and countries due to widespread criminality can weaken the social fabric. Human capital can be weakened by the direct effects of crime on victims, and by the associated atmosphere of fear that may encourage others (particularly better-off and skilled people) to leave. By limiting movements of people, crime may impede access to employment and educational opportunities (particularly in the case of females).

Crime worsens the business climate and discourages investment: Criminal activities are often directed against businesses and hence directly inflict losses on them, but more damaging is the harm crime and perceptions of it do to business investments. Foreign investors may be discouraged, domestic investors may not start activities, and more generally financial capital may flee from high-crime areas and countries. Corruption also can adversely affect the business climate in a major way.

Crime undermines the state and its ability to promote development: Finally, crime can become closely linked to corruption (itself a form of criminal activity), with very harmful consequences for development and public finance management. Trust between people and the state is destroyed and/or is prevented from being built. Corruption and other forms of crime can erode the revenue base of the state and thereby its effective functioning.

Criminality, and corruption in particular, can drive business activity into the informal sector, and keep most businesses small (so as to avoid visibility vis-a-vis criminals and/or corrupt officials). This has adverse consequences for investment, technology, productivity growth, and more generally the competitiveness of the economy, reducing prospects for sustained rapid economic growth which is the only way countries can develop and reduce poverty. The unfavorable effects of conflict and insecurity, and often of crime as well, tend to be disproportionately felt by the poor, minorities, and other vulnerable groups. This is partly because as in the case of many other public goods, the better-off can use their own resources to insulate themselves at least to some extent from insecurity (private security, physical protection through fences etc., mobility), while minorities and vulnerable groups are at higher risk of being targeted in situations of conflict or breakdown of law and order when the state no longer is able to protect its citizens. However, where insecurity is generalized and long-lasting, as was the case in Afghanistan in the 1980s and 1990s, the effects reach all levels of society, and many assets of the rich may get lost or devalued. Nevertheless, the poor are invariably more vulnerable to conflict and insecurity as they have fewer assets and weaker coping mechanisms to start with. Even if they lose many of their assets, better-off people have a greater chance to escape conflict and tend to be in a better position in terms of livelihoods where they flee to.

Conflict and insecurity can have an especially damaging effect from a gender perspective, notably in the form of escalated violence against women. Rape and sexual assault against women of opposing groups in community-based conflicts are frequently used as an ultimate means of dishonoring entire communities and reducing people's capacities to resist military advances, causing serious social and psychological disruptions. Any children resulting from such encounters will often be rejected by society and lead a pariah existence. In addition to violence directly against women, the environment of insecurity associated with conflict or a post-conflict situation can have a disproportionate adverse effect on women, as women's higher vulnerability in conflict may lead to imposition of stricter social norms resulting in limited or no access to education and basic health care due to their reduced mobility. Prolonged periods of conflict, high levels of social violence, and lack of security can also be reflected in increased levels of domestic violence, in which women and children are the primary victims. Conflict and insecurity have profoundly damaging effects on children. The loss of one or both parents, homelessness, the need to shoulder economic responsibilities in childhood, exposure to violence and abuse, disruption of elementary education, and lack of access to health services and immunization are examples of conflict-induced consequences which have profound and life-long impacts on children.

Positive synergies between security and development. From a more positive perspective, "The security of persons, property and assets, and the protection of human rights are fundamental to sustainable development and a pre-condition for people to improve their lives, particularly the poor.". Assets should be broadly interpreted to include public goods such as roads, common water points, and public infrastructure as well as social infrastructure and private assets such as property.

POTENTIAL CONSEQUENCES OF A TERRORIST ATTACK

The consequences of an attack on the industrial control systems of critical infrastructure could vary widely. It is commonly assumed that a successful cyber attack would cause few, if any, casualties, but might result in loss of infrastructure service while control was wrested from the attacker and damage repaired. For example, a successful cyber-attack on the public telephone switching network might deprive customers of telephone service while technicians reset and repaired the switching network. An attack on a chemical or liquid natural gas facility's control systems might lead to more widespread physical damage.

Lower probability events include catastrophic infrastructure failure, where the failure of one part of the infrastructure leads to the failure of other parts, causing widespread effect. Such failure might occur due to the synergistic effect of infrastructure industries on each other. A simple example might be an attack on electrical utilities where electricity distribution was disrupted; sewage treatment plants and waterworks could also fail, as perhaps the turbines and other electrical apparatuses in these facilities shut down. On August 5, 2002, the faulty closure of an emergency valve at one of Singapore's two natural gas suppliers blocked the flow of natural gas to seven electrical power plants. As an immediate result, power levels dropped 30%, and even after reserve power was employed, there was still a 8% shortfall. The power outage lasted up to 90 minutes. Several chemical production plants were forced to shutdown their facilities during the power outage, and required several days to restore full production.

Some experts warn of a cascade event, where a terrorist is able to manipulate control systems and cause catastrophic failure within an infrastructure. Cascade events can be very damaging, causing widespread utility outages. Twice in 1996, arcing between high voltage transmission lines and trees resulted in widespread power outages. On July 2, 1996, a cascade event left 2 million customers in 11 states and 2 Canadian provinces without power. Most service was restored within 30 minutes. On August 10, 1996, a similar event caused 7.5 million customers in seven western states and part of Canada to be without power for up to nine hours. The August 2003 blackout of the northeastern United States and parts of Canada, also a cascade event, has been invoked as indicative of the potential effects a successful terrorist cyber-attack on electrical utility control systems.

While it was quickly determined that the power outage was not caused by terrorism, there were questions whether control system failure, computer viruses or worms, or operatorerror played roles in the outage. It has been suggested by some that the Blaster worm, which had been contributing to congestion of the Internet, might have exacerbated the problems faced by utilities leading up to the blackout event. The scenario which causes the highest degree of concern among experts is the combined use of a cyber-attack on critical infrastructure in conjunction with a physical attack. This use of cyber-terrorism could result in an amplification of the physical attack's effects. An example of this might be a conventional bombing attack on a building combined with a temporary denial of electrical or telephone service. The resulting degradation of emergency response, until back-up electrical or communication systems can be brought into place and used, could increase the number of casualties and public panic.

Others believe that the consequences of a cyber-attack on critical infrastructure would be very limited, and that excessive focus has been given to an unsubstantiated terrorist threat. Cyber-security experts who doubt the effectiveness of such an attack range in opinion regarding an attack's impact. Some believe that a cyberattack on critical infrastructure control systems, while having some effect, would not be devastating, but rather only have minor impact. For example, security managers in some electric utilities reportedly believe that experience in dealing with natural disasters and power outages may translate well to recovering quickly from a cyberattack. Other believe that there could be significant impacts from a successful attack on control systems, but that such success would be very unlikely. Finally, some believe that while it is possible to use computers to generate high consequence attacks, it would be much more likely that a terrorist group would resort to a simpler conventional attack which would yield results of a similar magnitude.

CURRENT INITIATIVES DEPARTMENT OF HOMELAND SECURITY

The creation of the Department of Homeland Security has centralized within the Directorate of Information Analysis and Infrastructure Protection a number of offices related to critical infrastructure control system security: the Critical Infrastructure Assurance Office (CIAO), the National Infrastructure Protection Center, the National Infrastructure Simulation and Analysis Center (NISAC), and part of the Department of Energy's Office of Energy Assurance. CIAO and NIPC were created in response to Presidential Decision Directive No. 63, issued in 1998. CIAO coordinated the federal government's initiatives on critical infrastructure assurance and promotes national outreach and awareness campaigns about critical infrastructure protection. NIPC was a national critical infrastructure threat assessment, warning, vulnerability, and law enforcement investigation and response agency. Among other programs, NIPC developed the InfraGard program, which serves as a clearinghouse for information sharing and analysis for members of critical infrastructure industries. NISAC was created in 2001 through the passage of the USA PATRIOT Act. It is charged to "serve as a source of national competence to address critical infrastructure protection and continuity through support for activities related to counterterrorism, threat assessment, and risk mitigation." This center is to provide modeling and simulation capabilities for the analysis of critical infrastructures, including electricity, oil, and gas sectors. It is located at Sandia National Laboratories and Los Alamos National Laboratory. The Department of Homeland Security created a National Cyber Security Division, located in the Information Analysis and Infrastructure Protection

Directorate, to identify, analyze, and reduce cyber-threats and vulnerabilities; disseminate threat warning information; coordinate incident response; and provide technical assistance in continuity of operations and recovery planning.

This division has the responsibility for implementing programs for research and development in cyber-security, using expertise from the Science and Technology Directorate to provide research and development functions and execution. The President's Critical Infrastructure Protection Board has released *The National Strategy to Secure Cyberspace*, in which a general strategic overview, specific recommendations and policies, and the rationale for these actions are presented. This document addresses concerns regarding digital control systems and SCADA networks, rates SCADA network security as a national priority, and recommends joint public/private efforts in discovering solutions to potential vulnerabilities. This strategy identifies the Department of Homeland Security, in coordination with other federal agencies, as the department responsible for developing best practices and new technologies to increase SCADA security. Some cyber-security experts have criticized this plan, claiming that vulnerabilities will remain because of its lack of enforcement regulations.

Department of Energy

The Department of Energy's Office of Energy Assurance has also been involved in developing techniques to secure energy production and availability. Part of this effort has been the development of "simple, common-sense approaches to improve the overall level of protection in SCADA and digital control networks." A document describing a general approach to improving cyber-security in SCADA systems has been released.

Department of Energy National Laboratories

The Department of Energy National Laboratories have developed a series of test bed facilities to test security measures developed for critical infrastructure. The Idaho National Engineering and Environmental Laboratory, in conjunction with Sandia National Laboratory, are developing a SCADA test bed to help identify vulnerabilities and improve the security and stability of SCADA systems.

This test bed is part of an integrated Critical Infrastructure Test Range, which includes cyber security, wireless communications, power transmission, and physical security testbeds. The Pacific Northwest National Laboratory has developed a Critical Infrastructure Protection Analysis Laboratory where, among other things, the vulnerability of SCADA systems can be determined. Research into advanced technologies is currently underway at Department of Energy laboratories to address process control system security.

For example, Sandia National Laboratory under the Laboratory Directed Research and Development program has been developing secure control systems for the energy industry. Research includes new information architectures, cryptographic methods, and information system security assessments. Much of this work arises from needs discovered through partnerships with systems manufacturers. While a prototype system to demonstrate proof of principle has been implemented at the Sandia National Solar Thermal Test Facility, this system has not been widely implemented in the field. Similar security efforts, though less directly focused on industrial control systems, are being developed at both Lawrence Livermore National Laboratory and Los Alamos National Laboratory.

National Institute of Standards and Technology

The National Institute of Standards and Technology (NIST) has initiatives in industrial control system security. NIST, in conjunction with a number of industry groups, federal government agencies, and professional societies, have created the Process Control Security Requirements Forum to develop process control information security requirements. Through their Critical Infrastructure Protection program, the National Institute of Standards and Technology is developing information security requirements, best-practice guidelines, and test methods for the process control sector. Scientists at NIST are also actively involved in many industry-standards forums.

Department of Defense

The Department of Defense, through the Combating Terrorism Technology Support program, provides support for the protection of infrastructure elements. As part of this program, encryption algorithms for SCADA systems are being developed and tested with the end goal of providing recommendations to industry regarding their use.

FEDERAL ENERGY REGULATORY COMMISSION

The Federal Energy Regulatory Commission (FERC) is an independent regulatory agency within the Department of Energy that, among other duties, regulates interstate commerce in oil, natural gas, and electricity.

FERC has published a final rule related to critical energy infrastructure information. In this rule, critical energy infrastructure information (CEII) is defined as:

> *... information about proposed or existing critical infrastructure that: (i) Relates to the production, generation, transportation, transmission, or distribution of energy; (ii) Could be useful to a person in planning an attack on critical infrastructure; (iii) Is exempt from mandatory disclosure under the Freedom of Information Act, 5 U.S.C. 552; and (iv) Does not simply give the location of the critical infrastructure. Whether or not information falls under the CEII categorization is initially determined by the companies submitting the information to FERC. Categorization of select information as CEII may lead to greater information sharing between industry and the federal government.*

The FERC has also published a notice of public rulemaking which includes cyber-security standards for the electric industry.

This proposed regulation would require the electric industry to self-certify that they are meeting minimum cybersecurity standards. It has been reported that FERC will likely adopt standards developed by the North American Electric Reliability Council in the final version of this regulation. The final version of this regulation has not been issued.

Industry Initiatives

Some industry groups have taken steps towards addressing control system security, generally as part of an overall cyber-security initiative.

Some groups have launched initiatives in developing infrastructure security programs. The North American Electric Reliability Council has developed a set of minimum cyber-security standards for the electricity industry, as well as guidelines for securing remote access to critical electric infrastructure. Another approach is to develop voluntary best-practices for process control system security. Several organizations are taking part in such initiatives. For example, the Instrument Society of America has formed a committee, ISA-SP99, to develop a series of reports on best-practices and procedural improvements which would enhance control system security. Similar efforts are underway in other technical societies, including the Institute of Electrical and Electronics Engineers and the International Electrotechnical Commission, where working groups on process control systems and their security are established.

Some industry groups have focused on developing near-term solutions to the legacy equipment security vulnerabilities. For example, the Gas Technology Institute has focused on developing cryptographic protection of SCADA communications and developing a mechanism for retrofitting legacy equipment to handle these encrypted signals. Other groups have increased outreach efforts to improve understanding of security issues relating to cybersecurity and process control systems.

Policy Options

The vulnerability of industrial control systems may be reduced through a range of federal actions. These include the development of standards, either voluntary or mandatory, for cybersecurity of control systems; identifying and addressing critical infrastructure interdependencies; developing encryption methods for control systems; identifying and establishing technologies to address existing vulnerabilities; funding long-term research into secure SCADA systems; providing for free exchange of risk information between the federal government, private industry, and other critical infrastructure sectors; and assessing federal activities in this area.

Developing Standards

The federal government could mandate and enforce a uniform security standard for cybersecurity of industrial control systems, or support the development of industry developed and based standards. Because of the national importance of critical infrastructure systems, a uniform standard might be developed, with the input of advocates, industries and the federal government, which would include the functionality necessary to protect industrial control systems, while providing for more secure operation. A voluntary, standards-based approach has been developed for server operating systems with some success, and a similar mechanism might be used to develop standards for commercial off-the-shelf control systems. Alternately, processes and specifications currently being developed through industry-led programs might be generalized across critical infrastructure industries and established as a voluntary standard. Critics of this approach cite the many different uses of industrial control systems in different industry sectors as making such a standard unwieldy. Some experts have expressed concerns that a mandated standard would be less effective than a voluntary standard, as solutions to new problems could not be implemented immediately, but would wait for changes to the standard, and that such a standard may not be uniformly applicable across industry sectors. Others have stated that there is a need for federal requirements to assure that appropriate attention is focused on process control system security.

IDENTIFYING SECTORAL INTERDEPENDENCIES

Identifying the dependencies between critical infrastructure sectors, the vulnerabilities that are present in information technologies in these sectors, and the possible cross-sectoral impacts of a control system attack may lead to a greater understanding of the scale of the control system threat. As shown by the August 2003 blackout, the loss of a single infrastructure sector, here the energy sector, may have serious effects in other critical infrastructures, such as public health and transportation. Both the

Department of Homeland Security, in its role of protecting infrastructure, and the Department of Energy, in its role of ensuring a robust and reliable energy infrastructure, perform activities in determining sectoral dependencies and commonalities. Policymakers may wish to enhance current funding into SCADA security research, test bed modeling, or critical infrastructure vulnerability assessment to further clarify the current vulnerability.

Securing Control System Communications

Another option would involve supporting encryption research to protect industrial control system data transfer. Encrypting the information transmitted between remote units and their controllers would inhibit inclusion of false information to and from industrial control systems. Current encryption technology may not be compatible due to the time required to process the encrypted data and the level of technology built into control system components. Industrial control systems have stringent timing requirements and tend to be built out of less computationally robust components, which complicate the use of current encryption technologies. While a prototype encryption method for industrial control systems has been developed, it is still in the validation process and is only recently being evaluated for implementation in industry. Further research into encryption techniques for these processes could provide efficient, market-driven technology for securing industrial control systems information. Some experts highlight that securing data transfer does not assure the security of the control system itself. They assert that other routes of attack exist that do not rely on the security of the control system communications. Thus, securing those communications, while lowering system vulnerability, may not be addressing the most likely threat.

Securing Legacy Equipment

Further research and development into methods for retrofitting existing SCADA systems with more secure components or communications may be another method to reduce system vulnerability. This approach has been taken by researchers in both industry and federal government laboratories. While potentially addressing short term needs to reduce vulnerability, retrofit solutions are not likely to solve inherent shortfalls in SCADA security especially with respect to the inclusion of COTS equipment potentially vulnerable to cyber attack. Critics of retrofit solutions cite high costs and potential compatibility concerns as barriers to easy implementation of such solutions.

Increasing Research and Development Funding

A long term approach to limiting the vulnerability of SCADA systems is to provide further targeted investment into developing "next-generation" secure control systems. Development of a secure SCADA architecture may provide incentives to replace components in a secure manner during the normal replacement cycle, incrementally reducing the present vulnerability. While some argue such product research and development is a responsibility of private industry, others may assert that control system security is of national import, requiring enhanced federal investment.

Several National Laboratories have developed complementary testbed facilities to investigate potential vulnerabilities and solutions to SCADA systems. Such testbed facilities could be used to evaluate and validate the security of commercial SCADA systems, act as a proving ground for new technologies, or be dedicated to the development of federal efforts in secure process control systems.

Increasing Information Sharing

The new FOIA exemptions created in the Homeland Security Act of 2002 (P.L. 107-296) may provide a higher volume, freer exchange of information between the federal government and industry, as industry may become more forthcoming about potential vulnerabilities. The Critical Energy Infrastructure Information category for electrical infrastructure information may provide a model for how regulatory agencies might craft regulations protecting critical infrastructure information within a sector. Comments from various groups on the proposed implementation of the Homeland Security FOIA exemption have indicated that industry concern still remains over the potential release of information given to the federal government by private industry. Policymakers may wish to inquire into whether vulnerabilities transmitted to the federal government are eventually reduced, and how the information being provided to the federal government is used.

OVERSIGHT OF DEPARTMENT OF HOMELAND SECURITY COORDINATION

Policymakers may also wish to assess the effectiveness of the Department of Homeland Security in coordinating security enhancements to control systems, promoting government/industry partnerships, and performing risk and vulnerability assessments. With the concentration of previously existing agencies into the Directorate of Information Analysis and Infrastructure Protection, previous duplication of effort may be removed, but critics have suggested that difficulties in integrating these agencies may lead to a reduction in effectiveness. Some policymakers have expressed concern that the priorities DHS have placed on physical and cyber-security are not appropriate for the risks involved. Oversight of DHS's efforts to rectify this potential homeland security vulnerability may provide insight into successful models used within critical infrastructure sectors which might be used across multiple sectors.

2

Global Response to Terrorism

Since terrorism is not restricted to any one jurisdiction, it mandates a global response. Repercussions are felt everywhere, and at some point, counterterrorism must require more than the ability of one state to combat terrorism. Extradition and deportation schemes have been the traditional global counterterrorism tools. Extradition is the surrender by one state to another of an individual accused or convicted of an offence outside its own territory and within the territorial jurisdiction of the other, which, being competent to try and punish him, demands the surrender.

Political offenses, however, are normally exempt from extradition, and death penalty concerns are an additional complication. Deportation procedures, likewise, rely upon cooperation, and usually create problems for whatever country the terrorist is deported to. Deportation is often used in the United States whenever a defendant is not allowed to view classified material against them. Aliens convicted of serious crimes are regularly deported.

The G-8 countries (which include Canada, the United States, Britain, Germany, France, Italy, Japan, and Russia) have long made counterterrorism an agenda item at their summits. Most of their proposals rest on using Interpol as a formal association of police agencies everywhere, or more recently Europol, the embryonic Europe-wide police agency. Other recommendations involve military installations, municipal operations, defence contractors, and the private sector. Most well-known, however, is the call for a permanent International Criminal Court (ICC), an idea spawned in 1993 by a U.N. committee and ratified by the Rome Statute in 1998 and taking effect in 2002.

As an entity created by the U.N. treaty process, the ICC's jurisdiction would be any international crime like war crime, genocide, unprovoked aggression, crimes against humanity, and (theoretically) terrorism. States consent to participate on a case-by-case basis. The forum is supposed to be neutral and 18 judges are elected for nine-year terms. The court may sentence convicted offenders to incarceration for terms of up to 30 years or, in cases of extreme gravity, life imprisonment

Another basic problem of course is the questionable status of detainees in a war on terrorism. Captured terrorists may be held by one nation as "unlawful combatants" and deprived of POW (prisoner of war) status and Geneva convention protections. Such protections require viewing the terrorists as legitimate armies. Rule 117 of the ICC's *Rules of Procedure and Evidence* provides for detention in a "custodial state" and allows for a hearing on pretrial conditional release.

By definition, terrorists do not meet the four requirements necessary for combatant status (wear uniforms or other distinctive insignia, carry arms openly, be under command of a person responsible for group actions, and conduct their operations in accordance with laws of war). For this reason, *captured terrorists are not usually afforded prisoner of war status*" (Joint Chiefs of Staff Publication 3-07.2, Joint Tactics, Techniques and Procedures for Antiterrorism, Washington, DC: 17 March 1998).

DEFINITIONS OF TERRORISM

There is no one, good definition of terrorism. In fact, it might be impossible to define because it is intangible and fluctuates according to historical and geographical contexts. Some forms of it are indistinguishable from crime, revolution, and war. Other forms of it are easily distinguishable. Each and every person knows that they would in some way, some day, under some back-against-the-wall condition, support some form of terrorism (as a tactic of last resort) in the name of some deeply cherished cause or value. You may already be a supporter of terrorism, or you may live under a government that practices terrorism, and not know it. There is no universally accepted definition of terrorism (Long 1990).

The Christian Science Monitor's special report, Exactly What is Terrorism? draws the user into a quiz over what they think qualifies as terrorism, and what does not. Here are some excerpts (think about how strongly you feel that each case is terrorism or not, and the answers will be hidden in the following paragraph).

The nature of terrorism is always changing. What is called terrorism one year may be called something else next year. Terrorism is an emotionally charged word that is frequently used to politically and socially denigrate one's opponents. It seems, if you sympathize or side with the perpetrator, then it is not terrorism, but if you sympathize or side with the victim, then it is terrorism. A lot of people think they know terrorism when they see it. Now, for the answers from the earlier quiz - Case #1 is an example of inadvertent terrorism, at best, and if you think it's clearly terrorism, then all that's important to you is the harming of innocents, and motives don't matter. You're also confusing assassination, accident, and manslaughter with terrorism. Case #2 is an example of reckless terrorism, at best, and you'll probably recognize it as Sherman's march to the sea. If you thought it was a clear-cut case of terrorism, then you're confusing war with terrorism. War is hell, but terrorism is less than war.

However, if you thought it was clearly not a case of terrorism, then you're too focused too much on body counts, and have neglected to consider that property sabotage may be the most common form terrorism, especially with insurgency and counter-insurgency operations. Case #3 probably comes closest to a clear-cut example of terrorism because the hostages were originally put in harm's way by the revolutionaries; that is, unless the embassy employees did something to cause the revolutionary reprisal against them. If the employees are totally innocent (say an embassy from Sweden), then it is the case that noncombatants were deliberately targeted. If the employees were involved in espionage or something that had to do with the political prisoners, then it's a different matter. With terrorism as a criminal justice topic, you've really got to stretch the legal concepts of causation and intent.

Don't worry if you're confused on the whole good/bad, motive/act thing. Philosophers have debated it for years, and there are experts in criminal justice who say the act, not the motivation, should define terrorism (Jenkins 1985), and then there are experts who say the motivation, not the act, should define terrorism (Hoffman 1999). Those who write encyclopedias of terrorism state that an adequate working definition ought to have three parts: method, target, and purpose (Kushner 2003). You'll also note that three different branches of the U.S. government use three different definitions, as follows:

The State and Defence Departments conceive of terrorism as war — "the *premeditated*" or "the *calculated* use of violence". On the other hand, the Justice Department conceives of terrorism as crime — "the *unlawful* use of force or violence".

The State Dept. definition is the one used to officially count terrorism, and it is important to note that a "significant" terrorist event is one which meets the requirements of being "politically motivated" and "intended to influence an audience." This means that an "official" act of terrorism must be directed toward a symbolic target that is important to the political interests of a government somewhere. By contrast, the FBI definition (which is most often used in law enforcement training because it treats terrorism as crime) would classify random acts of violence and acts for personal gain as terrorism. The State Dept. definition comes closest to the FBI definition by the inclusion of an economic cost estimate, the threshold for economic harm being $10,000.

Simonsen and Spinlove (2000) do a good job of comparing and contrasting the different constructs, and note that the State approach emphasizes motives, the DOD approach emphasizes goals, and the FBI approach emphasizes methods. Combining the three would produce some overly complex definition like "Terrorism is the clandestine, criminal resort to violence or threat of violence on the part of a group toward innocent bystanders which seeks to accomplish some purpose against some recognized authority. The purpose is usually political and the target is usually civilian."

Alex Schmid (1988) has attempted to analyse the frequency of different emphases in at least 109 definitions of terrorism, and finds that, in rank order, most definitions emphasize goals (political), purposes (fear), targets (victim reactions), and methods (combat strategy or tactic). Only a small number of definitions emphasize the publicity aspect, covert nature, or criminal character of terrorism.

It is undoubtedly that case that political motivation ranks as the leading element in most definitions of terrorism. In fact, some years ago, the National Advisory Commission on Criminal Justice Standards and Goals (1976) recommended calling any crime that is politically motivated an act of terrorism. However, the problem with making something political into criminal goes beyond motivation (endless debates can be had over the presence or absence of instrumental or expressive motives in terrorism) as well as methods (*Historical note*: assassination was common in the 19th Century; bombing in the 20th; and techno-exotic forms such as cyber-, narco-, and eco- in the 21st). The idea of terrorism as crime rests upon having an adequate legal framework (which doesn't exist) as well as an understanding of the costs or impact of terrorism. Yet, that doesn't stop agencies from trying. The FBI has primary responsibility for the criminal investigation of terrorism. The Anti-Terrorism and Effective Death Penalty Act of 1996 authorizes them to (1) oversee detention and deportation of aliens suspected of terrorist activities; and (2) search and seize any fund-raising activities by foreign groups suspected of engaging in terrorist activity. Other countries have stronger criminal laws. In France and Great Britain, for example, suspected terrorists can be held for indefinite amounts of time. U.S. police are severely restricted in how they can interrogate and use electronic surveillance, and in addition, the U.S. Bill of Rights, to a certain degree, protects extremism (strongly held political beliefs) and fanaticism (strongly held religious beliefs) — two underlying causes of terrorism.

The U.S.A. Patriot Act (October 26, 2001) allows for longer detention of suspects, expanded surveillance and intelligence gathering powers by federal authorities. Congress passed additional anti-terrorism laws in the wake of September 11, and at least three states (Michigan, New Jersey, and New York) have passed their own anti-terrorism statutes.

The CIA has primary responsibility to preempt, disrupt, and defeat terrorism. Presidential Directives signed in 1995 and 1998 authorize them to treat terrorism as a crime, use all-source information, apprehend offenders, and bring them to justice wherever they can worldwide. The head of the CIA (DCI) coordinates the Intelligence Community (IC), and the National Security Council coordinates the nation's counterterrorism efforts. The CIA maintains a War on Terrorism website.

The Department of State has primary responsibility to use its diplomatic efforts with foreign governments to thwart terrorism. It also helps to develop, coordinate, and implement counterterrorism policy. On the State Department's website, one can find the Top Ten List of Most Wanted Terrorists as well as other lists, data, and resources, such as the List of Entities which constitute terrorist groups.

The newly-formed Department Homeland Security is charged with coordinating protection strategies against terrorism. A Nationwide Threat Level Warning (five level color coded) System is maintained at the Office of Homeland Security, and state variations exist (e.g. Virginia) which tell citizens what to do.

DHS is made up of units from 22 pre-existing agencies comprising four divisions: (1) Border, transportation and security — the Customs Service, Transportation Security Administration, Immigration and Naturalization Service, Border Patrol, the Agriculture Department's Animal and Plant Health Inspection Service and the U.S. Coast Guard; (2) Emergency preparedness — the Federal Emergency Management Agency, the Justice Department and the Department of Health and Human Services; (3) Weapons of mass destruction — research laboratories, such as the Lawrence Livermore National Laboratory, would coordinate research, develop vaccines, and plan for other countermeasures; (4) Information analysis — the CIA, the National Security Agency, the FBI, INS and other organizations with responsibility for evaluating the country's critical infrastructure and its vulnerabilities, including food and water systems, energy, transportation and national monuments.

The Department of Defence has unmatched resources for dealing with dangerous, unstructured situations, and they also have their own extensive intelligence apparatus. Yet the military is severely limited by what they can do legally. For one thing, the Posse Comitatus Act (18 U.S.C. 1385) prohibits the use of soldiers to enforce criminal laws against American citizens. Other Executive Orders and Presidential Directives (some secret; some not) similarly limit the use of military intelligence, such as Executive Order 12333 and PDD 39 (Presidential Decision Directive 39 - "US Policy on Counterterrorism"). One of the basic tenets of the law of war is established in the doctrine of *jus ad bellum* which defines whether the conflict has a legal basis to happen in the first place, and *jus in bello* which outlines what actions in war are legal in and of themselves.

The thing that most clearly distinguishes military from law enforcement action is that the military has mostly a free hand at preemption (preemptive first strike) while the best that the criminal justice system can do is harass and thwart (given exclusionary rule and entrapment constraints). One cannot overemphasize the importance of the rules of war since they have been around beginning in the early 17th Century when they were first proposed by Hugo Grotius and subsequently codified in the Geneva and Hague Conventions of 1860, 1899, 1907, and 1949. They consist of five (5) basic rules: civilians cannot be taken as hostages; POWs cannot be treated inhumanely; reprisals cannot be launched against innocents; and diplomats and ambassadors are off-limits. When the rules of war are broken, the term "war crime" is used to describe the act, and steps are taken to hold the perpetrators accountable by an international tribunal. If there is to be some kind of enforcement mechanism, it will most likely be an outgrowth of military tribunals.

Another approach might be to distinguish terrorists from others of their kind or how they perceive themselves. No group has openly admitted they were terrorists since the 1940s, and the most commonly preferred self-terminology includes guerrilla, fighter, or warrior. What follows is an alphabetical listing of the many terms terrorists use to call themselves (with the proviso that any errors or mistakes in definition are my own):

- Avengers — those who evoke the image of righteous vengeance (on behalf of others)
- Crusaders — those who engage in extremes to set the pace for others
- Defenders — those who think of themselves as vigilantes (defenders of self and others)
- Dissidents — those who want to defeat or overthrow an existing government
- Extremists — those with strongly held political beliefs out of the ordinary
- Fanatics — those with strongly held religious beliefs out of the ordinary
- Fighters — those who usually claim the other side are terrorists
- Guerrillas — those who fight a stronger opponent with hit-and-run tactics
- Insurgents — those who use propaganda, guerrilla tactics, and irregular fighting forces
- Insurrectionists — those who are in armed opposition to the laws of a government
- Liberators — those who consider themselves on the vanguard of freedom fighting
- Lunatics — those on the extreme fringes of left or right ideologies
- Nationalists — those fighting for the whole of their homeland
- Radicals — those with left-wing opinions (right-wingers are called reactionaries)
- Rebels — those who champion a cause not always their own, but the people's cause
- Revolutionaries — those who are committed to a certain ideology to bring about change

- Separatists – those fighting for a separate division of their homeland
- Soldiers – those who say they belong to an army or other military organization.

There are, of course, many other terms that one would encounter in studying terrorism. What is left out from the list would be terms such as: Liberationists; Pirates; Resisters; Propagandists; and Mercenaries. These may be terms that have some special meaning, but the process quickly gets redundant after awhile. Redundancy is evident in the phrase Freedom Fighter, because no side to every clash fights for anything but freedom. As an aside, it's often argued that parts of the American Revolution, like the Boston Tea Party, involved terrorist acts, and that this illustrates "one person's terrorist is another person's freedom fighter." However, this argument misses the fact that the groundwork for the American Revolution was already underway in a variety of directions, and *"legitimate" freedom fighting always contains advance warning, follows a warrior code, obeys the rules of war, prohibits certain kinds of weapons, does not use outlaw tactics, and takes steps to select targets that harm the least number of innocents.*

Critiques of definitions are also easier than making them. An illustrative example here is William Dyson's (2001) approach to dissecting terrorism. He starts by criticizing dictionary definitions of "terror," and most certainly, some of the worst definitions of terrorism confuse it with fear, fright, alarm, being shocked, or scared. It is also easily distinguishable from acts of civil disobedience, marches, demonstrations, leafleting, picketing, protesting, and rioting. It is less distinguishable from guerilla warfare or revolutionary wars (which can be restricted or unrestricted, as Martin calls it). In fact, terrorism often escalates into war, a phenomenon that experts call the Sarajevo Effect (Lacquer 1999) in which the 1914 assassination led to World War I. Dyson (2001) adds that terrorism can evolve into insurrection (which is the same as civil war), and he speculates that a terrorist situation becomes revolutionary whenever 25% of the population is engaged in the violence.

The most widely used definitions in criminal justice are simple ones created by Brian Jenkins (1985), Bruce Hoffman (1999), and Walter Laqueur (1999), all resting upon the idea of *illegitimate force to achieve political ends by targeting innocent people.* These simple definitions suffice for understanding complex social factors, but it should also be realized that we may never be able to define terrorism. It is important to note that the means used by terrorists are always illegitimate, even though their ends may be sometimes legitimate. Most of the terms similar to terrorism like freedom fighter and revolutionary often make use of the argument that the End Justifies the Means. To a terrorist, there's no such thing as innocent bystanders.

One of the main objectives of terrorism is usually to gain publicity for some cause, and public fear, roused thru the media, may contain a key to understanding the psychology of terrorism. It may also be important in producing a criminological definition of terrorism. The threat of harm to innocent bystanders is what makes terrorism powerful. In this sense, it is the same as what makes military operations powerful - striking terror in the hearts of the enemy. Terrorists are particularly concerned with invoking fear in those who identify with the victims of their action. In this fashion, terrorism is always symbolic, and "media-motivated", so targets likely to be reported on by prominent media organizations are especially vulnerable.

Terrorism should be distinguished from guerilla warfare since the latter is an acceptable form of combat. A terrorist should be distinguished from a guerilla (a term meaning "little war") because terrorists tend to have an urban focus and operate in small bands. An active terrorist organization is usually made up of "cadres" or "teams" of 3-5 members (the 9/11 attackers were organized in five-man teams) which themselves consist of "cells" of 1-2 members (who live and travel together).

Guerillas are organized differently, and generally have quite larger cadres and cells. Terrorism is generally a short-lived affair, while guerilla warfare is a long, drawn-out process. In addition (although this is debatable), terrorists tend to come from upper- rather than lower class backgrounds, as in the vigilante groups that make up right-wing, pro-government "death squads" in Latin America and Asia. Terrorists also tend (arguably) to be the products of over-permissive, wealthy families with whom they were in conflict, had inconsistent mothering, or were isolated from their parents in some way (Martin and Romano 1992). Terrorists also tend to use religion as a context or cover for their activities, a characteristics they share with extremists. Fanatics believe they must purify the world, destroy others in the name of righteousness, or advance a religious cause of some sort. Even environmental terrorists have some kind of pseudo-religious belief system.

Terrorism should also be distinguished from crime, at least in the sense that a war on terrorism is different from a war on crime or war on drugs. There are at least five good reasons for this, but the obvious one is that no law enforcement or criminal justice system needs to be nudged in the direction of becoming more like the military. There is also a long-standing tradition in the field of legal studies which only considers certain criminological aspects of terrorism (e.g., those aspects of terrorism which hold that the phenomenon is a sociological manifestation of societal structures and processes and not some "essentialist" phenomenon of "real" terrorism beyond the definitional powers of authorities). On the crime-terrorism distinction, Geraghty (2002) is a good guide, as is Deflem (2005). Fuller (2006) outlines the primary differences between a war on terrorism versus a war on crime or other social problems:

- a war on terrorism has (or should have) a clear and identifiable enemy (social problems are more diffuse)
- a war on terrorism is political (rather than social, or solved by tinkering with social service delivery systems)
- a war on terrorism uses military weapons (police have little need for military weapons and equipment)
- a terrorist enemy does not enjoy U.S. legal protections (at least fewer constitutional protections)
- a terrorist firmly believes their cause is just (most criminals admit they're deviant)

Deflem (2005) makes some good points about the current status of criminology on terrorism. He says that criminologists should not be embarrassed to learn from other research disciplines, but they must also seek to provide a distinctive contribution to the scholarship. Some issues, such as terrorism and the media and terrorism and foreign policy have already been well-explored by social scientists other than criminologists. But the relations between terrorism and counterterrorism in connection with criminal activity as well as with crime control remain at present *underexplored and form a field rich with potential* for criminological research and theory.

It is the specific province of criminology to study the patterns and dynamics of crime and social control from a social-scientific viewpoint in relation to their conditions and implications at a societal level. Terrorism is often connected with political, legal and military issues, often with deep-seated moral resonance. Counterterrorism is likewise a complex constellation much broader than police activities alone. However, issues of crime and social control are always and inevitably present in the reality and discourse on terrorism. The fact that the connection between terrorism and crime, on the one hand, and counterterrorism and social control, on the other, is not always neatly drawn nor evident does not mean that criminologists have no legitimate stake in their study. On the contrary, by bridging criminological scholarship with the existing literature on terrorism and counter-terrorism, a criminology of terrorism-related phenomena can be meaningfully connected to what is known from other social sciences and, at the same time, reveal the merits of its unique scientific focus and orientation.

CURRENT TRENDS

In addition to the activities of individuals and groups, two other factors, the growing interest in the acquisition of weapons of mass destruction by terrorists and other groups and the potential use of the Internet and cyberspace to commit acts of terrorism, are factors that contribute to the current terrorist threat to the United States.

Weapons of mass destruction. The trend toward high-profile, high-impact attacks comes at a time when interest is growing among both international and domestic terrorist groups in acquiring weapons of mass destruction (WMD). Currently, there is no credible information that a terrorist group has acquired, developed, or is planning to use chemical, biological, or radiological agents in the United States. However, there has been an increase in the number of cases or incidents involving use or threatened use of such agents in the United States. Between 1997 and 2000, the FBI investigated 779 WMD-related reports, generally involving individuals or small groups. The vast majority of these cases were found to be false or fabricated reports. The biological toxin ricin and the bacterial agent anthrax are emerging as the most prevalent agents involved in investigations. In 2000, 90 of II 5 biological threats investigated by the FBI involved threatened use of anthrax. While actual ricin toxin has been involved in a limited number of cases, anthrax agents have not been uncovered in any law enforcement investigation in the United States to date. Given the potential for inflicting large-scale injury or death, the efforts of international and domestic terrorists to acquire WMD remains a significant concern and priority of the FBI.

Terrorist use of emerging technology. Terrorist groups are increasingly using new information technology and the Internet to formulate plans, recruit members, communicate between cells and members, raise funds, and spread propaganda. Last year, in his statement on the Worldwide Threat in 2000, DCI Tenet testified before Congress that terrorist groups, "including Hizballah, Hamas, the Abu Nidal Organization, and bin Laden's Al-Queda Organization are using computerized files, e-mail, and encryption to support their operations." While these terrorist groups have not employed cyber-tools as a weapon to use against critical infrastructures, the reliance, accessibility, and expertise of these groups with computer and information technology networks and systems represents a clear warning sign.

Other terrorist groups, such as the Internet Black Tigers, who are reportedly affiliated with the Tamil Tigers, have engaged in attacks on foreign government web-sites and e-mail servers. During the unrest on the West Bank in the Fall of 2000, Israeli Government sites were subjected to e-mail flooding and "ping" attacks. These attacks allegedly originated with Islamic elements and were an attempt to inundate the systems with e-mail messages and degrade or deny services.

The FBI believes cyber-terrorism, the use of cyber-tools to shut down, degrade, or deny critical national infrastructures, such as energy, transportation, communications, or government services, for the purpose of coercing or intimidating a government or civilian population, is clearly an emerging threat for which its must develop prevention, deterrence, and response capabilities.

FBI Counterterrorism Jurisdiction and Role

The FBI is the lead federal agency for investigating terrorism. Under statutory authority granted by Title 28, United States Code, Section 533, the Attorney General has specifically assigned the FBI "lead agency responsibilities in investigating all crimes for which it has primary or concurrent jurisdiction and which involve terrorist activities or acts in preparation of terrorist activities within the statutory jurisdiction of the United States". In the United States, this would include the collection, coordination, analysis, management and dissemination of intelligence and criminal information as appropriate. If another federal agency identifies an individual who is engaged in terrorist activities or acts in preparation of terrorist activities, that agency is requested to promptly notify the FBI.

In addition, the FBI's role as a lead agency for investigating terrorism matters is supported by various Presidential Decision Directives (PDD). For example:

- PDD-3 9 sets forth the U.S. counterterrorism policy and outlines the FBI's jurisdictional responsibilities in relation to terrorism: "unless otherwise specified by the Attorney General, the FBI shall have lead responsibility for operational response to terrorist incidents that take place within U.S. territory or that occur in international waters and do not involve the flag vessel of a foreign country. Within this role, the FBI functions as the on-scene manager for the U.S. Government." Moreover, "the FBI shall have lead responsibility for investigating terrorist acts planned or carried out by foreign or domestic terrorist groups in the U.S. or which are directed at U.S. citizens or institutions abroad."

- PDD-62 grants the Department of Justice, acting through the FBI, lead agency or operational response authority to a incident.
- PDD-63 directs that the National Infrastructure Protection Center (NIPC) serve as a national critical infrastructure threat assessment, warning, vulnerability, and law enforcement investigation and response entity and that its mission "will include providing timely warnings of intentional threats, comprehensive analyses and law enforcement investigation and response." Under the directive, the Department of Justice/FBI have been given the responsibility for the Emergency Law Enforcement Services Sector. Helping assure the security of law enforcement agencies across the United States greatly increases preparedness to deal with terrorist incidents.
- PDD-77 set forth requirements for returning suspected terrorists to stand trial in the United States.

Various statutes give the FBI authority to investigate terrorist crimes committed overseas. Chief among these are the Comprehensive Crime Control Act of 1984, which created a new section in the U.S. Criminal Code for Hostage Taking, and the Omnibus Diplomatic Security and Anti-terrorism Act of 1986, which established a new statute pertaining to terrorist acts conducted abroad against U.S. nationals and/or its interests (Extraterritorial Terrorism Statute).

FBI Counterterrorism Strategy

The strategic goal of the FBI's Counterterrorism Program is to identify, prevent, deter, and respond to acts of terrorism. In the area of responding to terrorist incidents after they occur, the FBI, with the support of the Congress and the Administration, has greatly improved its crisis response capabilities since the World Trade Center bombing in 1993 and the Oklahoma City bombing in 1995. One can look to such investigative successes, as the indictment of 22 individuals in connection with the bombings of the U.S. Embassies in Kenya and Tanzania in 1998 to understand the FBI's far reaching capability to respond to terrorist incidents abroad as well as at home.

Even though the FBI has realized successes in responding to acts of terrorism, the FBI recognizes that the underlying political/religious/social movements which produced recent acts of terrorism are beyond its control- therefore, the FBI will never be able to prevent all acts of terrorism. International terrorists have demonstrated their willingness and ability to strike against citizens and facilities of the United States not only in foreign lands, but also here at home. Fast-paced global changes, such as the widespread growth in international trade and commerce; greater international openness and exchange of ideas brought about by improvements in communications and the Internet; shifts in the balance of political/social/economic forces in developing and established countries; and a growing international financial dependence, among others, continue to present the FBI with new challenges in the area of terrorism prevention.

In an effort to keep pace with the changing terrorist threat to the United States, the FBI is implementing a new management and operational initiative to further strengthen its ability to combat terrorism. This initiative, referred to as MAXCAP05, has as its goal the achievement by Fiscal Year 2005 of five core competencies or capacities for its Counterterrorism Program: investigative, intelligence, communications, liaison, and program management.

- Investigative Capacity is the extent to which each FBI Field Office is appropriately staffed, trained, equipped, and managed to prevent and effectively respond to acts of terrorism based on the known terrorist threat in that field office.
- Intelligence Capacity is the ability to produce, use, and appropriately disseminate on a timely basis strategic, operational, and tactical Counterterrorism intelligence products.
- Communications Capacity is the capability to fully utilize and integrate FBI resources throughout the Bureau in

support of Counterterrorism programs and initiatives through the use of appropriate information technology.

- Liaison Capacity is the capacity to prioritize, establish, and maintain sound and productive relationships with external counterparts in the intelligence community, law enforcement communities, other federal agencies, defense establishments, foreign services, private industry and non-governmental organizations, State and local agencies, legislative and executive bodies, the media, and academia to obtain maximum information and support.
- Program Management Capacity is the capacity to effectively direct, measure, and manage the Counterterrorism Program's progress toward identifying and achieving its core competencies.

The FBI recently completed a field-wide assessment of investigative capacity. This assessment has been used to establish operational priorities. More importantly, the baseline assessments can serve as a starting point upon which progress towards achieving core competencies can be measured. Field office assessments will be updated semiannually.

THE GLOBALIZATION THEORY OF TERRORISM

Nassar (2004) has probably written the most interesting piece on globalization theory as it relates to terrorism, and the ideas are fairly robust precisely because globalization can be a complex subject at times. Globalization contributes to dreams, fantasies, and rising expectations, but at the same time, it leads to dashed hopes, broken dreams, and unfulfilled achievements. Terrorism breeds in the gap between expectations and achievements.

The thinking is very similar to strain theory in criminology or the rising expectations theory of prison riots, and about the only thing unique about globalization theory is that it adds a rich-poor dichotomy. Rich people (or nations) are seen as wanting power and wealth, and poor people (or nations) are seen as wanting justice.

From this perspective, then, rich people are part of the causal factor or root cause of terrorism, since they contribute to the conditions which give rise to it. Perpetrators of "terrorism" (always treated as an ill-defined concept in globalization theory) are never seen as born or raised with any specific predispositions toward it. In brief, globalization theory holds that if the oppressed and disgruntled poor people of the world were simply given the chance to find peaceful means for achieving justice, terrorism would not thrive.

Globalization theory is further tied into ideas about colonialism, imperialism, and neocolonialism. The first two words are often used interchangeably to describe a set of conditions (technically, extensions of sovereignty) where the mores, values, and beliefs of the colonizers are considered superior to those of the colonized. However, when the assumption is made that (imperial) power is a necessary thing to maintain cultural superiority, this is the usual meaning of imperialism.

Neocolonialism is a concept developed by Marxists and holders of certain conspiracy theories to refer to allegations about First World nations, international organizations, and/or multinational corporations employing economic, financial and trade policies to dominate less powerful countries. Onwudiwe (2001) is typical of the criminological approach taken when globalization ideas are incorporated into theories about terrorism, and it is probably safe to say that the approach remains relatively underdeveloped.

THE POLITICAL THEORY OF FASCISM AS A THEORY OF TERRORISM

Fascism is the one form of government with the most disagreement about a definition for it, which Passmore (2002) attempts to consolidate as an ultranationalist ideology that is unabashedly racist. The word comes from the Latin "fasces" which means to use power to scare or impress people. It generally refers to the consolidation of all economic and political power into some form of super-patriotism that is devoted to genocide or endless war with one's enemies. Benito Mussolini, who practically invented the term in 1922, said it is the merger of state and corporate power. Adolf Hitler said that it is the clever and constant application of propaganda so that people can be made to see paradise as hell, and the other way around. So-called Islamo-Fascism can also be traced to the same time period as the birth of the Nazi ("national socialist") fascism in 1928 when the Muslim Brotherhood (Al Ikhwan Al Muslimun), parent organization of numerous terrorist groups, was formed in reaction to the 1924 abolition of the caliphate by the Turks.

Fascism supports terrorism at home and abroad. Charismatic leaders are usually given supreme powers to crack down on dissidents, peacemakers, and anyone who doesn't abide by the "cult of the individual" which worships a He-man mentality and the party line. With the frequent wars and militaristic ventures that come with fascism, an effort is made to demonize the enemy as sub-humans who deserve extinction. These enemies are also made into scapegoats for all the past problems a country has had. Fascism appeals to the frustrations and resentments of a race of people who think they ought to have a bigger place at the global table. When combined with an anti-western slant (the United States as Great Satan), fascism becomes a means of social identity (Pan-Africanism, Pan-Arabism, Islamo-Fascism) as well as a facilitator of terrorism against all western interests. Frustrated fascists who fail to gain control in their own countries have historically turned to terrorism.

They are most likely to turn to domestic terrorism since fascists do not believe that citizen rights are bestowed merely because someone inhabits a country. Nor do they believe that all human beings are possessed of equal rights. "Foreign" families and businesses (as they define them) are usually targeted for extermination by fascists. The enemies who are seen as the greatest threat are those who fascists see as corrupting or poisoning family and property relations.

Fascism is full of ironies and contradictions. On the one hand, it is anti-modern in its glorification of the land, a return to country life, and its fascination with peasant dress or costume. On the other hand, it is pro-modern in its worship of military technology, favoritism of big business, mass mobilization of people, promotion of commercialized sport, and its surprisingly liberal attitude toward the involvement of women in the movement. Science and scholarship also take on interesting twists under fascism. "Hard" sciences like biology and chemistry usually advance significantly, especially in areas such as genetic research. "Soft" sciences like sociology and psychology usually become usurped into mumbo-jumbo pseudoscientific ideas about a glorified folk culture and reasons for hating the enemy.

Just as anarchists have their May Day (May 1st) celebrations, fascists also tend to celebrate anniversaries. Many terrorists, of course, have been known to time their attacks to coincide with the date for an historical event or the birthday of someone special to them. For example, with ecoterrorism, that day is October 16, which coincides the the United Nation's World Food Day, and is usually when McDonald's restaurants are targeted for vandalism.

However, *the most important date in the study of terrorism is April 19*. A number of significant events have happened on that date. Right-wing domestic terrorist groups call it "Militia Day" because it was when the siege at Waco ended, it was when surveillance began at the Ruby Ridge compound in Idaho, and it marks the anniversary of the Oklahoma City bombing of the federal building. Neo-Nazi fascist groups celebrate April 19 because it was the day German Nazis started wiping out Jewish ghettos across Europe, as well as the following day being Adolf Hitler's birthday. Internationally, terrorist groups who regard themselves as "freedom fighters" and trace at least part of this justification to the American Revolution, take heart in the fact that the American Revolution started on April 19, 1775 at the Battle of Lexington. It remains to be seen if September 11 will replace April 19 as the most popular date for terrorism.

TERRORISM—A THREAT TO DEMOCRACY

The terrorism according to United Nations can be defined as:-

"Any action that is intended to cause death or serious bodily harm to civilians or non-combatants, when the purpose of such an act, by its nature or context, is to intimidate a population, or to compel a Government or an international organization to do or to abstain from doing any act.

"Terrorism" is an ambiguous term whose definition implies a political act. Over the years, the term has been used more frequently, and today it often seems to be synonymous with "evil". Generally speaking, the term "terrorism" can be used to describe a "systematic use or threat of violence in order to achieve political goals". But this definition does not address some of the problematic aspects of the phenomenon, and does not differentiate between terrorism and other forms of political violence, such as revolution, uprising and guerrilla warfare. Terrorism is subjective. One person's terrorist is another's revolutionary crusader. Terrorism in its modern interpretation is a new word for cruel criminal acts. Terror can be committed in the name of Good – but basically it is a way to fight for political goals in a criminal manner. Indeed, disputing the claim that it is important to define terrorism in order to effectively battle it, some argue that clearly defining terrorism and making it a singular criminal offense may serve to authorize the deprivation of the human rights of the suspects. Regardless of the definition of terrorism, democracies must be beware of the danger of transforming the war on terrorism from a means of defending democracy to one that undermines its foundations.

Terrorists have killed people of all nationalities, faiths and backgrounds. Terrorists aim to achieve objectives through intimidation and fear. They assert that "end justify means", no matter what the cost in human life and suffering.

Since past, we have encountered several main types of terrorism:

1. Acts of terrorism committed by the state against internal or external opposition.
2. Acts of terrorism committed in order to oppose the state or in order to promote national independence.
3. Acts of fundamentalist terrorism, which is an expression of a struggle between religions or cultures.

Some examples of terrorist acts involve:

- The use of explosive devices and suicide bombers

- The assassination of political, military or media figures
- Hostage taking
- The hijacking of airplanes or other vehicles
- The destruction of infrastructure and communications
- The use of chemical, biological and nuclear weapons

Their methods, too, are different. Because they recognize no common bonds with people who have different beliefs, they are prepared to kill indiscriminately. Indeed, mass murder is their explicit objective, their measure of success in their terms, and their methods of recruitment bear more comparison with self-destructive cults than political movements.

Democracy lies in the hearts and minds of people. It permeates those hearts and minds, so that no one allows them to be usurped by force or in any other way. Democracy is a condition in which the vast numbers of people who comprise a nation — and ultimately the world — submit themselves to institutions of law of their own making, and in which they care about each other and the planet on which they live. Democracy is not only an idea; it is also a set of values (freedom, equality and brotherhood) and a way of governing."Terror" in the sense of a "terror-regime" is originally another way of governing - without democratic values. It is a thread against democracy which is not threaded as criminal acts but as something, that can suspend democratic rights in societies.

Democracy is not a form of government but a set of principles that guide how we govern ourselves. Terrorism is merely a method of utilizing fear as a means to an end. Therefore, Terrorism cannot destroy the principles of democracy. Terrorist can and indeed are attempting to cause us to ignore those principles as we cater to our fears that terrorism brings. It is when we abandon the principles, even in the short term that will bring the ultimate demise of Democracy. So we should not allow ourselves to publically fear terrorism but instead, we should discipline ourselves to allow the principles of Democracy and peace to prevail. I believe that even a terrorist desires peace. The question is who gets to lead the peace, the people or the terrorist?

Terrorism poses a direct and indirect threat to democracy. The direct threat is a result of terrorism's capability to undermine the fundamental security that nations and international organizations are supposed to provide their citizens, which is the foundation of the legitimacy of a government. Terrorism also poses a direct threat to the basic human rights of life and property. But the indirect threat to democracy is by far the most dangerous. The war on terrorism challenges the democratic institutions of the nations and their ability to ensure the security of their citizens without harming innocent people. The terrorist attacks signal a turning point not only in the intensity of global terrorism, but also a warning to any enlightened democracy that wishes to combat the threat of terrorism.

Democracy is traditionally seen as a panacea to provide security and civil liberties to citizens and avoid political extremism or terrorism provoked by un-redressed grievances. The oft-cited theory of democratic peace holds that democracies do not wage war against each other. Democracy is in crisis; insecurity is on the rise and the threat of terrorism is equally menacing in newly democratizing and long-democratic countries.

Terrorism, and equally the fight against terrorism, pose a dual challenge to recent and long-established democracies: terrorism undermines a cherished goal and objective of democracy, that of providing citizens with security and the rule of law; and in responding to terrorism, democracies risk undermining the values of democracy such as the rule of law and human rights that are central to their existence and legitimacy.

Terrorism's greatest power lies in the arbitrary nature of its victims and in the large amount of coverage it receives in the media. Today, in addition to "conventional" terrorism, there are also the risks of the use of weapons of mass destruction and cyber-terrorism. The ability to use diverse methods in order to wreak havoc indicates that although terrorism has not yet become an existential world threat, if we didn't wake up then, that day is not far-off.

In my views, Terrorism can both destroy and build democracy. Throughout past, the oppressed and abused have used such means as were available to them to strive to attain social justice and gain individual dignity based on liberty, freedom and full access to democratic rights of citizenship. The means have often been inhumane but the character of the struggle is as much determined by the resistance of those in power as the selected means of the terrorist. In Zimbabwe the threats of the Zanu-PF thugs against all opposition voters destroyed the validity of the last two- three elections there. But making the most inspiring sights in the modern world for democracy to be seen, the peoples rose above the threats of terrorists and millions queued patiently to cast their ballots despite the physical perils involved in going to polling stations. This happened in Afghanistan after the fall of the Taliban and of course then again in Iraq in December 2005.

While Islamic fundamentalist terrorists see an undemocratic religious state as the fulfillment of their earthly goals, this is one type of terrorism. Other types of terrorism can create democracy - for example, the African National Congress had an armed wing, led by Nelson Mandela, which easily falls under the category of terrorist. Indeed, 'Free Nelson Mandela' records and T-shirts could fall under the category of glorification of terrorism. Yet this very organization and this very terrorist leader were responsible for leading South Africa to democracy.

In Sri Lanka, the ongoing war between the Tamil Tigers and the Colombo administration is in danger of undermining the nation's fragile democracy. Similarly, in the Gaza strip, Algeria and most obviously Pakistan, terror and the threat of terror are a serious impediment to nurturing a viable, democratic state. By contrast, the voters of Spain responded to the Madrid train bombings with a bravura display of popular sovereignty. And in Northern Ireland it was the ballot box and not the Armalite that brought the struggle to an end.

We cannot rely exclusively on military power to assure our long-term security. Lasting peace is gained as justice and democracy advance. In democratic and successful societies, men and women do not swear allegiance to malcontents and murderers; they turn their hearts and labor to building better lives. And democratic governments do not shelter terrorist camps or attack their peaceful neighbors; they honor the aspirations and dignity of their own people. In our conflict with terror and tyranny, we have an unmatched advantage, a power that cannot be resisted, and that is the appeal of freedom to all mankind."

Freedom of speech, freedom of the press, and the right to peaceably assemble, serve to empower citizens, legitimize debate, and provide alternatives to violence. The fair and independent judicial systems present in liberal democracies play a similar role. A truly independent judiciary is a vital check on executive power and a protector of those exercising their rights to free expression. Ensuring that no group is above the law also gives average citizens a greater stake in their political systems. Absent these democratic attributes, we find conditions that in some instances give rise to sympathy for terrorism. This is especially true in nations where demagogues who preach the language of hate under the guise of religion are the only alternatives to corrupt or brutal elite. Today, the danger to us comes not exclusively from dictators who make war directly upon us, our allies, and our interests — it also Proceed from dictators who create an atmosphere so poisonous and so brutal that evil sprouts and motivates a small but radicalized cadre to terrorism.

To counter terrorism, we seek genuine representative government that brings liberty and democracy to all of a country's citizens, including those who often have been excluded — especially women. Women have a critical role to play in democracy, in civil society, and in ensuring that democratic ideals are instilled in future generations. Our long-term strategy is to strike at the heart of terrorism by depriving it of its shelter, its recruitment grounds, and its foot soldiers. We will do this in no small measure through the avid promotion of democracy and freedom. I believe that this can be achieved because we have developed a highly successful model of integration which enables people of all backgrounds and faiths to prosper and live together within the safeguard of common values. Our society is itself an affront, and a reproach, to the ideologues who believe that only their way of living life is the right one. And make no mistake: The threat we face is ideological. It is not driven by poverty, or by social exclusion, or by racial hatred. Those who attacked London in July, those who have been engaged in terrorist networks elsewhere in the world, and those who attacked New York in 2001 were not the poor and dispossessed. They were, for the most part, well educated and prosperous.

Unlike the liberation movements of the post-World War II era, these are not political ideas like national independence from colonial rule, or equality for all citizens without regard for race or creed, or freedom of expression without totalitarian repression. Such ambitions are, at least in principle, in many cases have actually been negotiated. However, there can be no negotiation about the re-creation of the Caliphate; there can be no negotiation about the imposition of Sharia law; there can be no negotiation about the suppression of equality between the sexes; there can be no negotiation about the ending of free speech. These values are fundamental to our civilization and are simply not up for negotiation. It is equally wrong to claim, as some do, that the motivation of terrorists and their allies is driven by some desire to seek justice in the Middle East—the part of the world where progress has been most difficult to achieve in the past 30 years. I do not accept this in any respect.

I suggest that the best way to contest this threat is by building and strengthening the democracy of our society, by isolating extremism in its various manifestations, by strengthening the legal framework within which we contest terrorism, and by developing more effective means to protect our democracy.

First, in each of our societies, we need to strengthen our democracy. That means promoting a society which is based upon the true respect of one individual for another, one culture for another, one faith for another, one race for another. It means promoting the view that democracy is the means of making change in our societies, and it means working to strengthen our democracy so that young people from all communities can see the ways in which their engagement in our societies can bring about democratic change and reduce the alienation which can make individuals prey to those who seek to destroy us.

Second, we need to take steps to isolate extremist organizations and those individuals who promote extremism. In so doing, it is essential for us to work closely with the mainstream faith communities and to understand their preoccupations. In our country, we need legislation which outlaws incitement to religious or race hatred and makes it clear that glorification of terrorism is not a legitimate political expression of view. We wish to encourage faiths to pursue their faith openly and directly. We should intend to attack the foci of extremist organization, whether they are in training camps, in prisons, in bookshops, or in places of worship. We should, work with international allies where appropriate, to identify the networks and individuals who are promoting extremism, and use legal power to disrupt and weaken them. We should intend to remove from the India those foreign citizens who are using their time in our country to promote extremism, though this course is not legally straightforward. All of these measures will further isolate and weaken those extremists who wish to promote terrorism as an appropriate form of activity.

Third, we need to strengthen the legal framework within which we can address these issues. I assert throughout all this the need to retrain and strengthen our human rights and the values which underlie them. But I say at the same time that the right to be protected from the death and destruction caused by indiscriminate terrorism is at least as important as the right of the terrorist to be protected from torture and ill-treatment. I believe that our peoples expect not only the protection of individual rights, but also the protection of democratic values such as safety and security under the law. We need a legal framework which seeks to address the difficult balance in these rights. We cannot properly fight terrorism with one legal hand tied behind our back, or give terrorists the unfettered right to defend themselves as they promote and prepare violent attacks on our society. For that reason, we should propose legal changes in our country which outlaw acts preparatory to terrorism and terrorist training.

Fourth, we need to strengthen our ability to control our borders. That means doing our best to harmonize the biometric data on passports, visas, ID cards where they exist, and perhaps even driving licenses. This is a substantial agenda to contest the threats we face, but I believe it to be essential for us.

Democracy is the strongest form of society and the most resilient. It is the aspiration of peoples throughout the world.

Through democracy, extremist terrorism will be defeated. As we face the challenge of terrorist attack, most recently in Delhi again last Saturday, it is our duty to analyze and then determine the means by which this threat can be best contested. We have to clarify the values and society which we are defending; identify the threat with which we have to deal; and set out the central means by which we need both to contest those who seek to destroy us and to build the solidarity and determination which we need to succeed.

The most important conclusion to draw from this analysis is that there is not some particular government policy decision, or even some overall policy stance, which we could change and thus somehow remove our society from the terrorist firing line. Their nihilism means that our societies would only cease to be a target if we were to give up all those values of freedom and liberty which we have fought to extend over so many years.

We all know that our society, based on these values, will continue to evolve and develop. But we also know that the achievements we do have are based on centuries of struggle. The societies which we have built, with the values which they embody, are not slight or passing. They are deeply rooted and profound. However, it is the case that these are absolutely enormous changes in one generation, which proves that change for the good can happen and, moreover, that it can happen in very many cases without violence or bloodshed. And the fight for democracy is at the core of this change.

It can be lastly concluded that terrorism can not be a threat to democracy but democracy can be a weapon to fight against terrorism. I assert that the single most important weapon that we have in defending the societies from which we come is our determination and our solidarity.

THE POLITICAL THEORY OF ANARCHISM AS A THEORY OF TERRORISM

Terrorism is most definitely not a form of governance, but anarchism is. Most anarchists reject terrorism in its vanguard varieties (for nationalist or religious purposes), but in a theoretical sense, anarchism justifies terrorism as a form of criminal action that attacks the values of an organized, complacent society. Anarchism is a theory of governance that rejects any form of central or external authority, preferring instead to replace it with alternative forms of organization such as shaming rituals for deviants, mutual assistance pacts between citizens, syndicalism (any non-authoritarian organizational structure that gives the greatest freedom to workers), iconoclasm (the destruction of cherished beliefs), libertarianism (a belief in absolute liberty), and plain old rugged individualism. Anarchism is often referred to as the nineteenth century roots of terrorism, the term first being introduced in 1840 by Pierre-Joseph Proudhon. *Anarchism defined* is the rejection of the state, of any form of coercive government, of any form of domination and exploitation. It is the notion of free and equal access to all the world's resources to enable positive freedom (*freedom to*) in place of negative freedom (*freedom from*, or the basis of most constitutional rights).

As a theory, anarchism holds a unique place in history because it was the first revolutionary movement to come up with systematic ideas about the purpose of agitation. You'll recognize some of these ideas as terrorist tactics, but it's important first to understand them in the context of anarchism. Proudhon contributed the idea of finding the "moment" as in when the moment is ripe for revolutionary action. Another anarchist, Mikhail Bakunin, popularized the idea of "propaganda by deed" or letting your actions speak for themselves, which was a theory originally developed by Carlo Pisacane, an Italian revolutionary who argued that ideas spring from deeds and not the other way around. Over the years, this notion has evolved into a fairly competent philosophy of the bomb as part of a propaganda campaign to stimulate awareness and sympathy with the cause, and in this respect has been noted as a defining feature of terrorism (Georges-Abeyie & Hass 1982). Bakunin's ideas strongly influenced anarchism because his concept of propaganda by deed also included a prohibition against large scale group action (it being better, he thought, for anarchist action to be individualized or done in small groups). Most anarchists operate on the principle of leaderless resistance, or acting on your own, with little knowledge or support of the groups they may belong to. Major anarchist figures, like Karl Heinzen and Johann Most, contributed the idea that murder, especially murder-suicide, constituted the highest form of revolutionary struggle. Both advocated the use of weapons of mass destruction. Other anarchists contributed different ideas, such as Peter Kropotkin's notion of "propaganda by word" or radicalizing the public by use of subversive publications. Anarchism (like fascism) has also had some influential female figures, and Emma Goldman (1869-1940) comes to mind as a early founder of free speech (the ACLU) and sexual freedom movements. Minor figures in the history of anarchism, like Charles Gallo, Auguste Vaillante, Emile Henry, and Claudius Konigstein advocated the idea that to have the most effect, the targets must be innocents (in places such as crowded dance halls or shopping centers) or symbols of economic success (like banks and stock exchanges). It may be worth noting, in passing, that the famous Italian criminologist, Cesare Lombroso, developed his notion of the "born criminal" in part by being called in to examine the physical features of some minor anarchists who were really nothing more than criminals justifying their behaviour with anarchist talk.

Between 1875 and 1912, anarchists alone or in small groups managed to assassinate or attempt to assassinate the leaders of nine (9) different countries, including the U.S. (with President William McKinley in 1901). These crimes were just the most well-known acts of anarchism, as anarchists were involved in numerous ordinary crimes such as theft, robbery, murder, kidnapping, assault, and bombing. The most famous incident was the Haymarket riot in Chicago during 1886. During these peak years for classic anarchism, May Day celebrations became famous as all-out crime-rampant days. Police departments around the world became convinced there was an international conspiracy, and suspicious foreigners were locked up by the hundreds in many countries. Perfunctory trials were held, and many defendants were hanged or deported. The most famous of these trials was the 1920 case of Sacco and Vanzetti who were more antiwar and labor activists than anarchists. Anarchism in the classical sense was largely erased from the face of the earth by 1917 via a number of factors: the rise of communism and fascism (both of which are opposed to anarchism), strong xenophobic deportation (Red Scare) laws in democratic countries, and the fact that classic anarchism never became an organized movement. Twentieth-century terrorist groups which came later and claimed an ancestry with anarchism include: the Japanese Red Army, the British Angry Brigade, the German Baader-Meinhof Gang, the Weatherman in the United States, and the Mexican Zapatista movement (Kushner 2003). During the Spanish revolution of 1936, something called anarcho-syndicalism developed, which is a loose confederation of various protest groups. Those who call themselves anarchists today are more likely to be environmentalists or part of the anti-globalization movement who target for attack such institutions as the World Bank, International Monetary Fund, or World Trade Organization.

For purpose of balance, it is important to point out that anarchism today does not support terrorism. It has historically supported terrorism and even today might support assassination, but there are only weak theoretical links between the two, most strongly with the propaganda by deed concept. Anarchists hold to a doctrine that anarchy must be created in the act of self-liberation from oppressive and coercive relationships. You don't blow up the relationship as terrorists do; instead, you convince others that grounds for the existing relationship must be blown up. Anarchism is not about mad bombing or chaos. *Terrorists target people; anarchists target things* such as institutions and structures. Bakunin did not want the death of people but the destruction of things and positions of authority. Only a small minority of terrorists have ever been anarchists, and only a small minority of anarchists have ever been terrorists.

In fact, there is an area of study called anarchist criminology, a controversial subfield of critical criminology which celebrates the fact anarchism really has no workable definition. Anarchist criminology advocates the abolishment of criminal justice systems. It argues that much harm has been committed in the name of reasonableness, and anarchist criminology is committed to promoting the unthinkable and unreasonable. Like other subfields of critical criminology, anarchist criminology views the state as an inherently oppressive entity, and anarchist justice not only promotes social justice (equal access to all resources), but protects diversity and difference among people (Ferrell 1999).

TERRORISM AND WEAPONS OF MASS DESTRUCTION

The potential use of nuclear, biological, or chemical weapons by a terrorist group remains the nightmare scenario of our times. The fear that the use of any of these weapons in an urban environment might be catastrophic is probably well founded, particularly given the demonstrated willingness of some groups, such as Al Qaeda, to sacrifice its members in performing violence against civilian populations. This paper will examine the potential use of non conventional weapons by terrorists that are not surrogates of a state. Some States that have sponsored or supported terrorism in the past have current programs to develop weapons of mass destruction (WMD). Though the number of these terrorist sponsors has diminished since the collapse of the Soviet Union, there are serious concerns about the WMD programs and the suspected intentions of Iraq, Iran and North Korea to actually use these weapons. The possibility that any of these states might provide non-conventional weapons to terrorists that are not adjuncts of the state will also be considered.

In the past, most terrorist groups have had a political objective in wielding their violence, seeking to obtain a desired outcome through force. The employment of WMD would appear at first look to be inimical to the political agendas of such groups, whether that agenda was territorial concessions, the reversal of a state policy or another goal. Usually, the appeal of the group carrying out dramatic violence was to a broader audience beyond the immediate target. Traditional terrorists sought to benefit politically from their violence, drawing sympathy from the wider audience. This set of objectives argued against the use of WMD by the group, even when such weapons were available. Groups in the past that attempted to use of variety of WMD, e.g. Aum Shinrikyo in Tokyo, not only failed in causing mass casualties (only 12 people were killed in the subway attack) but discredited themselves internationally and failed to achieve any political objective whatsoever. To be sure, conventional attacks in the past could have catastrophic effects and often undercut the stated political goals of the perpetrators. The killing of 168 persons in the Oklahoma City bombing by Timothy McVeigh is an example. McVeigh, influenced by ethnic supremacists and radical groups such as Christian Identity, seriously miscalculated the effect of his violence on the wider audience, thereby diminishing support for white supremacists and his political objectives. And Al Qaeda itself, which has defined specific political goals for its actions, carried out the attacks on the American Embassies in Kenya and Tanzania in August 1998 which killed 224 and injured nearly 5000, mostly Africans. We can see that inflicting mass casualties using conventional weapons is a feature of the past several years. This era of trying to achieve mass casualties is characterized by Hezbollah's use of suicide bombers in Lebanon to attack the French and American military barracks and the American Embassy.

Osama bin Laden articulated the political goals for his terrorism on several occasions. His public issuance of a "Fatwa" or declaration of struggle, on 12 October 1996, stated:

> *"The people of Islam have suffered from aggression, iniquity and injustice imposed by the Zionist-Crusader alliance and their collaborators...It is the duty now on every tribe in the Arabian Peninsula to fight jihad and cleanse the land from these Crusader occupiers. Their wealth is booty to those who kill them. My Muslim brothers: your brothers in Palestine and in the land of the two Holy Places are calling upon your help and asking you to take part in fighting against the enemy – the Americans and the Israelis. They are asking you to do whatever you can to expel the enemies out of the sanctities of Islam."*

Later in the same year Bin Laden said that *"terrorizing the American occupiers of Islamic Holy Places is a religious and logical obligation."*

In February 1998 bin Laden issued and signed another Fatwa which included a decree to all Muslims:

> "...the killing of Americans and their civilian and military allies is a religious duty for each and every Muslim to be carried out in whichever country they are until Al Aqsa

mosque has been liberated from their grasp and until their armies have left Muslim lands." In the same 'fatwa' he called on Muslim scholars and their leaders and their youths to "launch an attack on the American soldiers of Satan."

He concluded, finally:

"We – with God's help – call on every Muslim who believes in God and wishes to be rewarded to comply with God's order to kill Americans and plunder their money whenever and wherever they find it. We also call on Muslims... to launch the raid on Satan's US troops and the devil's supporters allying with them, and to displace those who are behind them."

When asked, in 1998, about obtaining chemical or nuclear weapons, he said: *"acquiring such weapons for the defense of Muslims was a religious duty."*

We must understand not only the nature of the threat from religious extremes but its possible evolution. In America, in addition to the presence of some Islamic fanatics, we also have fundamentalists such as Christian Identity, and other religious extremists who kill or maim in the name of God, blowing up abortion clinics and gay bars. Comprehending the danger and the mind-set of these groups is a first step to deterring their violence. But it is also important to understand their willingness to employ so-called "doomsday" weapons if they believe they are carrying out the will of God. This is the common thread from Islamic fanatics, to Jewish extremists and Christian radicals: the belief they are carrying out divine instruction.

Terrorism has evolved significantly over the past twenty years to the point that most contemporary terrorism originates from these extremist religious groups and ethnic and sub-national elements. Whether the political goal is the expulsion of Western influence from the Middle East and the Persian Gulf, or the resistance to Israeli occupation in Palestine, extremist religious groups such as Hezbollah, Hamas, Palestinian Islamic Jihad and Al Qaeda are in the forefront. Radical, secular groups' pursuit of violent means to achieve ends is, of course, very much present in today's world but overall these secularists are in a long decline dating back to the collapse of the Soviet Union. Here we can cite groups such as the Red Army faction, the Brigate Rosse, and even the 17 November group in Greece. There are, of course, ethnic and regional conflicts fueled by political violence that have flared with varying intensity. Groups with a non-religious perspective formed the base of the Chechen resistance although the Chechens are slowly being influenced by religious extremists who provided the only real international support to the struggle against Russia. There are also the secular elements of the Palestinian resistance (in partnership with religiously based parties) that pursue the use of terrorism as a political tactic. And the major conflicts in Sri Lanka and Northern Ireland have had a non-religious character. In general, the major threat facing Western democracies today comes from fundamentalist religious groups.

Religious extremism includes Hindu, Muslim, and Jewish groups as well as Christian Identity and similar White Supremacy groups derived from fundamentalist Christian origins. Al Qaeda, Hezbollah, Hamas and the Palestinian Islamic Jihad are examples of religious militants that have used suicide bombings regularly as a political weapon. Hamas and the Jihad, which has become increasingly sophisticated in its capabilities recently, use violence to demoralize the Israeli people to the point that the groups hope they will achieve their proximate goals of ending Israeli occupation. They have not, until now, considered the use of WMD because of the congested geography in which both Israelis and Palestinians live but the possibility that their calculus will change is growing especially as the frustration level of their constituencies rises. At some point, terrorist tactics will evolve and limited use of some kinds of WMD could be attempted within Israel. Already these groups are experimenting with chemical additives to their explosive devices and it is not a leap to expect them to use other and more deadly forms of biological and chemical weaponry. Israeli weapons technology, advanced as it is, will provide little deterrence to the use by extremist religious groups willing to use WMD in suicide operations.

A number of terrorist groups that have been active in the past several years have shown significant interest in acquiring weapons of mass destruction. In addition to the well known development of nerve gas by Aleph, the new name for Aum Shinrikyo, that was demonstrated in Japan to minimal effect, groups such as Al Qaeda have conducted active experiments with poison gases, as at the Darunta Camp in Afghanistan; they have also developed plans for the construction of a radioactive explosive device (the so-called dirty bomb) and pursued attempts to acquire weapons grade uranium. While the efforts of non-state sponsored terrorist groups to independently develop WMD have been limited by lack of infrastructure and resources that are usually only available to nation states, there is among some groups a highly developed appreciation of the effect the use of WMD would have on the Western audience. During the war against the Taliban and Al Qaeda inside Afghanistan, a number of Al Qaeda training camps yielded information on the group's experiments with WMD and its exploration of various operations using some elements of WMD designed not only to cause mass casualties, but to inflict a significant psychological blow on its Western audience. Documents recovered from Al Qaeda facilities in Afghanistan show that Bin Laden was pursuing a sophisticated biological weapons research program. Terrorist groups worldwide have ready access to information on chemical, biological, and even nuclear weapons via the Internet, and we know that Al Qaeda was working to acquire some of the most dangerous chemical agents and toxins.

It has been speculated by U.S. government officials that Al Qaeda or other terrorist groups might try to launch conventional attacks against the chemical or nuclear industrial infrastructure of Western nations to cause widespread toxic or radiological damage. Complementary to this fear is the suspicion that terrorists might use cyber warfare attacks. September 11 demonstrated the western world's dependence on critical infrastructure systems that rely on electronic and computer networks. Attacks of this nature will become an increasingly viable option for terrorists as they and other foreign adversaries become more familiar with these targets, and the technologies required to attack them.

Al Qaeda, and most transnational groups that are not the surrogate of a state, lack necessary resources on their own to develop WMD. Ironically, the very lack of resource infrastructure has impelled Al Qaeda to consider new and imaginative uses of conventional weapons with elements of WMD that are more easily obtainable. The use of radioactive substances, such as found in medical equipment, can be used in a conventional explosive to disseminate low level radiation over the blast area. Another example is the possible use of the chemical Chlorine. Chlorine has a legitimate civilian use but it is also the raw material for the synthesis of precursor chemicals used to produce blister and nerve agents. Chlorine can be employed in its gaseous state as a deadly poison and can be disseminated by crop duster aircraft and other techniques over a wide area. Although aerial dispersion is often an ineffective delivery system for a poison gas, it can generate hysteria when the gas in employed in a congested urban environment. The psychological effect would likely be many more times the actual physical damage, but this is often precisely what the terrorist group intends. Bin Laden, who has shown a strong interest in acquiring WMD, has had some of his operatives trained to conduct attacks with commonly available chemicals.

The use of a nuclear weapon is, of course, the most lethal tool that could be used by a terrorist group. The technology of building a nuclear weapon is understood by some terrorist groups, particularly including Al Qaeda, but also by some Pakistani radical Muslims. Yet the key to actually building a nuclear device is the availability of fissile material. This would mean the acquisition of plutonium or highly enriched uranium. Indicators of al Al Qaeda's interest in WMD and its pursuit of these capabilities include the following taking from Congressional testimony in the United States:

Well conceived schematics detailing the construction of a nuclear device were discovered in Afghanistan. Al Qaeda so far has not succeeded in constructing such a weapon. Several attempts by the group to acquire nuclear materials since the 1990's have been documented. In September 1998, Mamdouh Mahmud Salim, an Al Qaeda operative, was arrested for attempting to purchase "enriched uranium" in Western Europe. Enriched uranium is defined in terms of its concentration of uranium-235 molecules. The more uranium-235 molecules that are in uranium, the more enriched is the unranium. Weapons grade uranium or HEU is enriched to over 90%. In February 2001, Jamal Ahmad al-Fadl, a bin Laden aid, testified that he participated in a deal to acquire uranium. Al Qaeda 's bid for enriched uranium may indicate their interest in developing conventional nuclear weapons. Enriched uranium would probably be used in a gun-assembly device similar to the "Little Boy" device that was dropped on Hiroshima.

Approximately 25 Kg of highly enriched uranium (HEU) is needed to build a gun-assembly device, and there is no evidence that Al Qaeda ever acquired any highly enriched uranium or other radioactive substances that could be used to develop conventional nuclear weapons.

Al Qaeda has also attempted to purchase spent nuclear fuel. In September 2001, a Bulgarian businessman claimed that aides to bin Laden approached him to purchase spent fuel from a local plant. The businessman said he first met with "the Saudi dissident," taken to mean Osama bin Laden, and the next day a young Arab chemical engineer contacted him to ask if he would serve as an intermediary for the transaction. According to the businessman, no deal ever took place. Spent fuel could be used to develop both conventional nuclear weapons and dirty bombs. If it were to be used in nuclear weapons, it would require reprocessing. Spent fuel is reprocessed by separating neutron-absorbing fission products from unused fissile uranium 235 and plutonium 239, and fertile uranium 238. This task requires extensive knowledge of chemical processes and reactions, access to various chemicals not commonly available in industry, laboratories with hot cells, shielding to protect against radioactivity, and other equipment to complete the task. Al Qaeda does not appear to have any of these. Spent fuel could be more easily used in a dirty bomb. In this case, the substance would be combined with a conventional explosive that when set off would spread highly radioactive material over a wide area. Evidence pointing to Al Qaeda 's interest in developing dirty bombs can be found in the June 2002 arrest of suspected Al Qaeda associate Abdullah al Muhajir, also known as Jose Padilla. Muhajir was arrested by U.S. authorities for scheming to develop and use a dirty bomb in an American city. Another piece of evidence is a set of containers found in Afghanistan that were marked with skull and cross bones and filled with a liquid registering a slight radioactive signature. Investigators believe that Al Qaeda members were duped into thinking that this substance was actually highly radioactive material that could be used to develop a nuclear or radiological weapon.

In Pakistan, a number of nuclear scientists were arrested for allegedly assisting Al Qaeda with nuclear technologies. Media accounts do not detail the scientists' assistance to Al Qaeda, but they do cite one scientist, Sultan Bashiruddin Mahmood, admitting that he met with Al Qaeda and helped the organization through his non-profit "humanitarian" organization. Mahmood is believed to have been a senior member of Pakistan's nuclear weapons program, "with broad access to classified information." Western experts are concerned that he and others may have transferred nuclear knowledge, equipment, or materials to the Taliban, which in turn would have been passed to Al Qaeda.

Reports also claim that Al Qaeda attempted to purchase whole nuclear weapon assemblies. In 1998, the Paris-based Arabic paper Al-Watan Al-Arabi ran a story about a "nuclear warhead deal," where Al Qaeda members and Chechen crime figures met to exchange two tons of opium and $30 million in cash for 20 nuclear warheads. There is no evidence that this exchange ever took place, nor is it likely that Al Qaeda has ever possessed nuclear warheads.

In reviewing the information publicly available, we can conclude that one of Al Qaeda 's objectives is to develop a nuclear capability. However, to the present there is no evidence that the organization ever acquired enough nuclear material to develop a nuclear weapon, nor does it appear that they were able to acquire whole nuclear weapon assemblies. The more immediate risk is that Al Qaeda has succeeded in obtaining a limited amount of enriched uranium or other radioactive material from Central Asia or Russia and intends to employ it as the core of a conventional explosive device. It has been estimated that if such device were detonated in an urban environment, depending on the lethality of the core material, the blast area would be uninhabitable for several years until all of the soil was physically removed.

According to CIA public declarations, Al Qaeda has aggressively pursued a chemical and biological weapon (CBW) capability. The organization appears to have made more progress in these fields than in the nuclear realm. Although it is difficult to point to physical evidence of Al Qaeda's CBW capability, several hints suggest the likelihood that Al Qaeda has produced small amounts of some type of agent. One comes from the ten volume "Encyclopedia of Afghanistan Resistance" which was found while coalition forces were inspecting a camp close to Jalalabad in Afghanistan. The encyclopedia contains precise formulas for manufacturing toxins, botullinum, and ricin. The document also instructs would-be perpetrators in methods of disseminating the deadly materials. From the American investigation of the September 11 tragedy it was discovered that some Al Qaeda wanted to purchase crop dusters that analysts believe would have been used to disseminate anthrax and chemical or biologic agents.

Another indicator of Al Qaeda's chemical weapons interest comes from a recently discovered videotape that records experiments involving dogs that were exposed to vapors from a "white liquid." In the tape, the dogs struggle, vomit, have trouble breathing, and finally die. Some experts speculate that the gas was a nerve agent such as sarin. The last hint of Al Qaeda's chemical weapons capability comes from Ahmed Ressam, the Algerian convicted of planning to bomb the Los Angeles airport during the Millennium celebrations. Ressam testified that Al Qaeda taught him to poison people by putting toxins on door knobs, and that he engaged in experiments in which dogs were injected with a mixture containing cyanide and sulphuric acid. Although a stock of agents or their precursors has not been found, it is apparent that some quantity of an agent was obtained by Al Qaeda personnel.

How did Al Qaeda acquire CBW materials in the first place? One possibility is outlined in a September 2001 British media report alleging that operatives may have acquired samples of anthrax, salmonella, and e-coli through Czech facilities. However, this has not been proven and Czech officials deny the allegations. What we can conclude from captured documents, media reports, and U.S. government statements is that Al Qaeda has obtained chemical agents, albeit probably in small quantities, and performed experiments on live subjects to determine the lethality of the substances. Manuals and testimony also indicate that Al Qaeda has determined how to operationalize chemical and biological warfare.

Notwithstanding the above, there are significant obstacles to terrorist groups in acquiring a WMD stockpile. For example, terrorists working outside a state-run laboratory would have to overcome extraordinary technical and operational challenges to effectively and successfully weaponize and deliver a biological agent to cause mass casualties. While many biological agents can be obtained or grown with relative ease, several significant steps remain on the way to weaponization and effective use of these agents. The main challenge is effective dissemination, which requires an aerosol form. The formulation of agents for airborne dispersal requires dissolving optimal amounts of weaponized agents in a specific combination of different chemicals (with each agent requiring a unique formulation). This is possibly the major remaining secret of the former U.S. and Soviet BW programs. Moreover, aerosol disseminators need to be operated effectively and suitable meteorological conditions must be present to carry out a successful BW attack. Despite the fact that the Aum Shinrikyo sect had substantial resources, members who were trained chemists and bioscientists, motivation, and ample time for research, they failed to carry out an effective BW attack despite several attempts.

Some experts in the field believe that less efficient aerosol techniques may be obtained by capable non-state groups, and that even a crude delivery system could still cause casualties or injuries in the thousands, especially if the attack is carried out against a large indoor population. Toxic industrial chemicals such as chlorine or phosgene, as noted above, are easily available and do not require great expertise to be adapted into chemical weapons. Nerve agents are more difficult to produce, and require a synthesis of multiple precursor chemicals. They also require high-temperature processes and create dangerous byproducts, which makes their production unlikely outside of an advanced laboratory. Aerosol or vapor forms are the most effective for dissemination, which can be carried out by sprayers or an explosive device. However, agents are vulnerable to temperature, moisture and wind, and are unreliable in the open air. Their most effective use as a terrorist weapon would be on an indoor population.

If transnational terrorist groups have only a limited capability to develop and exploit WMD as tools for their violent acts, states that have sponsored terrorism in the past do have a marked capability in this area. These states include Iran, North Korea, Iraq and Libya. Among these countries, the CBW threat continues to grow for a variety of reasons but the dual-use nature of many CW and BW agents complicates any assessment of offensive programs. Many CW and BW production capabilities are hidden in plants that are virtually indistinguishable from genuine commercial facilities. There have been reports of dubious reliability indicating that Iraq has acquired Smallpox strains from a Russian laboratory that are impervious to inoculation. Iraq may have had access to some strains of common smallpox although there is no confirmation that such stocks exist in Iraqi inventories. Yet the possibility of a smallpox scourge unleashed on a world where inoculations against the disease no longer exist is terrifying to modern societies. A repressive government such as the one headed by Saddam Hussein that has demonstrated a willingness to employ chemical weapons in the past against its own Kurdish population will probably be willing to use the most deadly chemical and biological agents at its disposal when the government is placed in extremis. But would Saddam Hussein or another leader with stockpiles of WMD release these weapons to a terrorist group such as Al Qaeda? Certainly we have no evidence that this is the case right now. We will consider the future possibilities.

Iraq is the poster child for states that have developed weapons of mass destruction, at least in the past, and which has also harbored terrorist groups such as the 15 May Group, the Abu Nidal Organization, and others. According to public dossiers issued by the United Kingdom and the United States, Baghdad has been producing chemical warfare agents, including mustard, sarin, cyclosarin and VX. The Iraqis have experience in manufacturing CW bombs, artillery rockets and probably possess CW bulk fills for SRBM warheads, including warheads mounted on extended-range Scuds. Iraq has also developed incapacitating BW agents and has been able to weaponize such agents, including Anthrax, for delivery by bombs, missiles, aerial sprayers and covert operatives. Iraq has also used chemical weapons in the past. Some examples:

- August 1983, mustard gas used against Iranians and Kurds.
- February 1986, mustard/taban gas used against Iranians (8,000 casualties).
- October 1987, mustard gas and other nerve agents used against Iranians.

Western intelligence analysis assumes that Iraq is unlikely to produce enough weapons-grade material for a deliverable nuclear weapon until the end of this decade. Iraq could, in this analysis, produce a nuclear bomb if it were able to acquire weapons-grade fissile material abroad. But the question remains: If Iraq has a WMD capability, how likely would it be that it provides some of these weapons to terrorist groups for their own use?

There is no precedent among the states that have sponsored or support terrorism to provide WMD materials to non-state groups. The Libyans, who for years provided safe haven and support to the Abu Nidal Group, never provided chemical or biological agents to the group. Iran, which is the sponsor of the Lebanese Hezbollah, has provided that group with significant assistance, including rockets and other sophisticated conventional weaponry. But there is no record that Iran has provided any components of WMD to the Hezbollah, nor does it appear likely to do so in the future.

There are significant obstacles to states, which by and large are attempting to conceal their WMD programs, in providing these weapons to groups they do not entirely control.

Once the weapons are ceded to such a terrorist group, the state loses operational control and has potentially incriminated its own clandestine WMD program. There are few incentives for states with a WMD capability to loosen control over weapons programs developed in great secrecy and considered an essential component of the nation's political and military strategy.

WMD programs are also becoming more advanced and effective as they mature, and as some countries become more aggressive in pursuing them.

This is exacerbated by the diffusion of technology over time– which enables proliferators to draw on the experience of others and to develop more advanced weapons more quickly than they could otherwise. Proliferators are also becoming more self-sufficient.

And they are establishing advanced production capabilities by taking advantage of both foreign assistance and the dual-use nature of WMD– and missile-related technologies. This also allows them to conduct WMD– and missile-related research under the guise of legitimate commercial or scientific activity.

Iran remains a serious concern because of its across-the-board pursuit of WMD and missile capabilities.

Tehran may be able to indigenously produce enough fissile material for a nuclear weapon by late this decade. Iran may also flight-test an ICBM later this decade, using either Russian or North Korean assistance. It also continues to pursue dual-use equipment and expertise that could help to expand its BW arsenal, and to maintain a large CW stockpile.

Syria has a longstanding chemical warfare program and is pursuing the development of biological weapons. It has signed but not ratified the BWC and is not a state party to the CWC. Damascus has a stockpile of the nerve agent sarin that can be delivered by aircraft or ballistic missiles.

It is trying to develop the more toxic and persistent nerve agent VX and will likely continue to improve its chemical agent production and delivery infrastructure. Iraq made extensive use of chemical weapons (CW) during the 1980s, both against Iranian troops and Kurdish civilians in Iraq. Iraq probably retained a stockpile of CW munitions in the form of aerial bombs, rockets, and artillery shells, as well as precursor chemicals and agents, including mustard gas, VX, and other nerve agents. Iraq may have built new agent and munitions production facilities since 1998. UN weapons inspectors are currently in the process of determining whether Iraq has retained CBW stockpiles. Iraq is not a signatory of the Chemical Weapons Convention.

Libya remains dependent on foreign suppliers for precursor chemicals and other key CW-related equipment, and may be re-establishing contacts with sources of expertise, equipment and precursors now that sanctions have been suspended. Tripoli has not given up its goal of establishing its own offensive CW capability and continues to pursue an indigenous production capability for the weapons. Libya also may use its new procurement opportunities to develop an indigenous BW capability.

Libya is not a signatory of the CWC and probably retains an inventory of nerve and blister agents. In 1987, Libya used small quantities of mustard gas munitions against Chadian troops. Because of its reliance on foreign suppliers for precursor chemicals, Libya's chemical weapons (CW) program was severely hampered by UN sanctions in the 1990s.

It is important to note when considering the use of non-conventional weapons by terrorists that attacks using WMD need not be directed only at humans. Plant and animal pathogens may be used against agricultural targets, creating both potential economic devastation and the possibility that a criminal group might seek to exploit such an attack for economic advantage. As deadly as they now are, BW agents could become even more sophisticated.

Rapid advances in biotechnology present the prospect of a new array of toxins or live agents that require new detection methods, preventative measures, and treatments. Particularly with respect to chemical weapons, there is a growing risk that new and difficult-to-combat agents will become available to hostile countries or sub-national groups.

Countries are taking advantage of denial and deception techniques, concealing and protecting BW and CW programs. BW in particular lends itself to concealment because of its overlap with legitimate research and commercial biotechnology. The technologies used to prolong our lives and improve our standard of living can quite easily be adapted to cause mass casualties.

The terrorist threat in the modern world goes well beyond Al Qaeda. The situation in the Middle East continues to fuel terrorism and anti-US sentiment worldwide, but other Western nations are not immune to the threat. Groups like the Palestine Islamic Jihad and Hamas have escalated their violence and have attracted support from radical secular Palestinian groups. There is increasingly a convergence of common interest among anti-Western and anti-democratic elements in striking at Europe and America.

The war on terrorism may have crippled Al Qaeda and its leadership and the group seems no longer able to run large-scale training and recruitment programs in Afghanistan. Yet the group remains dispersed throughout the world, certainly entrenched in some societies, and retains the loyalty of a fanatical cadre. This cadre is willing to use violence against those who do not share their religious fervor and it heeds what it believes to be the voice of God as interpreted by charismatic fanatics such as Bin Laden.

Poverty, alienation, territorial occupation and ethnic and religious tensions are factors that terrorist groups exploit, and these conditions may grow more acute over the next decade. This will especially be the case in those parts of the world that have served as the most fertile recruiting grounds for Islamic extremist groups. We have already seen–in Afghanistan and elsewhere–that domestic unrest and conflict in weak states is one of the factors that create an environment conducive to terrorism.

Importantly, demographic trends suggest that the world's poorest and most politically unstable regions–which include parts of the Middle East and Sub-Saharan Africa–will have the largest youth populations in the world over the next two decades and beyond.

Most of these countries will lack the economic institutions or resources to effectively integrate these youth into society. One of the places where they converge that has the greatest long-term impact on any society is its educational system. Primary and secondary education in parts of the Muslim world is often dominated by an interpretation of Islam that teaches intolerance and hatred. The graduates of these schools–"Madrassas" –provide the foot soldiers for many of the Islamic militant groups that operate throughout the Muslim world. The current conflict between Israel and the Palestinians has been raging for almost a year and a half and has been deteriorating.

The peace seekers are difficult to find. The violence has hardened the public's positions on both sides and increased the longstanding animosity between Israeli Prime Minister Sharon and Palestinian leader Yasser Arafat. Moderates on both sides admit that ultimately the conflict can only be resolved through negotiations.

But there is an absence of any meaningful security cooperation between Israel and the Palestinian Authority, there is escalating and uncontrolled militancy by the Islamic Jihad and Hamas, and there is an increasingly harsh and repressive occupation inflicted by the Israeli military over Palestinian territories. All this makes any meaningful progress extremely difficult. In this environment there are many opportunities for state sponsors of terrorism to escalate the violence and for terrorist groups to appeal for support from a wider audience.

3

Alleged Nuclear Terrorism Attempts and Plans

In June 2002, U.S. citizen Jose Padilla was arrested for allegedly planning a radiological attack on the city of Chicago; however, he was never charged with such conduct. He was instead convicted of charges that he conspired to "murder, kidnap and maim" people overseas. In November 2006, MI5 warned that al-Qaida were planning on using nuclear weapons against cities in the United Kingdom by obtaining the bombs via clandestine means.

In June 2007, the FBI released to the press the name of Adnan Gulshair el Shukrijumah, allegedly the operations leader for developing tactical plans for detonating nuclear bombs in several American cities simultaneously. The Alexander Litvinenko poisoning with radioactive polonium "represents an ominous landmark: the beginning of an era of nuclear terrorism," according to Andrew J. Patterson. Security specialist Shaun Gregory argued in an chapter that terrorists have attacked Pakistani nuclear facilities three times in the recent past; twice in 2007 and once in 2008.

OBAMA ADMINISTRATION

Nuclear weapons materials on the black market are a global concern, and there is concern about the possible detonation of a small, crude nuclear weapon by a terrorist group, in a major U.S. city, with significant loss of life and property. The Obama administration says they will focus on reducing the risk of such nuclear threats and aims to strengthen homeland nuclear security.".

Pakistan

After several incidents in Pakistan in which terrorists attacked three of its military nuclear facilities it became clear that there emerged a serious danger that they would gain access to the country's nuclear arsenal, according to a journal published by the US Military Academy at West Point. In January 2010 it was revealed that the US army was training a specialised unit *"to seal off and snatch back"* Pakistani nuclear weapons in the event that militants would obtain a nuclear device or materials that could make one. Pakistan supposedly possesses about 80 nuclear warheads. US officials refused to speak on the record about the American safety plans.

Recovering Lost Weapons & Material

In August 2002, the United States launched a program to track and secure enriched uranium from 24 Soviet-style reactors in 16 countries, in order to reduce the risk of the materials falling into the hands of terrorists or "rogue states". The first such operation was *Project Vinca,* "a multinational, public-private effort to remove nuclear material from a poorly secured Yugoslav research institute." The project has been hailed as "a nonproliferation success story" with the "potential to inform broader 'global cleanout' efforts to address one of the weakest links in the nuclear nonproliferation chain: insufficiently secured civilian nuclear research facilities."

In order to reduce the danger of attacks using nuclear waste material, European Union Commissioner Loyola de Palacio suggested in November 2002 the creation of common standards in the European Union, especially in the new member states operating Soviet-era reactors, for subterranean nuclear waste disposal. In November 2007, burglars with unknown intentions infiltrated the Pelindaba nuclear research facility near Pretoria, South Africa. The burglars escaped without acquiring any of the uranium held at the facility.

NUCLEAR SECURITY AND THE PROTECTION AGAINST NUCLEAR TERRORISM

With nuclear proliferation concerns as a backdrop, the security of nuclear and other radioactive material has taken on dramatically heightened significance in recent years. The IAEA has been active in the field of nuclear security for many years, but as you are all aware, the events of September 2001 propelled the rapid and dramatic re-evaluation of the risks of terrorism in all its forms — whether related to the security of urban centers, sports arenas, industrial complexes, harbors and waterways, oil refineries, air and rail travel, or nuclear and radiological activities. For those of us in the nuclear sphere, it became rapidly apparent that "the lesson of Chernobyl", in the safety sphere, should be applied to security as well: that is, that nuclear security should be urgently strengthened, without waiting for a "watershed" nuclear security event to provide the impetus for needed security upgrades.

International cooperation has become the hallmark of these security efforts. While nuclear security is and should remain a national responsibility, some countries still lack the programmes and the resources to respond properly to the threat of nuclear and radiological terrorism. International efforts are focused both on assisting these countries in strengthening their programmes, and on building regional and global networks for combating transnational threats.

Understanding the Threats

The IAEA has categorized four potential nuclear security threats (or, more accurately, nuclear security risks): the acquisition of nuclear weapons by theft; the creation of nuclear explosive devices using stolen nuclear materials; the use of radioactive sources in radiological dispersal devices (RDDs); and the radiological hazards caused by an attack on, or sabotage of, a facility or a transport vehicle. The threat of nuclear terrorism is real and current. Some experts share the view of the Director General of the United Kingdom Security Service, who said in August 2003: "It will only be a matter of time before a crude version of a [chemical, biological, radiological or nuclear] attack is launched at a major Western city." To date, the IAEA's own database on illicit trafficking has recorded, since 1993, approximately 630 confirmed incidents of trafficking in nuclear or other radioactive material. Sixty incidents were reported in 2003, and it is clear that the total for this year will be even higher. While the majority of trafficking incidents do not involve nuclear material, and while most of the radioactive sources involved are of limited radiological concern, the number of incidents shows that the measures to control and secure nuclear and other radioactive materials need to be improved. They also show that measures to detect and respond to illicit trafficking are essential.

A strategy to counter the potential threats needs to be comprehensive. It must encompass not only power and research reactors and their related fuel cycle facilities; not only waste storage sites and vehicles used in domestic and international transport; but also relevant research and academic institutions; and agricultural, industrial and medical institutions and applications where nuclear or radioactive materials are involved. This is a tall order.

Asia and the Pacific Region

In Asia and the Pacific region, interest has been expanding in a broad range of nuclear technologies. The reliance on nuclear power as a source of electricity is already substantial, with well established programmes in China (including Taiwan, China), Japan, the Republic of Korea, India and Pakistan — and when compared to any region in the world, Asia holds the strongest current growth market for nuclear power. In addition, more than 50 research reactors and accelerators are operating in 15 Asian countries. Nuclear applications are also playing a strong role in development. Nuclear and isotopic techniques are being used, inter alia: to diagnose and treat cancer patients; to study and improve child nutrition; to produce higher yielding, disease resistant crops; to manage drinking water supplies; to eradicate disease-bearing pests; to increase industrial productivity; and to help address many other development issues.

Effective and credible national and regional approaches to security are therefore essential — not only for nuclear power plants, but also for research reactors, accelerators, and the ubiquitous array of radioactive sources that support these nuclear applications. To optimize the effectiveness of these efforts, it will be important for efforts to be prioritized by focusing on those facilities where the risk is greatest — and to maintain a balance between security needs and the many peaceful applications of nuclear technology. For example, the recent increase in the denial of shipments of radioactive material, while driven by perceived security issues, can be a matter of significant humanitarian concern — particularly when such shipments involve radionuclides intended for use in medical applications. While we should be strongly focused on ensuring the security of nuclear and other radioactive materials globally, we should equally seek solutions that will ensure the continued delivery of the benefits that these materials and related applications provide.

For nuclear installations such as nuclear power plants and fuel cycle facilities, it is also important to understand how safety and security aspects come together in the identification and protection of vulnerabilities. The IAEA has increasingly been asked to provide guidance on how to reconcile the need for transparency, in matters of nuclear and radiation safety, with the need for confidentiality, from a security perspective. Effective risk management requires striking a balance that protects the security of sensitive information while ensuring that safety concerns are addressed in a transparent manner, and that lessons learned, relating to both safety and security, are shared for the benefit of the entire nuclear community.

IAEA Nuclear Security Plan of Activities

The IAEA's nuclear security plan is founded on measures to guard against thefts of material and to protect related facilities against malicious acts. Our work has three main points of focus: *prevention, detection and response*. Our first objective is to assist States in *preventing* any illicit or non-peaceful use of nuclear or other radioactive materials — including acts of terrorism. This requires: effective physical protection of these materials in use, storage and transport; protection of related nuclear facilities; strong State programmes for accounting and control of nuclear material; and continued efforts to convert research reactors to use low enriched uranium — as the necessary funding and technological solutions become available.

The IAEA has been providing a range of international advisory service missions — as well as training workshops — on nuclear security, physical protection, "design basis threat" assessments, and nuclear material accounting, to assist States in these prevention measures. In Asia and the Pacific region, this has included advisory missions in China, Indonesia, Malaysia and the Philippines, as well as many national and regional training courses on nuclear security topics. The Agency's technical guidance documents provide the foundations for many of these preventive measures.

A *preventive* focus has also been given to finding and securing vulnerable nuclear and other radioactive material. Working with Russia and the United States, 15 missions were conducted just last year in 11 countries of the former Soviet Union, to identify and secure high activity disused sources. Over 20 000 curies of sealed sources from Bolivia, Cote d'Ivoire, Haiti, the Islamic Republic of Iran, Malaysia, Sudan and Thailand have been conditioned for long term storage or shipped back to the original suppliers. We expect the volume of these and other high priority assistance efforts to increase.

The second objective relates to *detection* — ensuring that we have systems in place that can help countries to identify, at an early stage, illicit activity related to nuclear materials or radioactive sources. To this end, we have been assisting countries from many regions in training customs officials, installing better equipment at border crossings, and ensuring that information on trafficking incidents is shared effectively. The Agency database on illicit trafficking, now with a total of 80 participating countries, has proven helpful in identifying patterns of trafficking activity.

Third, we have been working with national governments and international organizations to ensure that, in the event that illicit activity occurs — including acts of terrorism involving nuclear material or radioactive sources — we can *respond*rapidly and cooperatively. To date, most such responses have involved helping governments with the recovery of radioactive sources.

The bulk of this activity has occurred in the past three years, progressing at an exceptionally fast pace on multiple fronts. Since September 2001, working in Europe, Asia, Latin America and

Africa, we have conducted more than 50 security advisory and evaluation missions, and convened more than 60 training courses, workshops and seminars.

And in an effort relevant to all three areas of focus — prevention, detection and response — the IAEA has strengthened its own cooperation with relevant international and regional organizations, such as Interpol, Europol, OSCE, the Universal Postal Union, the World Customs Organization and specialized United Nations Agencies.

IAEA Member States have been very supportive in providing financial and in-kind resources to fund the Agency's security related activities.

Australia, Japan and the Republic of Korea have contributed significant sums to the Agency's Nuclear Security Fund, and China´s recent pledge of extrabudgetary funding includes provisions for supporting nuclear security. Throughout Asia and the Pacific, IAEA Member States have hosted workshops and regional training courses, participated in source recovery missions, provided technical insights on how engineered safety features at nuclear facilities can enhance security against sabotage, and contributed to the development of Agency guidelines and recommendations.

NUCLEAR NON-PROLIFERATION TREATY

At present, 189 countries are States Parties to the *Treaty on the Nonproliferation of Nuclear Weapons,* more commonly known as the Nuclear Nonproliferation Treaty or NPT. These include the five Nuclear Weapons States (NWS) recognized by the NPT: the People's Republic of China, France, Russian Federation, the UK, and the United States.

Notable non-signatories to the NPT are Israel, Pakistan, and India (the latter two have since tested nuclear weapons, while Israel is considered by most to be an unacknowledged nuclear weapons state). North Korea was once a signatory but withdrew in January 2003. The legality of North Korea's withdrawal is debatable but as of 9 October 2006, North Korea clearly possesses the capability to make a nuclear explosive device.

International Atomic Energy Agency

The IAEA was established on 29 July 1957 to help nations develop nuclear energy for peaceful purposes. Allied to this role is the administration of safeguards arrangements to provide assurance to the international community that individual countries are honouring their commitments under the treaty. Though established under its own international treaty, the IAEA reports to both the United Nations General Assembly and the Security Council.

The IAEA regularly inspects civil nuclear facilities to verify the accuracy of documentation supplied to it. The agency checks inventories, and samples and analyses materials. Safeguards are designed to deter diversion of nuclear material by increasing the risk of early detection. They are complemented by controls on the export of sensitive technology from countries such as UK and United States through voluntary bodies such as the Nuclear Suppliers Group. The main concern of the IAEA is that uranium not be enriched beyond what is necessary for commercial civil plants, and that plutonium which is produced by nuclear reactors not be refined into a form that would be suitable for bomb production.

Scope of Safeguards

Traditional safeguards are arrangements to account for and control the use of nuclear materials. This verification is a key element in the international system which ensures that uranium in particular is used only for peaceful purposes.

Parties to the NPT agree to accept technical safeguard measures applied by the IAEA. These require that operators of nuclear facilities maintain and declare detailed accounting records of all movements and transactions involving nuclear material. Over 550 facilities and several hundred other locations are subject to regular inspection, and their records and the nuclear material being audited. Inspections by the IAEA are complemented by other measures such as surveillance cameras and instrumentation. The inspections act as an alert system providing a warning of the possible diversion of nuclear material from peaceful activities. The system relies on;

1. Material Accountancy-tracking all inward and outward transfers and the flow of materials in any nuclear facility. This includes sampling and analysis of nuclear material, on-site inspections, and review and verification of operating records.
2. Physical Security-restricting access to nuclear materials at the site.
3. Containment and Surveillance-use of seals, automatic cameras and other instruments to detect unreported movement or tampering with nuclear materials, as well as spot checks on-site.

All NPT non-weapons states must accept these full-scope safeguards. In the five weapons states plus the non-NPT states (India, Pakistan and Israel), facility-specific safeguards apply. IAEA inspectors regularly visit these facilities to verify completeness and accuracy of records.

The terms of the NPT cannot be enforced by the IAEA itself, nor can nations be forced to sign the treaty. In reality, as shown in Iraq and North Korea, safeguards can be backed up by diplomatic, political and economic measures.

While traditional safeguards easily verified the correctness of formal declarations by suspect states, in the 1990s attention turned to what might not have been declared. While accepting safeguards at declared facilities, Iraq had set up elaborate equipment elsewhere in an attempt to enrich uranium to weapons grade. North Korea attempted to use research reactors (not commercial electricity-generating reactors) and a reprocessing plant to produce some weapons-grade plutonium. The weakness of the NPT regime lay in the fact that no obvious diversion of material was involved.

The uranium used as fuel probably came from indigenous sources, and the nuclear facilities were built by the countries themselves without being declared or placed under safeguards. Iraq, as an NPT party, was obliged to declare all facilities but did not do so. Nevertheless, the activities were detected and brought under control using international diplomacy. In Iraq, a military defeat assisted this process. In North Korea, the activities concerned took place before the conclusion of its NPT safeguards agreement.

With North Korea, the promised provision of commercial power reactors appeared to resolve the situation for a time, but it later withdrew from the NPT and declared it had nuclear weapons.

Additional Protocol

In 1993 a program was initiated to strengthen and extend the classical safeguards system, and a model protocol was agreed by the IAEA Board of Governors 1997. The measures boosted the IAEA's ability to detect undeclared nuclear activities, including those with no connection to the civil fuel cycle. Innovations were of two kinds. Some could be implemented on the basis of IAEA's existing legal authority through safeguards agreements and inspections. Others required further legal authority to be conferred through an Additional Protocol. This must be agreed by each non-weapons state with IAEA, as a supplement to any existing comprehensive safeguards agreement. Weapons states have agreed to accept the principles of the model additional protocol.

Key elements of the model Additional Protocol:

- The IAEA is to be given considerably more information on nuclear and nuclear-related activities, including R & D, production of uranium and thorium (regardless of whether it is traded), and nuclear-related imports and exports.
- IAEA inspectors will have greater rights of access. This will include any suspect location, it can be at short notice (e.g., two hours), and the IAEA can deploy environmental sampling and remote monitoring techniques to detect illicit activities.
- States must streamline administrative procedures so that IAEA inspectors get automatic visa renewal and can communicate more readily with IAEA headquarters.
- Further evolution of safeguards is towards evaluation of each state, taking account of its particular situation and the kind of nuclear materials it has. This will involve greater judgement on the part of IAEA and the development of effective methodologies which reassure NPT States.

As of 9 October 2008, 127 countries have signed Additional protocols, and 88 have brought them into force. The IAEA is also applying the measures of the Additional Protocol in Taiwan. Among the leading countries that have not signed the Additional Protocol are Egypt, which says it will not sign until Israel accepts comprehensive IAEA safeguards, and Brazil, which opposes making the protocol a requirement for international cooperation on enrichment and reprocessing, but has not ruled out signing.

Limitations of Safeguards

The greatest risk from nuclear weapons proliferation comes from countries which have not joined the NPT and which have significant unsafeguarded nuclear activities; India, Pakistan, and Israel fall within this category. While safeguards apply to some of their activities, others remain beyond scrutiny.

A further concern is that countries may develop various sensitive nuclear fuel cycle facilities and research reactors under full safeguards and then subsequently opt out of the NPT. Bilateral agreements, such as insisted upon by Australia and Canada for sale of uranium, address this by including fallback provisions, but many countries are outside the scope of these agreements. If a nuclear-capable country does leave the NPT, it is likely to be reported by the IAEA to the UN Security Council, just as if it were in breach of its safeguards agreement. Trade sanctions would then be likely. IAEA safeguards, together with bilateral safeguards applied under the NPT can, and do, ensure that uranium supplied by countries such as Australia and Canada does not contribute to nuclear weapons proliferation. In fact, the worldwide application of those safeguards and the substantial world trade in uranium for nuclear electricity make the proliferation of nuclear weapons much less likely.

The Additional Protocol, once it is widely in force, will provide credible assurance that there are no undeclared nuclear materials or activities in the states concerned. This will be a major step forward in preventing nuclear proliferation.

Other Developments

The Nuclear Suppliers Group communicated its guidelines, essentially a set of export rules, to the IAEA in 1978. These were to ensure that transfers of nuclear material or equipment would not be diverted to unsafeguarded nuclear fuel cycle or nuclear explosive activities, and formal government assurances to this effect were required from recipients. The Guidelines also recognised the need for physical protection measures in the transfer of sensitive facilities, technology and weapons-usable materials, and strengthened retransfer provisions. The group began with seven members – the United States, the former USSR, the UK, France, Germany, Canada and Japan – but now includes 46 countries including all five nuclear weapons states.

According to Kenneth D. Bergeron's *Tritium on Ice: The Dangerous New Alliance of Nuclear Weapons and Nuclear Power*, tritium is not classified as a 'special nuclear material' but rather as a 'by-product'. It is seen as an important litmus test on the seriousness of the United States' intention to nuclear disarm. This radioactive super-heavy hydrogen isotope is used to boost the efficiency of fissile materials in nuclear weapons. The United States resumed tritium production in 2003 for the first time in 15 years. This could indicate that there is a potential nuclear arm stockpile replacement since the isotope naturally decays.

In May 1995, NPT parties reaffirmed their commitment to a Fissile Materials Cut-off Treaty to prohibit the production of any further fissile material for weapons. This aims to complement the Comprehensive Test Ban Treaty of 1996 and to codify commitments made by the United States, the UK, France and Russia to cease production of weapons material, as well as putting a similar ban on China. This treaty will also put more pressure on Israel, India and Pakistan to agree to international verification.

On 9 August 2005, Ayatollah Ali Khamenei issued a fatwa forbidding the production, stockpiling and use of nuclear weapons. Khamenei's official statement was made at the meeting of the International Atomic Energy Agency (IAEA) in Vienna. As of February 2006 Iran formally announced that uranium enrichment within their borders has continued. Iran claims it is for peaceful purposes but the United Kingdom, France, Germany, and the United States claim the purpose is for nuclear weapons research and construction.

NUCLEAR JIHAD

However, in sharp contrast with the optimism and confidence of the "Indian-and-Pakistani-states-as-rational-actors" proponents, the anti-state actors could care less if nuclear prevention breaks down and results in large-scale and unprecedented death and destruction. To understand their perspective in its proper context, a brief historical overview is in order before we examine the views and impact of anti-state actors on nuclear prevention in South Asia.

Much like other worldwide ideologies, Islam and its followers also divide the world into two regions: the world of believers, *Dar-ul-Islam*, or the House of Islam, and *Dar-ul-Harb*, or the House of Infidels and non-believers containing all territories ruled by non-Muslims, against whom no-holds-barred jihad is to be waged by the believers (true followers of Islam) who are destined to dominate and rule over the non-believers. Such concepts promote ideas of "us versus them" and generate hatred, hostility, enmity and a permanent state of war. Interestingly, this concept of continuous struggle (holy war against non-believers) bears remarkable resemblance to Mao's concept of permanent revolution against his perceived enemies—rightists and capitalists—during the Great Proletarian Cultural Revolution (1967–76) in China. The division of the world into two blocs is also similar to the one made by the followers of other totalitarian ideologies—Fascism and Communism—which ruled out peaceful coexistence with other belief systems. As Cathy Young observes: "Perhaps every belief system that lays claim to the ultimate truth carries the seeds of violent fanaticism and intolerance. This is true not only of religions but of secular ideologies such as Communism." The Islamists see the growing economic interdependence, globalization, Western cultural penetration, and the notions of liberty (freedom of speech, expression, and movement) and equality (especially equality of religions and sexes) as posing a serious threat to the basic tenets of Islam.

Historically, jihad in the Indian subcontinent was primarily waged against Hindus, Sikhs and Buddhists and later against the Christians during and after the British rule. In the nineteenth century, Sayyid Ahmad Barelvi took the struggle one step further and launched an "eternal jihad" against *kafirs* (infidels) with his call to Muslims: "Fill the uttermost ends of India with Islam, so that no sounds may be heard but Allah Allah Allah!" The long-term objective of Islamists is to spread the frontiers of Islam eastward to the whole continent of Asia and beyond. During the 1980s and 1990s, Afghanistan and Pakistan became the jihadis' destination of choice, as Islamist warriors coalesced in the two countries to battle the enemies of the faith (first the Soviet Union, then the United States, Israel, and India). As noted earlier, Saudi Arabia, in its self-appointed mission to protect and promote Islam, especially the puritanical Wahabi version, has been providing much of the financial and ideological support to religious schools, charities and organizations around the world at which students are taught to develop their hatred for non-believers such as Christians, Jews and Hindus. They are taught that Islam cannot coexist with other religions and that to kill in the interests of Islam and the Shariat is a religious obligation and not a sin, even if the killing involves the use of WMD. Verse 191, Sura 2, of the Holy Quran explicitly enjoins upon the Ummah to punish enemies of the faith in this fashion: "And slay them wherever ye catch them, and turn them out from where they have turned you out." Coupled with "the Medina Syndrome" (the perception that Islam is perennially in danger from powerful enemies), the only answer for pious Muslims in despair is "unity, faith and war." To put it simply, solidarity for jihad and jihad for solidarity. As Therese Delpech observes:

> Their declared ambition is to annihilate not just religions other than Islam (the destruction of the ancient Bamiyan's Buddhist statutes in February 2001 is an eloquent testimony), but also anyone who does not accept its perverse version of Islam (bin Laden's people have burnt Shi'ites alive in Afghanistan)...No concession, however great, would be enough to end [their] "mission" because, unlike many previous terrorist organizations, *it does not intend to create a state nor does it wish to introduce political reforms. Its objective is metaphysical: a titanic struggle between "good" and "evil" forces, in which any means can be used to achieve the end.*

In the India-Pakistan context, the Islamists argue that Kashmir is a symbol, not the root cause of the India-Pakistan conflict. They point to General Parvez Musharraf 's statement made as the Chief of Army Staff in April 1999: "Even a settlement of the Kashmir issue will not usher in peace in the region.

Low intensity conflict against India will continue because India is a large hegemonic power." This reinforces the view that the India-Pakistan conflict is rooted in history, religion, culture, and the politics of revenge, epitomizing clashing worldviews and a divide along religious, civilizational fault lines.

Many Islamists are convinced that India, like its erstwhile friends, the Soviet Union and Yugoslavia, is doomed to further partition and Balkanization. In the aftermath of the Soviet collapse in the early 1990s, there was great optimism in Pakistan about "the coming collapse of India," which would enable the creation of a large Islamic state in Central and South Asia with Pakistan as its core.

The leader of *Jamaat-i-Islami* Pakistan, Qazi Hussain Ahmad, speaking in Rawalpindi in February 1992, declared, "a great Islamic State spreading from Kashmir to Central Asia would emerge after the independence of Kashmir." Islamists contend that Prophet Muhammed is said to have singled out India as a special target for jihad—the land of idol worshippers: "Slay the idolaters wheresoever you find them" (Sura 9:5). "Whosoever will take part in jihad against India," *Markaz* leader Muhammad Ibrahim Salafi claims that the Prophet had declared, "Allah will set him free from the pyre of hell."

Interestingly, notwithstanding their conflicting perspectives and interests, both Hindu and Islamist fundamentalists seem to have an identical interpretation of Indian history: that the ultimate game plan is not limited to "liberating Kashmir" but to subsume "Hindu India" into Islamic civilization. In this context, they point out that Zulfiqar Ali Bhutto's threat in 1971 of a thousand-year war with Hindustan (repeated by his daughter at the height of the 1990 crisis) was not hyperbole. Since the beginning of the second millennium, Hindu India has been subjected to repeated invasions by the armies of Islamic faith. As a result of Islam's eastward march over the last one thousand years, ancient India has already been successfully broken up into four states—Afghanistan, Pakistan, Bangladesh and India. Hopefully in another one thousand years, so the argument goes, the objective of either an Islamic India or the creation of more Islamic states will be achieved by the end of the third millennium.

Indians oppose this by saying that their country, one of the oldest civilizations in the world, has not only survived but thrived during millennia of invasions, whereas Pakistan could not survive the first twenty-five years of its existence and is unlikely to survive over the next twenty-five years if it continues with its self-destructive policies. The Islamists respond by saying that Ghauri and Ghaznavi may have lost war several times but they won eventually to subjugate Hindu India. Likewise, Pakistan may have lost to India in 1971 and 1999 but that does not mean the end of their attempts to expand Islam's frontiers eastwards. Islam, *if not Pakistan,* will eventually prevail. To this end, "pro-*jihadi* cells" armed with weapons are being established throughout India's minority regions ready to unleash terror and communal bloodbath at an appropriate time in the future when India is faced with a series of domestic crises and/or external aggression and is headed by a weak leader (in the mold of Indonesia's B. J. Habibie) unable to resist international pressure. Islamists also note that Pakistan still draws inspiration from the medieval period when Muslim warriors from Afghanistan used to invade ancient India, evident by the fact that all of its nuclear-capable ballistic missiles— Ghauri, Ghaznavi and Abdali—are named after the three prominent Afghan warlords who attacked India frequently between the eleventh and eighteenth centuries in an attempt to expand their empires. As Zaffar Abbas notes: "he symbolism highlights the official mindset in the country. For Islamabad, the present conflict with India is a continuation of the battles of the past, wars that are described in Pakistani history books as the just causes of Muslim invaders against infidels."

From the perspective of Hindu nationalists, nothing could be more provocative than Pakistanis (including Bhattys, Chaudharys, Dhillons, Khokars, Naiks, Ranas, Shahs, Sethis, among others) seeing themselves as "direct descendants" of Muslim invaders and plunderers (such as Ghauris, Ghaznavis, Abdalis and Babbars who looted Lahore, Multan, and laid waste to the cities in Sindh—all now in Pakistan) and wanting to wage a no-holds-barred holy war.

In Hindutva's discourse, Islamic religion and people are portrayed as intolerant, hostile to Hindu values, proselytizing, expansionist, repressive, and violent. The Indian response is articulated by a former chief of the Indian Army: "If a nuclear war can bring an end to the thousand years of invasions of India by the armies of Islamic faith, so be it.

Let's fight a nuclear war and destroy Pakistan once and for all." Apparently, both countries have become infected with the virus of religious-based nationalism, increasing the "death or glory" spirit within their armed forces.

For their part, right-wing Hindu nationalists have also not given up their dream of regaining the "lost territories" ("the sacred lands of Hinduism and Buddhism lost to Islam during the second millennium," as the *Vishwa Hindu Parishad* or World Hindu Council puts it) and restoring the Hindu supremacy over the entire *Akhand Bharat* (Undivided India). The growing ascendancy of Hindutva forces in Indian politics is an indication of the radicalization of Indian society as a result of a two-decade long, Pakistan-backed proxy war.

Meanwhile, Islamist extremism continues to haunt Pakistani state and society. Pakistan is, in the words of former Italian foreign minister Gianni De Michelis, "the fuse of the world." The provinces close to the Afghan border and home to the U.S. armed bases are now controlled by Islamist parties that created the Taliban and are openly sympathetic to the aims and ideals of al-Qaeda.

The concern is that the radical Islamist worldview of groups like the *Jamiat Ulema Islam*, which is supportive of both the Taliban and al-Qaeda, could become the country's leitmotif.

Violence levels in Indian Kashmir also continue to rise. Many observers believe that Washington may have to rethink its strategy vis-à-vis Islamabad if the war on terrorism is to be won decisively.

The complete dismantling of the al-Qaeda terrorist infrastructure in Pakistan seems unlikely because of the apprehension within Pakistani armed that doing so would devalue Pakistan's importance in the U.S. security strategy and once again make the United States turn its back on the country and make the country vulnerable to Western pressure and sanctions over Islamabad's WMD proliferation activities. It would also deprive Pakistan of invaluable Western aid and leverage vis-à-vis Washington and New Delhi.

As long as anti-state actors donate to to the "Islamic Caliphate" and Pakistan to the two-nation theory, and as long as political power in Pakistan is exercised by the army, the mullahs, and the feudal lords in the name of jihad, Islam, and Kashmir, there cannot be peace in the region.

A noted author and commentator, M.J. Akbar, in his book, *The Shade of Swords,* concedes that Pakistan's anger against India is larger than the problem over Kashmir, but contends that the anger of the "Muslim Street" is not merely socio-economic, as some are positing. Muslim anguish is essentially about departed glory, contrasted to Hindu resurgence after one thousand years and Jewish revival after two thousand years backed by the secular, but Christian, West. As has often happened in the past, Muslim radicals have latched on to certain enemies to explain the current decay because they need someone to blame, apart from themselves.

This partly explains why and how Pakistan, a homeland for Muslims, "turned jihad into an instrument of state policy from its inception and became the breeding ground for the first international Islamic brigade in the modern era."

The fall of the Taliban has transformed the frontline state of Pakistan in the war on terrorism into its next battlefield, as fleeing al-Qaeda/Taliban jihadis and their supporters take refuge in Pakistan's Wild West with many slipping down into the cities, using networks of associated groups and sympathizers to reorganize to fight another battle another day. The Islamist fundamentalist groups have repeatedly demonstrated their power with a series of terrorist attacks in

India and Pakistan seen as warnings to Musharraf that abandoning militants in Kashmir and siding with the infidel West would have disastrous consequences. In the worst-case scenario, radical Islamic extremists, especially those who sympathize with al-Qaeda in the armed establishment, could gain control of the nuclear weapons and delivery systems and launch nuclear strikes.

The threatened use of nuclear weapons by irrational anti-state actors will carry greater credibility than the threatened use of nuclear weapons by nation-states.

India's nuclear deterrent can deter neither nuclear attacks nor cross-border terrorism conducted by anti-state actors. Interestingly, one perceptive commentator has argued that in Pakistan's destruction lies al-Qaeda's salvation because anti-state actors can survive and thrive only in failed, collapsed and war-torn states:

[Since] al-Qaeda has long used Pakistan as an ongoing base for its command and control and training functions, it has a deep interest in Pakistan's future. Paradoxically, al-Qaeda's and Pakistan's national security interests are not at all the same. From al-Qaeda's point of view, a war with India—even one that led to the destruction of an independent Pakistan— would be highly desirable for three reasons:

1. As al-Qaeda sees it, the government of President Pervez Musharraf has become a tool of the United States, supporting U.S. efforts to destroy al-Qaeda in Pakistan. While Musharraf 's support has been far from wholehearted, al-Qaeda is aware that Musharraf cannot be relied upon to protect the network, particularly while under heavy pressure from the United States and India.
2. A stable Pakistan with a strong central government poses a threat to al-Qaeda's security [because] a strong government is less manipulable ...[and] less predictable. It can turn its power against al-Qaeda quite easily. *A Pakistan whose armed has been smashed and whose government ceases to function creates a situation in which al-Qaeda can stake out* and defend remote areas of the country from encroachment. From a geographic point of view, India has the ability to smash Pakistan. Occupying and pacifying the country, particularly the regions that al-Qaeda uses for its bases, is far more difficult...With an Indian army stretched to the

limit and no meaningful Pakistani force to face, al-Qaeda becomes more secure. Even U.S. operations against al-Qaeda in remote areas without Pakistani collaboration would become extremely difficult.

3. Al-Qaeda has, as its core argument, the idea that Islam is under attack from other religions. *If India were to attack Pakistan, al-Qaeda would be able to make the argument—convincingly in the Islamic world—that the Jews, the Christian West and the Hindus have allied to strangle Islam.* The plausibility of this argument would, al-Qaeda hopes, galvanize the Islamic world into united resistance. That unification is al-Qaeda's goal.

From al-Qaeda's viewpoint, an Indian attack on Pakistan would be highly desirable. *Even an attack involving nuclear weapons would be acceptable…That is why Pakistani-based Islamic militants aligned with al-Qaeda have persistently exacerbated the crisis between the two countries. In the long run, they see a war, even one that is ruinous to Pakistan, as an acceptable price to pay for their ultimate goals.* What is unacceptable is a settlement between India and Pakistan that would leave the United States in a dominant position in both countries as broker and arbiter. Islamic militants have done everything possible to foment a conflict.

The perspectives and interests of state and anti-state actors and this, in turn, makes India-Pakistan nuclear prevention highly unstable.

In fact, the two frameworks are so markedly different that mere institution of confidence-building measures alone will not address the problem.

None of the political, technical or situational conditions identified by Lewis Dunn apply to anti-state actors. Thus, the entry of anti-state actors makes the situational context vastly different from that of the Cold War era. Undoubtedly, the greatest disruption to the equilibrium of the nuclear balance of terror emanates from anti-state actors that may come to acquire "a level of power and technological sophistication once associated only with nation-states." The multinational mercenary terror network that al-Qaeda and others have assembled could be regarded as a malignant and mutated form of the "virtual state" that requires a reconsideration of conventional strategies of prevention based on retaliation.

The traditional theories of prevention may apply to other states but certainly do not apply to anti-state actors and rogue regimes. Nuclear weapons were never meant to deter transnational terrorists. Religious zealots bent on martyrdom have turned on its head a nuclear doctrine that was based on the deterrent value of mutually assured destruction.

4

Role of Nuclear Weapons in Terrorism

There's a strong connection between the maintenance of nuclear weapons in state arsenals and the risk of nuclear terrorism. Terrorists cannot build a nuclear weapon from scratch; they can't make the core of the bomb—the highly enriched uranium or plutonium required for the device. That requires massive factories and billions of dollars of investment plus Giga-Watts of energy.

But if they can get the material from a state that's already built it, or a bomb itself, then it's relatively easy for them to construct a primitive Hiroshima style device, smuggle it into an urban centre, and detonate it.

We know that Al-Qaeda is trying to do this. We know that Osama Bin Laden had meetings with Pakistani nuclear scientists in the months before 9/11. We know that Al-Qaeda has tried to buy highly enriched uranium and was foiled only when the purchase turned out to be a scam. We know that clerics within the Al-Qaeda movement have issued fatwa declaring it the duty of Muslims to acquire a nuclear weapon to strike back at the United States and other countries. So they are trying to do this. If the countries with nuclear weapons and nuclear weapons materials insist on keeping large stockpiles of these weapons and materials around, it's only a matter of time before the demand hooks up with the source. Many experts believe that if we keep on with our current policies, there is a high likelihood of a nuclear terrorist incident within the next ten years.

We see that terrorist groups are looking for high-impact events now. This is the era we are in—an era of apocalyptic terrorism. Fortunately, they are still somewhat limited in their capability, so it is hard for them even to carry out a bomb attack on cargo planes, but they are trying. As long as conflicts in highly volatile regions such as the Middle East and South Asia continue, and as economic conditions make it difficult, particularly for young men, to find alternative and gainful employment, then you are going to see a steady supply of radicalised individuals coming into these terrorist movements. Some even join with some of the skills that are required in the modern era, particularly computer skills, engineering, physics and others that can be applied to these terrorist strategies. I expect to see an increase in cyber-warfare. I wouldn't be surprised to see it linked with attempts to steal nuclear material—that is, a cyber attack to shutdown the security fences at a facility, allowing a truck to enter and scoop-up radioactive material. I'm personally surprised that we have not seen the detonation of a so-called "dirty bomb," which is a conventional bomb that is laced with radioactive material and that produces not a nuclear explosion (*a mushroom cloud*), but a cloud of radioactive dust that could contaminate tens of blocks of a downtown area. That kind of weapon is relatively simple for a terrorist group to make. I would expect to see that kind of nuclear terrorist attack before we see a full-on Hiroshima style explosion.

POLITICAL LANDSCAPE

The reasons countries don't get nuclear weapons turn out to be the mirror-images of why they do. That is, there are one hundred and eighty three countries in the world that have signed the non-proliferation treaty, and promised never to acquire nuclear weapons.

Well, if nuclear weapons were so great, why would they make that pledge? They calculate that it's in their own security interests not to have weapons, and to make sure that none of their neighbours have nuclear weapons. They've decided that their prestige is enhanced by being a non-nuclear state rather than being a nuclear-weapons state.

So you see all the countries that have declared their continents to be a nuclear weapons free zone—nobody has nuclear weapons or programmes there. It's the same in Africa and several other key regions of the world. What you realise is that we have two phenomena that are still promoting the illusion that nuclear weapons can provide security or prestige.

We have the Cold War over-hang: these twenty two or so thousand nuclear weapons we have left over from the Cold War. And we have major areas of unresolved conflict that are still giving rise to proliferation imperatives—in order to protect myself from attack I need to have a nuclear weapon. You see this in the arc-of-crisis that runs from the Middle East through South Asia to North East Asia.

There aren't really nuclear concerns outside that arc-of-crisis and that tells you something about how you have to convince other countries not to get nuclear weapons. You have to resolve the underlying crises that might motivate them. The efforts to reduce the desire and drive for nuclear weapons have been so successful over the past few years that we have gotten rid of most of the aspiring states.

More countries have given up nuclear weapons or programmes in the past twenty-five years than have tried to acquire them, and that includes Brazil, Argentina, Ukraine, Belarus, Kazakhstan, South-Africa, Libya, and Iraq. All of whom either had nuclear programmes or actual weapons and have given them up. We are down to the last two hard cases: Iran and North Korea. And they are really hard, which is where the concern is. If you can stop the programmes there, you can largely resolve the proliferation problem—you can largely resolve the risk of new countries getting these weapons. If you fail, and those countries do acquire or solidify their status as nuclear states, what you will likely see is a cascade of proliferation as their neighbours hatch their capabilities. There would be great pressure on South Korea or Japan to match the capability of North Korea. In the Middle East it's even worse, with the rivals of Iran that would try to match whatever nuclear capability Iran acquired. That would mean Egypt, Turkey, Saudi-Arabia, and maybe the U.A.E seeking to acquire at least a nuclear weapons capability and maybe even the bomb itself. We are at a tipping point. It will go one way or the other.

The nuclear weapons capability of any state always link to the greater strategic needs of that state. This goes back to the first nuclear power, the United States, who acquired the weapon first to prevail in a war, but secondly as an element necessary to project U.S. power around the world and to protect the empire the U.S. had built during the fighting of World War II. You see that now in the debate over whether to get rid of nuclear weapons. One of the major reasons countries don't want to get rid of nuclear weapons, whether that be the United States, or Russia, or France is the fear that this would weaken them globally or that they would be seen as a weaker power and would lose their edge over other nuclear and non-nuclear powers. These weapons are therefore still tied very closely to elite views of what national power is. This is weakening and it is becoming a smaller and smaller component of the assessment of power, but it's still there.

Israel has had nuclear weapons since about 1968. Israel acquired them because it thought they were absolutely necessary for its survival as a nation and as a counter-balance to the superior military force of its neighbours who were trying to destroy Israel. The security threat was real and they saw this as part of the solution. As it turns out, Israel has now got more conventional military power than any of its neighbours or any combination of its neighbours and so nuclear weapons are less of a security need for Israel and more of a security threat. It's the one weapon that could destroy Israel. When we consider nuclear weapons within Israel's security, they have not served their main purpose of defending the country against attack; Israel has been attacked since it acquired nuclear weapons and it bears no relationships to their main threat, which is the conflict with Palestine. It's coming to the point where Israel has to considertaking its nuclear bombs out of the basement and putting them on the negotiating table, using its nuclear arsenal as a tool for negotiating a security arrangement that would prevent any country in the Middle East from getting the one weapon that would destroy Israel. That won't happen any time soon, but I think it would eventually have to.

Nuclear weapons still have a very powerful psychological role in Israel even though they don't serve a strategic purpose. If we can make progress towards resolving the Israeli/Palestinian crisis and containing the Iranian programme, then I think in talks aimed at establishing a new security regime in the Middle East where each country respects the territorial integrity of the other countries, you will have to talk about nuclear weapons and it will become more likely that Israel will be willing to bargain away an arsenal that no longer serves its purpose for a security regime that does.

NUCLEAR WEAPONRY SIT ALONGSIDE NUCLEAR

There's no question that it would be far easier to eliminate nuclear weapons if there were no nuclear power—if there were no commercial use of nuclear technology. As long as nuclear power exists, we have to make sure that it's controlled in such a way that it does not allow countries to acquire nuclear weapons under the guise of a peaceful civilian programme. The problem isn't the reactors, it's what goes into and comes out of the reactors. The same facilities that can enrich uranium to low levels for reactor fuel can enrich them to high levels for bombs. This is the problem we have with Iran. They are building an enrichment facility that they say is for fuel, but do you trust them? Do you trust any nation? The answer has got to be to put greater controls over the fuel cycle, either by international ownership of all the uranium enrichment and plutonium reprocessing facilities of the world, or through multi-national control in the way Europe does it, where three countries (UK, Germany, and the Netherlands) share control over enrichment so that no one country can use it for weapons purposes. This is the way we have to go. If nuclear power is going to play a role in solving one of the great global threats—global warming—we have to make sure that the process doesn't exacerbate the threat of nuclear weapons.

Nuclear Weapons to be Eliminated

The answer is very simple. As long as any nation has nuclear weapons, other nations will want them. This is a finding of the recent Australia-Japan commission, which picks up on a theme first articulated by the Canberra commission of 1995. It is what some people call the "proliferation imperative". If you believe that the threat of nuclear terrorism and new nuclear states is the number one security threat to your security as a nation, then you have to do everything in your power to reduce or eliminate that threat, and you have got to move towards a world with zero nuclear weapons. There is no way to ensure that other countries will not acquire the weapons to destroy you, if you insist on holding on to hundreds of those weapons yourself. If NATO, for example, as the most powerful military alliance in history, insists that nuclear weapons are essential to its security, then why aren't nuclear weapons essential for other countries? Why exactly can't Iran have a nuclear weapon? Or Burma? Or Brazil even! The only way to stop a nuclear weapon from being detonated is to get rid of them. It is foolish to think that we can keep these weapons lying around indefinitely and that they won't be used, they will be.

Looking at global zero, this is absolutely a realistic target. Most of the world is already at global zero—one hundred and eighty three countries in the world don't have nuclear weapons and don't think that the other countries should have them either. There was a new poll published by the Associated Press in the United States just yesterday that found that 67% of the American public think all the countries in the world should eliminate nuclear weapons. When you ask them whether the United States and its allies should keep nuclear weapons but stop everyone else from getting them only 16% felt that that was a realistic policy; but that is in fact our existing policy, which is unrealistic! Getting to global zero is the more realistic and logical solution to the problem and we're heading in that direction. There is a growing bipartisan consensus that we have to reduce our nuclear weapons arsenals and move in the direction of eliminating nuclear weapons. We now see people who formerly built nuclear empires in their respective countries arguing that it is now the time to take it down. This includes people as respected as former Secretary of State George Schulz, Henry Kissinger, James Baker, and Colin Powell—all of whom say that we have to move towards eliminating nuclear weapons. The trend is clearly in that direction. There is, in fact, a great consensus on the goal of moving down to low hundreds of weapons in U.S. and Russian arsenals. After that, it becomes harder, and no one really knows how you get from low hundreds to zero, but that direction itself is enough for now. As long as we are moving down there, as we go to fewer and fewer nuclear weapons, it will become clear how to construct the verification and security regimes that would be require to eliminate those last few. I think nuclear weapons, just as we have for all practical purposes eliminated biological and chemical weapons from the major powers, must be eliminated too.

BASIC EFFECTS OF NUCLEAR WEAPONS

Nuclear explosions produce both immediate and delayed destructive effects. Blast, thermal radiation, and prompt ionizing radiation cause significant destruction within seconds or minutes of a nuclear detonation. The delayed effects, such as radioactive fallout and other possible environmental effects, inflict damage over an extended period ranging from hours to years. Each of these effects are calculated from the point of detonation.

Ground Zero

The term "ground zero" refers to the point on the earth's surface immediately below (or above) the point of detonation. For a burst over (or under) water, the corresponding point is generally called "surface zero". The term "surface zero" or "surface ground zero" is also commonly used for ground surface and underground explosions. In some publications, ground (or surface) zero is called the "hypocenter" of the explosion.

Blast Effects

Most damage comes from the explosive blast. The shock wave of air radiates outward, producing sudden changes in air pressure that can crush objects, and high winds that can knock objects down. In general, large buildings are destroyed by the change in air pressure, while people and objects such as trees and utility poles are destroyed by the wind. The magnitude of the blast effect is related to the height of the burst above ground level.

For any given distance from the centre of the explosion, there is an optimum burst height that will produce the greatest change in air pressure, called overpressure, and the greater the distance the greater the optimum burst height. As a result, a burst on the surface produces the greatest overpressure at very close ranges, but less overpressure than an air burst at somewhat longer ranges.

When a nuclear weapon is detonated on or near Earth's surface, the blast digs out a large crater.

Some of the material that used in be in the crater is deposited on the rim of the crater; the rest is carried up into the air and returns to Earth as radioactive fallout. An explosion that is farther above the Earth's surface than the radius of the fireball does not dig a crater and produces negligible immediate fallout. For the most part, a nuclear blast kills people by indirect means rather than by direct pressure.

Thermal Radiation Effects

Approximately 35 percent of the energy from a nuclear explosion is an intense burst of thermal radiation, i.e., heat. The effects are similar to the effect of a two-second flash from an enormous sunlamp. Since the thermal radiation travels at roughly the speed of light, the flash of light and heat precedes the blast wave by several seconds, just as lightning is seen before thunder is heard.

The visible light will produce "flashblindness" in people who are looking in the direction of the explosion. Flashblindness can last for several minutes, after which recovery is total. If the flash is focused through the lens of the eye, a permanent retinal burn will result. At Hiroshima and Nagasaki, there were many cases of flashblindness, but only one case of retinal burn, among the survivors. On the other hand, anyone flashblinded while driving a car could easily cause permanent injury to himself and to others.

Skin burns result from higher intensities of light, and therefore take place closer to the point of explosion. First-degree, second-degree and third-degree burns can occur at distances of five miles away from the blast or more.

Third-degree burns over 24 percent of the body, or second-degree burns over 30 percent of the body, will result in serious shock, and will probably prove fatal unless prompt, specialized medical care is available. The entire United States has facilities to treat 1,000 or 2,000 severe burn cases. A single nuclear weapon could produce more than 10,000.

The thermal radiation from a nuclear explosion can directly ignite kindling materials. In general, ignitable materials outside the house, such as leaves or newspapers, are not surrounded by enough combustible material to generate a self-sustaining fire. Fires more likely to spread are those caused by thermal radiation passing through windows to ignite beds and overstuffed furniture inside houses. Another possible source of fires, which might be more damaging in urban areas, is indirect. Blast damage to Stores, water heaters, furnaces, electrical circuits or gas lines would ignite fires where fuel is plentiful.

DIRECT NUCLEAR RADIATION EFFECTS

Direct radiation occurs at the time of the explosion. It can be very intense, but its range is limited. For large nuclear weapons, the range of intense direct radiation is less than the range of lethal blast and thermal radiation effects. However, in the case of smaller weapons, direct radiation may be the lethal effect with the greatest range. Direct radiation did substantial damage to the residents of Hiroshima and Nagasaki. Human response to ionizing radiation is subject to great scientific uncertainty and intense controversy. It seems likely that even small doses of radiation do some harm.

Fallout

Fallout radiation is received from particles that are made radioactive by the effects of the explosion, and subsequently distributed at varying distances from the site of the blast. While any nuclear explosion in the atmosphere produces some fallout, the fallout is far greater if the burst is on the surface, or at least low enough for the fireball to touch the ground. The significant hazards come from particles scooped up from the ground and irradiated by the nuclear explosion.

The radioactive particles that rise only a short distance (those in the "stem" of the familiar mushroom cloud) will fall back to earth within a matter of minutes, landing close to the centre of the explosion. Such particles are unlikely to cause many deaths, because they will fall in areas where most people have already been killed.

However, the radioactivity will complicate efforts at rescue or eventual reconstruction. The radioactive particles that rise higher will be carried some distance by the wind before returning to Earth, and hence the area and intensity of the fallout is strongly influenced by local weather conditions. Much of the material is simply blown downwind in a long plume. Rainfall also can have a significant influence on the ways in which radiation from smaller weapons is deposited, since rain will carry contaminated particles to the ground. The areas receiving such contaminated rainfall would become "hot spots," with greater radiation intensity than their surroundings.

TYPES OF NUCLEAR EXPLOSIONS

The effects of a nuclear explosion depend in part to the height of the detonation. There five general classifications of bursts: air, high-altitude, underwater, underground, and surface bursts. An air burst is defined as one in which the explosion occurs in the air at an altitude below 100,000 feet (30,480 meters), but at such a height that the fireball does not touch the surface of the earth. A detontation above that altitude is generally refered to as a high-altitude burst.

A nuclear explosion that occurs at or slightly above the actual surface of the land or water is known as a surface burst. If the explosion happens beneath the surface of the land or water, then it is known as underground or underwater respectively. The design of Robust Nuclear Earth Penetrator (RNEP) uses the charaterastics of an underground burst in an attempt to destroy buried targets. One of the greatest results of the type of burst is the amount of radioactive debris and fallout, and the force of the blast wave.

The Blast Wave

A fraction of a second after a nuclear explosion, the heat from the fireball causes a high-pressure wave to develop and move outward producing the blast effect. The front of the blast wave, i.e., the shock front, travels rapidly away from the fireball, a moving wall of highly compressed air. The air immediately behind the shock front is accelerated to high velocities and creates a powerful wind. These winds in turn create dynamic pressure against the objects facing the blast. Shock waves cause a virtually instantaneous jump in pressure at the shock front.

The combination of the pressure jump (called the overpressure) and the dynamic pressure causes blast damage. Both the overpressure and the dynamic pressure reach to their maximum values upon the arrival of the shock wave. They then decay over a period ranging from a few tenths of a second to several seconds, depending on the blast's strength and the yield.

NUCLEAR WEAPON

A nuclear weapon is an explosive device that derives its destructive force from nuclear reactions, either fission or a combination of fission and fusion. Both reactions release vast quantities of energy from relatively small amounts of matter. The first fission ("atomic") bombtest released the same amount of energy as approximately 20,000 tons of TNT. The firstthermonuclear ("hydrogen") bomb test released the same amount of energy as approximately 10,000,000 tons of TNT.

A thermonuclear weapon weighing little more than 2,400 pounds (1,100 kg) can produce an explosive force comparable to the detonation of more than 1.2 million tons (1.1 million tonnes) of TNT. Thus, even a small nuclear device no larger than traditional bombs can devastate an entire city by blast, fire, and radiation. Nuclear weapons are consideredweapons of mass destruction, and their use and control have been a major focus of international relations policy since their debut.

Two nuclear weapons have been used in the course of warfare, both times by the United States near the end of World War II. On 6 August 1945, a uranium gun-type fission bombcode-named "Little Boy" was detonated over the Japanese city of Hiroshima. Three days later, on 9 August, a plutonium implosion-type fission bomb code-named "Fat Man" was exploded over Nagasaki, Japan. These two bombings resulted in the deaths of approximately 200,000 people—mostly civilians—from acute injuries sustained from the explosions. The role of the bombings in Japan's surrender, and their ethical status, remain the subject of scholarly and popular debate.

Since the bombings of Hiroshima and Nagasaki, nuclear weapons have been detonated on over two thousand occasions for testing purposes and demonstrations. Only a few nationspossess such weapons or are suspected of seeking them. The only countries known to have detonated nuclear weapons—and that acknowledge possessing such weapons—are (chronologically by date of first test) the United States, the Soviet Union (succeeded as a nuclear power by Russia), the United Kingdom, France, the People's Republic of China, India, Pakistan, and North Korea. Israel is also widely believed to possess nuclear weapons, though it does not acknowledge having them. One state, South Africa, fabricated nuclear weapons in the past, but as its apartheid regime was coming to an end it disassembled its arsenal, acceded to the Nuclear Non-Proliferation Treaty, and accepted full-scope international safeguards. The Federation of American Scientists estimates there are more than 17,000 nuclear warheads in the world as of 2012, with around 4,300 of them considered "operational", ready for use.

Types

There are two basic types of nuclear weapons: those that derive the majority of their energy from nuclear fission reactions alone, and those that use fission reactions to begin nuclear fusion reactions that produce a large amount of the total energy output.

Fission Weapons

All existing nuclear weapons derive some of their explosive energy from nuclear fission reactions. Weapons whose explosive output is exclusively from fission reactions are commonly referred to as atomic bombs or atom bombs (abbreviated as A-bombs). This has long been noted as something of a misnomer, as their energy comes from the nucleus of the atom, just as it does with fusion weapons.

In fission weapons, a mass of fissile material (enriched uranium or plutonium) is assembled into a supercritical mass—the amount of material needed to start an exponentially growing nuclear chain reaction—either by shooting one piece of sub-critical material into another (the "gun" method) or by compressing a sub-critical sphere of material using chemical explosives to many times its original density (the "implosion" method). The latter approach is considered more sophisticated than the former and only the latter approach can be used if the fissile material is plutonium.

A major challenge in all nuclear weapon designs is to ensure that a significant fraction of the fuel is consumed before the weapon destroys itself. The amount of energy released by fission bombs can range from the equivalent of just under a ton of TNT, to upwards of 500,000 tons (500 kilotons) of TNT.

All fission reactions necessarily generate fission products, the radioactive remains of the atomic nuclei split by the fission reactions. Many fission products are either highly radioactive (but short-lived) or moderately radioactive (but long-lived), and as such are a serious form of radioactive contamination if not fully contained. Fission products are the principal radioactive component of nuclear fallout.

The most commonly used fissile materials for nuclear weapons applications have been uranium-235 and plutonium-239. Less commonly used has been uranium-233. Neptunium-237 and some isotopes of americium may be usable for nuclear explosives as well, but it is not clear that this has ever been implemented, and even their plausible use in nuclear weapons is a matter of scientific dispute.

Fusion Weapons

The other basic type of nuclear weapon produces a large proportion of its energy in nuclear fusion reactions. Such fusion weapons are generally referred to as thermonuclear weapons or more colloquially as hydrogen bombs (abbreviated as H-bombs), as they rely on fusion reactions between isotopes of hydrogen (deuterium and tritium). All such weapons derive a significant portion, and sometimes a majority, of their energy from fission.

This is because a fission weapon is required as a "trigger" for the fusion reactions, and the fusion reactions can themselves trigger additional fission reactions.

Only six countries—United States, Russia, United Kingdom, People's Republic of China, France and India—have conducted thermonuclear weapon tests. (Whether India has detonated a "true", multi-staged thermonuclear weapon is controversial.) Thermonuclear weapons are considered much more difficult to successfully design and execute than primitive fission weapons. Almost all of the nuclear weapons deployed today use the thermonuclear design because it is more efficient.

Thermonuclear bombs work by using the energy of a fission bomb to compress and heat fusion fuel. In the Teller-Ulam design, which accounts for all multi-megaton yield hydrogen bombs, this is accomplished by placing a fission bomb and fusion fuel (tritium, deuterium, orlithium deuteride) in proximity within a special, radiation-reflecting container. When the fission bomb is detonated, gamma rays and X-rays emitted first compress the fusion fuel, then heat it to thermonuclear temperatures. The ensuing fusion reaction creates enormous numbers of high-speed neutrons, which can then induce fission in materials not normally prone to it, such as depleted uranium. Each of these components is known as a "stage", with the fission bomb as the "primary" and the fusion capsule as the "secondary". In large, megaton-range hydrogen bombs, about half of the yield comes from the final fissioning of depleted uranium.

Virtually all thermonuclear weapons deployed today use the "two-stage" design described above, but it is possible to add additional fusion stages—each stage igniting a larger amount of fusion fuel in the next stage. This technique can be used to construct thermonuclear weapons of arbitrarily large yield, in contrast to fission bombs, which are limited in their explosive force. The largest nuclear weapon ever detonated—the Tsar Bomba of the USSR, which released an energy equivalent of over 50 million tons (50 megatons) of TNT—was a three-stage weapon. Most thermonuclear weapons are considerably smaller than this, due to practical constraints from missile warhead space and weight requirements. Fusion reactions do not create fission products, and thus contribute far less to the creation of nuclear fallout than fission reactions, but because all thermonuclear weapons contain at least one fission stage, and many high-yield thermonuclear devices have a final fission stage, thermonuclear weapons can generate at least as much nuclear fallout as fission-only weapons.

Other Types

There are other types of nuclear weapons as well. For example, a boosted fission weapon is a fission bomb that increases its explosive yield through a small amount of fusion reactions, but it is not a fusion bomb. In the boosted bomb, the neutrons produced by the fusion reactions serve primarily to increase the efficiency of the fission bomb.

Some weapons are designed for special purposes; a neutron bomb is a thermonuclear weapon that yields a relatively small explosion but a relatively large amount of neutron radiation; such a device could theoretically be used to cause massive casualties while leaving infrastructure mostly intact and creating a minimal amount of fallout. The detonation of any nuclear weapon is accompanied by a blast of neutron radiation. Surrounding a nuclear weapon with suitable materials (such as cobalt orgold) creates a weapon known as a salted bomb. This device can produce exceptionally large quantities of radioactive contamination.

Research has been done into the possibility of pure fusion bombs: nuclear weapons that consist of fusion reactions without requiring a fission bomb to initiate them. Such a device might provide a simpler path to thermonuclear weapons than one that required development of fission weapons first, and pure fusion weapons would create significantly less nuclear fallout than other thermonuclear weapons, because they would not disperse fission products. In 1998, the United States Department of Energy divulged that the United States had, "...made a substantial investment" in the past to develop pure fusion weapons, but that, "The U.S. does not have and is not developing a pure fusion weapon", and that, "No credible design for a pure fusion weapon resulted from the DOE investment".

Most variation in nuclear weapon design is for the purpose of achieving different yields for different situations, and in manipulating design elements to attempt to minimize weapon size.

Antimatter, which consists of particles resembling ordinary matter particles in most of their properties but having opposite electric charge, has been considered as a trigger mechanism for nuclear weapons. A major obstacle is the difficulty of producing antimatter in large enough quantities, and there is no evidence that it is feasible beyond the military domain. However, the U.S. Air Force funded studies of the physics of antimatter in the Cold War, and began considering its possible use in weapons, not just as a trigger, but as the explosive itself. A fourth generation nuclear weapon design is related to, and relies upon, the same principle as Antimatter-catalyzed nuclear pulse propulsion.

WEAPONS DELIVERY

Nuclear weapons delivery—the technology and systems used to bring a nuclear weapon to its target—is an important aspect of nuclear weapons relating both tonuclear weapon design and nuclear strategy. Additionally, development and maintenance of delivery options is among the most resource-intensive aspects of a nuclear weapons program: according to one estimate, deployment costs accounted for 57% of the total financial resources spent by the United States in relation to nuclear weapons since 1940.

Historically the first method of delivery, and the method used in the two nuclear weapons used in warfare, was as a gravity bomb, dropped from bomber aircraft. This is usually the first method that countries developed, as it does not place many restrictions on the size of the weapon and *weapon miniaturization* requires considerable weapons design knowledge. It does, however, limit attack range, response time to an impending attack, and the number of weapons that a country can field at the same time. With the advent of miniaturization, nuclear bombs can be delivered by both strategic bombers and tactical fighter-bombers, allowing an air force to use its current fleet with little or no modification. This method may still be considered the primary means of nuclear weapons delivery; the majority of U.S. nuclear warheads, for example, are free-fall gravity bombs, namely the B61.

More preferable from a strategic point of view is a nuclear weapon mounted onto a missile, which can use a ballistic trajectory to deliver the warhead over the horizon. Although even short-range missiles allow for a faster and less vulnerable attack, the development of long-range intercontinental ballistic missiles (ICBMs) and submarine-launched ballistic missiles (SLBMs) has given some nations the ability to plausibly deliver missiles anywhere on the globe with a high likelihood of success.

More advanced systems, such as multiple independently targetable reentry vehicles (MIRVs), can launch multiple warheads at different targets from one missile, reducing the chance of a successful missile defence. Today, missiles are most common among systems designed for delivery of nuclear weapons. Making a warhead small enough to fit onto a missile, though, can be difficult.

Tactical weapons have involved the most variety of delivery types, including not only gravity bombs and missiles but also artillery shells, land mines, and nuclear depth charges andtorpedoes for anti-submarine warfare. An atomic mortar was also tested at one time by the United States. Small, two-man portable tactical weapons (somewhat misleadingly referred to as suitcase bombs), such as the Special Atomic Demolition Munition, have been developed, although the difficulty of combining sufficient yield with portability limits their military utility.

NUCLEAR STRATEGY

Nuclear warfare strategy is a set of policies that deal with preventing or fighting a nuclear war. The policy of trying to prevent an attack by a nuclear weapon from another country by threatening nuclear retaliation is known as the strategy of nuclear deterrence. The goal in deterrence is to always maintain a second strike capability (the ability of a country to respond to a nuclear attack with one of its own) and potentially to strive for first strike status (the ability to completely destroy an enemy's nuclear forces before they could retaliate). During the Cold War, policy and military theorists in nuclear-enabled countries worked out models of what sorts of policies could prevent one from ever being attacked by a nuclear weapon, and developed weapon game theory models that create the greatest and most stable deterrence conditions.

Different forms of nuclear weapons delivery allow for different types of nuclear strategies. The goals of any strategy are generally to make it difficult for an enemy to launch a pre-emptive strike against the weapon system and difficult to defend against the delivery of the weapon during a potential conflict. Sometimes this has meant keeping the weapon locations hidden, such as deploying them on submarines or land mobile transporter erector launchers whose locations are very hard for an enemy to track, and other times, this means protecting them by burying them in hardened missile silo bunkers.

Other components of nuclear strategies have included using missile defence (to destroy the missiles before they land) or implementation of civil defence measures (using early-warning systems to evacuate citizens to safe areas before an attack).

Note that weapons designed to threaten large populations, or to generally deter attacks are known as *strategic weapons.* Weapons designed for use on a battlefield in military situations are called *tactical weapons.*

There are critics of the very idea of nuclear strategy for waging nuclear war who have suggested that a nuclear war between two nuclear powers would result in mutual annihilation. From this point of view, the significance of nuclear weapons is purely to deter war because any nuclear war would immediately escalate out of mutual distrust and fear, resulting in mutually assured destruction. This threat of national, if not global, destruction has been a strong motivation for anti-nuclear weapons activism.

Critics from the peace movement and within the military establishment have questioned the usefulness of such weapons in the current military climate. According to an advisory opinion issued by the International Court of Justice in 1996, the use of (or threat of use of) such weapons would generally be contrary to the rules of international law applicable in armed conflict, but the court did not reach an opinion as to whether or not the threat or use would be lawful in specific extreme circumstances such as if the survival of the state were at stake.

Another deterrence position in nuclear strategy is that nuclear proliferation can be desirable. This view argues that, unlike conventional weapons, nuclear weapons successfully deter all-out war between states, and they succeeded in doing this during the Cold Warbetween the U.S. and the Soviet Union. In the late 1950s and early 1960s, Gen. Pierre Marie Gallois of France, an adviser to Charles DeGaulle, argued in books like *The Balance of Terror: Strategy for the Nuclear Age* (1961) that mere possession of a nuclear arsenal, what the French called the *force de frappe*, was enough to ensure deterrence, and thus concluded that the spread of nuclear weapons could increase international stability. Some very prominent neo-realist scholars, such as the late Kenneth Waltz, formerly a Political Science at UC Berkeley and Adjunct Senior Research Scholar at Columbia University, and John Mearsheimer of University of Chicago, have also argued along the lines of Gallois. Specifically, these scholars have advocated some forms of nuclear proliferation, arguing that it would decrease the likelihood of total war, especially in troubled regions of the world where there exists a unipolar nuclear weapon state. Aside from the public opinion that opposes proliferation in any form, there are two schools of thought on the matter: those, like Mearsheimer, who favour selective proliferation, and those of Kenneth Waltz, who was somewhat more non-interventionist.

The threat of potentially suicidal terrorists possessing nuclear weapons (a form of nuclear terrorism) complicates the decision process. The prospect of mutually assured destruction may not deter an enemy who expects to die in the confrontation. Further, if the initial act is from a stateless terrorist instead of a sovereign nation, there is no fixed nation or fixed military targets to retaliate against. It has been argued by the New York Times, especially after the September 11, 2001 attacks, that this complication is the sign of the next age of nuclear strategy, distinct from the relative stability of the Cold War. In 1996, the United States adopted a policy of allowing the targeting of its nuclear weapons at terrorists armed with weapons of mass destruction.

Robert Gallucci, president of the John D. and Catherine T. MacArthur Foundation, argues that although traditional deterrence is not an effective approach toward terrorist groups bent on causing a nuclear catastrophe, Gallucci believes that "the United States should instead consider a policy of expanded deterrence, which focuses not solely on the would-be nuclear terrorists but on those states that may deliberately transfer or inadvertently lead nuclear weapons and materials to them. By threatening retaliation against those states, the United States may be able to deter that which it cannot physically prevent.".

Graham Allison makes a similar case, arguing that the key to expanded deterrence is coming up with ways of tracing nuclear material to the country that forged the fissile material. "After a nuclear bomb detonates, nuclear forensics cops would collect debris samples and send them to a laboratory for radiological analysis. By identifying unique attributes of the fissile material, including its impurities and contaminants, one could trace the path back to its origin." The process is analogous to identifying a criminal by fingerprints. "The goal would be twofold: first, to deter leaders of nuclear states from selling weapons to terrorists by holding them accountable for any use of their own weapons; second, to give leader every incentive to tightly secure their nuclear weapons and materials."

GOVERNANCE, CONTROL, AND LAW

Because of the immense military power they can confer, the political control of nuclear weapons has been a key issue for as long as they have existed; in most countries the use of nuclear force can only be authorized by the head of government or head of state.

In the late 1940s, lack of mutual trust was preventing the United States and the Soviet Union from making ground towards international arms control agreements. The Russell–Einstein Manifesto was issued in London on July 9, 1955 by Bertrand Russell in the midst of the Cold War. It highlighted the dangers posed by nuclear weapons and called for world leaders to seek peaceful resolutions to international conflict. The signatories included eleven pre-eminent intellectuals and scientists, including Albert Einstein, who signed it just days before his death on April 18, 1955. A few days after the release, philanthropist Cyrus S. Eatonoffered to sponsor a conference—called for in the manifesto—in Pugwash, Nova Scotia, Eaton's birthplace. This conference was to be the first of the Pugwash Conferences on Science and World Affairs, held in July 1957.

By the 1960s steps were being taken to limit both the proliferation of nuclear weapons to other countries and the environmental effects of nuclear testing. The Partial Test Ban Treaty (1963) restricted all nuclear testing tounderground nuclear testing, to prevent contamination from nuclear fallout, whereas the Nuclear Non-Proliferation Treaty (1968) attempted to place restrictions on the types of activities signatories could participate in, with the goal of allowing the transference of non-military nuclear technology to member countries without fear of proliferation.

In 1957, the International Atomic Energy Agency (IAEA) was established under the mandate of the United Nations to encourage development of peaceful applications for nuclear technology, provide international safeguards against its misuse, and facilitate the application of safety measures in its use. In 1996, many nations signed the Comprehensive Test Ban Treaty, which prohibits all testing of nuclear weapons. A testing ban imposes a significant hindrance to nuclear arms development by any complying country.The Treaty requires the ratification by 44 specific states before it can go into force; as of 2012, the ratification of eight of these states is still required.

Additional treaties and agreements have governed nuclear weapons stockpiles between the countries with the two largest stockpiles, the United States and the Soviet Union, and later between the United States and Russia. These include treaties such as SALT II (never ratified), START I (expired), INF, START II (never ratified), SORT, and New START, as well as non-binding agreements such as SALT Iand the Presidential Nuclear Initiatives of 1991. Even when they did not enter into force, these agreements helped limit and later reduce the numbers and types of nuclear weapons between the United States and the Soviet Union/Russia.

Nuclear weapons have also been opposed by agreements between countries. Many nations have been declared Nuclear-Weapon-Free Zones, areas where nuclear weapons production and deployment are prohibited, through the use of treaties.

The Treaty of Tlatelolco(1967) prohibited any production or deployment of nuclear weapons in Latin America and the Caribbean, and the Treaty of Pelindaba(1964) prohibits nuclear weapons in many African countries. As recently as 2006 a Central Asian Nuclear Weapon Free Zone was established amongst the former Soviet republics of Central Asia prohibiting nuclear weapons.

In the middle of 1996, the International Court of Justice, the highest court of the United Nations, issued an Advisory Opinion concerned with the "Legality of the Threat or Use of Nuclear Weapons". The court ruled that the use or threat of use of nuclear weapons would violate various articles of international law, including the Geneva Conventions, the Hague Conventions, the UN Charter, and the Universal Declaration of Human Rights. In view of the unique, destructive characteristics of nuclear weapons, the International Committee of the Red Cross calls on States to ensure that these weapons are never used, irrespective of whether they consider them lawful or not.

Additionally, there have been other, specific actions meant to discourage countries from developing nuclear arms. In the wake of the tests by India and Pakistan in 1998, economic sanctions were (temporarily) levied against both countries, though neither were signatories with the Nuclear Non-Proliferation Treaty. One of the stated *casus belli* for the initiation of the 2003 Iraq War was an accusation by the United States that Iraq was actively pursuing nuclear arms (though this was soon discovered not to be the case as the program had been discontinued). In 1981, Israel had bombed a nuclear reactor being constructed in Osirak, Iraq, in what it called an attempt to halt Iraq's previous nuclear arms ambitions; in 2007, Israel bombed another reactor being constructed in Syria.

In 2013, Mark Diesendorf says that governments of France, India, North Korea, Pakistan, UK, and South Africa have used nuclear power and/or research reactors to assist nuclear weapons development or to contribute to their supplies of nuclear explosives from military reactors.

Disarmament

Nuclear disarmament refers to both the act of reducing or eliminating nuclear weapons and to the end state of a nuclear-free world, in which nuclear weapons are completely eliminated.

Beginning with the 1963 Partial Test Ban Treaty and continuing through the 1996 Comprehensive Test Ban Treaty, there have been many treaties to limit or reduce nuclear weapons testing and stockpiles. The 1968 Nuclear Non-Proliferation Treaty has as one of its explicit conditions that all signatories must "pursue negotiations in good faith" towards the long-term goal of "complete disarmament". The nuclear weapon states have largely treated that aspect of the agreement as "decorative" and without force.

Only one country—South Africa—has ever fully renounced nuclear weapons they had independently developed. The former Soviet republics of Belarus, Kazakhstan, and Ukrainereturned Soviet nuclear arms stationed in their countries to Russia after the collapse of the USSR.

Proponents of nuclear disarmament say that it would lessen the probability of nuclear war occurring, especially accidentally. Critics of nuclear disarmament say that it would undermine the present nuclear peace and deterrence and would lead to increased global instability. Various American elder statesmen, who were in office during the Cold War period, have recently been advocating the elimination of nuclear weapons. These officials include Henry Kissinger, George Shultz, Sam Nunn, and William Perry. In January 2010, Lawrence M. Krauss stated that "no issue carries more importance to the long-term health and security of humanity than the effort to reduce, and perhaps one day, rid the world of nuclear weapons". In the years after the end of the Cold War, there have been numerous campaigns to urge the abolition of nuclear weapons, such as that organized by the Global Zero movement, and the goal of a "world without nuclear weapons" was advocated by United States President Barack Obama in an April 2009 speech in Prague. A CNN poll from April 2010 indicated that the American public was nearly evenly split on the issue. Some analysts have argued that nuclear weapons have made the world relatively safer, with peace through deterrence and through the stability–instability paradox, including in south Asia. Kenneth Waltz has argued that nuclear weapons have helped keep an uneasy peace, and further nuclear weapon proliferation might even help avoid the large scale conventional wars that were so common prior to their invention at the end of World War II. But former Secretary Henry Kissinger says there is a new danger, which cannot be addressed by deterrence: "The classical notion of deterrence was that there was some consequences before which aggressors and evildoers would recoil. In a world of suicide bombers, that calculation doesn't operate in any comparable way". George Shultz has said, "If you think of the people who are doing suicide attacks, and people like that get a nuclear weapon, they are almost by definition not deterrable".

United Nations

The UN Office for Disarmament Affairs (UNODA) is a department of the United Nations Secretariat established in January 1998 as part of the United Nations Secretary-General Kofi Annan's plan to reform the UN as presented in his report to the General Assembly in July 1997. Its goal is to promote nuclear disarmament and non-proliferation and the strengthening of the disarmament regimes in respect to other weapons of mass destruction, chemical and biological weapons.

It also promotes disarmament efforts in the area of conventional weapons, especially land mines and small arms, which are often the weapons of choice in contemporary conflicts.

CONTROVERSY

Ethics

Even before the first nuclear weapons had been developed, scientists involved with the Manhattan Project were divided over the use of the weapon. The role of the two atomic bombings of the country in Japan's surrender and the U.S.'s ethical justification for them has been the subject of scholarly and popular debate for decades. The question of whether nations should have nuclear weapons, or test them, has been continually and nearly universally controversial.

Notable nuclear weapons accidents

- February 13, 1950: a Convair B-36B crashed in northern British Columbia after jettisoning a Mark IV atomic bomb. This was the first such nuclear weapon loss in history.
- 7 June 1960: the 1960 Fort Dix IM-99 accident destroyed a Boeing CIM-10 Bomarc nuclear missile and shelter and contaminated the BOMARC Missile Accident Site in New Jersey.
- 24 January 1961: the 1961 Goldsboro B-52 crash occurred near Goldsboro, North Carolina. A B-52 Stratofortress carrying two Mark 39 nuclear bombs broke up in mid-air, dropping its nuclear payload in the process.
- 1965 Philippine Sea A-4 crash, where a Skyhawk attack aircraft with a nuclear weapon fell into the sea. The pilot, the aircraft, and the B43 nuclear bomb were never recovered. It was not until the 1980s that the Pentagon revealed the loss of the one-megaton bomb.
- January 17, 1966: the 1966 Palomares B-52 crash occurred when a B-52G bomber of the USAF collided with a KC-135 tankerduring mid-air refuelling off the coast of Spain. The KC-135 was completely destroyed when its fuel load ignited, killing all four crew members. The B-52G broke apart, killing three of the seven crew members aboard. Of the four Mk28 type hydrogen bombs the B-52G carried, three were found on land near Almería, Spain. The non-nuclear explosives in two of the weapons detonated upon impact with the ground, resulting in the contamination of a 2-square-kilometer (490-acre) (0.78 square mile) area by radioactiveplutonium. The fourth, which fell into the Mediterranean Sea, was recovered intact after a 2½-month-long search.
- January 21, 1968: the 1968 Thule Air Base B-52 crash involved a United States Air Force (USAF) B-52 bomber. The aircraft was carrying four hydrogen bombs when a

cabin fire forced the crew to abandon the aircraft. Six crew members ejected safely, but one who did not have an ejection seat was killed while trying to bail out. The bomber crashed onto sea ice in Greenland, causing the nuclear payload to rupture and disperse, which resulted in widespread radioactive contamination.

Nuclear Fallout

Over 500 atmospheric nuclear weapons tests were conducted at various sites around the world from 1945 to 1980. Radioactive falloutfrom nuclear weapons testing was first drawn to public attention in 1954 when the Castle Bravo hydrogen bomb test at the Pacific Proving Grounds contaminated the crew and catch of the Japanese fishing boat *Lucky Dragon*. One of the fishermen died in Japan seven months later, and the fear of contaminated tuna led to a temporary boycotting of the popular staple in Japan.

The incident caused widespread concern around the world, especially regarding the effects of nuclear fallout and atmospheric nuclear testing, and "provided a decisive impetus for the emergence of the anti-nuclear weapons movement in many countries".

As public awareness and concern mounted over the possible health hazards associated with exposure to the nuclear fallout, various studies were done to assess the extent of the hazard. A Centres for Disease Control and Prevention/ National Cancer Institute study claims that fallout from atmospheric nuclear tests would lead to perhaps 11,000 excess deaths amongst people alive during atmospheric testing in the United States from all forms of cancer, including leukemia, from 1951 to well into the 21st century. As of March 2009, the U.S. is the only nation that compensates nuclear test victims. Since the Radiation Exposure Compensation Act of 1990, more than $1.38 billion in compensation has been approved. The money is going to people who took part in the tests, notably at the Nevada Test Site, and to others exposed to the radiation.

Public Opposition

Peace movements emerged in Japan and in 1954 they converged to form a unified "Japanese Council Against Atomic and Hydrogen

Bombs". Japanese opposition to nuclear weapons tests in the Pacific Ocean was widespread, and "an estimated 35 million signatures were collected on petitions calling for bans on nuclear weapons".

In the United Kingdom, the first Aldermaston March organised by the Campaign for Nuclear Disarmament(CND) took place at Easter 1958, when, according to the CND, several thousand people marched for four days from Trafalgar Square, London, to the Atomic Weapons Research Establishment close to Aldermaston in Berkshire, England, to demonstrate their opposition to nuclear weapons. The Aldermaston marches continued into the late 1960s when tens of thousands of people took part in the four-day marches.

In 1959, a letter in the *Bulletin of Atomic Scientists* was the start of a successful campaign to stop the Atomic Energy Commission dumping radioactive waste in the sea 19 kilometres from Boston. In 1962, Linus Pauling won the Nobel Peace Prize for his work to stop the atmospheric testing of nuclear weapons, and the "Ban the Bomb" movement spread.

In 1963, many countries ratified the Partial Test Ban Treaty prohibiting atmospheric nuclear testing. Radioactive fallout became less of an issue and the anti-nuclear weapons movement went into decline for some years. A resurgence of interest occurred amid European and American fears of nuclear war in the 1980s.

COSTS AND TECHNOLOGY SPIN-OFFS

According to an audit by the Brookings Institution, between 1940 and 1996, the U.S. spent $8.75 trillion in present day terms on nuclear weapons programs. 57 percent of which was spent on building nuclear weapons delivery systems. 6.3 percent of the total, $549 billion in present day terms, was spent on Environmental remediation and nuclear waste management, for example cleaning up the Hanford site, and 7 percent of the total, $615 billion was spent on making nuclear weapons themselves.

NON-WEAPONS USES

Civil Engineering and Energy Production

Apart from their use as weapons, nuclear explosives have

been tested and used for variousnon-military uses. These have included large-scale earth moving and the creation of artificial bays. Due to the inability of the physicists to reduce the fission fraction of small, approximately 1 kiloton, yield nuclear devices that would have been required for many civil engineering projects, when long term health and clean-up costs from fission products were included in the cost, there was virtually no economic advantage over conventional explosives, except for potentially the very largest of projects.

At the peak of the Atomic Age, the United States Federal government initiated Operation Plowshare, involving "peaceful nuclear explosions". The United States Atomic Energy Commission chairman announced that the Plowshares project was intended to "highlight the peaceful applications of nuclear explosive devices and thereby create a climate of world opinion that is more favourable to weapons development and tests". The Operation Plowshare program included 27 nuclear tests designed towards investigating these non-weapons uses from 1961 through 1973.

The Qattara Depression Project, as developed by Professor Friedrich Bassler who during his appointment to the West German ministry of economics in 1968 put forth a plan to create a Saharan lake and hydroelectric power station by blasting a tunnel between the Mediterranean sea and the Qattara Depression in Egypt, an area that lies below sea level. The core problem of the entire project was the water supply to the depression. Calculations by Bassler showed that digging a canal or tunnel would be too expensive, therefore Bassler determined that the use of nuclear explosive devices, to excavate the canal or tunnel, would be the most economical. The Egyptian government declined to pursue the idea.

The Soviet Union's Nuclear Explosions for the National Economy was a program in the Soviet Union that investigated non-weapons uses of nuclear explosions. These included one 30 kiloton explosion being used to close the Uzbekistani *Urtabulak* gas well in 1966 that had been blowing since 1963, and a few months later a 47 kiloton explosive was used to seal a higher pressure blowout at the nearby *Pamuk* gas field.

The public records for devices that produced the highest proportion of their yield via fusion-only reactions are possibly the Soviet peaceful nuclear explosions of the 1970s, with 98% of their 15 kiloton explosive yield being derived from fusion reactions, a total fission fraction of 0.3 kilotons in a 15 kt device.

The repeated detonation of nuclear devices underground in salt domes, in a somewhat analogous manner to the explosions that power a car internal combustion engine (in that it would be a heat engine) has also been proposed as a means of fusion power, in what is termed PACER. Other investigated uses for peaceful nuclear explosions were underground detonations to stimulate, by a process analogous to fracking, the flow of petroleum and natural gas in tight formations, this was most developed in the Soviet Union, with an increase in the production of many well heads being reported.

Physics

The discovery and synthesis of new chemical elements by nuclear transmutation, and their production in the necessary quantities to allow the studying of their properties, was carried out in nuclear explosive device testing. For example, the discovery of the short lived einsteinium and fermium, both created under the intense neutron flux environment within thermonuclear explosions, followed the first Teller-Ulam thermonuclear device test - Ivy Mike. The rapid capture of so many neutrons required in the synthesis of einsteinium would provide the needed direct experimental confirmation of the so-called r-process, the multiple neutron absorptions needed to explain the cosmic nucleosynthesis (production) of all heavy chemical elements heavier than nickel on the periodic table, in supernova explosions, before beta decay, with the r-process explaining the existence of many stable elements in the universe.

In 2008 the worldwide presence of new isotopes from atmospheric testing beginning in the 1950s was developed into a reliable way of detecting art forgeries, as all paintings created after that period may contain traces of caesium-137 and strontium-90, isotopes that did not exist in nature before 1945. Fission products like Cs-137 and Sr-90 did occur in nature prior to 1945, being produced in the natural nuclear fission reactor at Oklo, but almost all traces of them had long since decayed away before the rise of even the earliest known human painting.

Both climatology and particularly aerosol science, a subfield of atmospheric science, were largely created to answer the question of how far and wide fallout would travel. Similar to radioactive tracersused in hydrology and materials testing, fallout and the neutron activation of nitrogen gas served as a radioactive tracer that was used to measure and then help model global circulations in the atmosphere by following the movements of fallout aerosols.

After the Van Allen Belts surrounding Earth were published about in 1958, James Van Allen suggested that a nuclear detonation would be one way of probing the magnetic phenomenon, data obtained from the August 1958 Project Argus test shots, a high altitude nuclear explosion investigation, were vital to the early understanding of Earth's magnetosphere.

Soviet nuclear physicist and Nobel peace prize recipient Andrei Sakharov also proposed the idea that earthquakes could be mitigated and particle accelerators could be made by utilizing nuclear explosions, with the latter created by connecting a nuclear explosive device with another of his inventions, the explosively pumped flux compression generator, to accelerate protons to collide with each other to probe their inner workings, an endeavour that is presently done at much lower energy levels with non-explosive superconducting magnetsin CERN. Sakharov suggested to replace the copper coil in his MK generators by a bigsuperconductor solenoid to magnetically compress and focus underground nuclear explosions into a shaped charge effect. He theorized this could focus 10^{23} positively chargedprotons per second on a 1 mm^2 surface, then envisaged making two such beams collide in the form of a supercollider.

Underground nuclear explosive data from peaceful nuclear explosion test shots have been used to investigate the composition of Earth's mantle, analogous to the exploration geophysics practice of mineral prospecting with chemical explosives in "deep seismic sounding" reflection seismology.

Project A119, proposed in the 1960s, which as Apollo scientist Gary Latham explained, would have been the detonating of a "smallish" nuclear device on the Moon in order to facilitate research into its geologic make-up. Analogous in concept to the comparatively low yield explosion created by the water prospecting (LCROSS) Lunar Crater Observation and Sensing Satellite mission, which launched in 2009 and released the "Centaur" kinetic energy impactor, an impactor with a mass of 2,305 kg (5,081 lb), and an impact velocity of about 9,000 km/h (5,600 mph), releasing the kinetic energy equivalent of detonating approximately 2 tons of TNT (8.86 GJ).

Propulsion Use

Although likely never achieving orbit due to aerodynamic drag, the first macroscopic object to obtain Earth orbital velocity was a "manhole cover" propelled by the detonation of test shot Pascal-B, beforesputnik obtained orbital velocity, and also successfully became the first satellite, in October 1957. The use of a subterranean shaft and nuclear device to propel an object to escape velocity has since been termed a "thunder well".

The direct use of nuclear explosives, by using the impact of propellant plasma from a nuclear shaped charge acting on a pusher plate, has also been seriously studied as a potential propulsion mechanism for space travel.

Edward Teller, in the United States, proposed the use of a nuclear detonation to power an explosively pumped *soft* X-ray laser as a component of a ballistic missile defence shield, this would destroy missile components by transferring momentum to the vehicles surface by laser ablation. This ablation process is one of the damage mechanisms of a laser weapon, but it is also the basis of pulsed laser propulsion for spacecraft.

Ground flight testing by Professor Leik Myrabo, using a non-nuclear, conventionally powered pulsed laser test-bed, successfully lifted a lightcraft 72 meters in altitude by a method similar to ablative laser propulsion in 2000. A powerful solar system based *soft* X-ray, to ultraviolet, laser system has been calculated to be capable of propelling an interstellar spacecraft, by the light sail principle, to 11% of the speed of light. In 1972 it was also calculated that a 1 Terawatt, 1-km diameter x-ray laser with 1 angstrom wavelength impinging on a 1-km diameter sail, could propel a spacecraft to Alpha Centauri in 10 years.

NUCLEAR WEAPONS IN THE TWENTY-FIRST CENTURY

Nuclear weapons played a pivotal role in international security during the latter half of the twentieth century. Despite rapid increases in communications, transportation, and weapons technology, there has been no large-scale strategic conflict since the Second World War.

Nuclear weapons, as the most destructive instruments ever invented, had a stabilizing effect on superpower relations by making any conflict unacceptably costly.

However, geopolitical change and the evolution of military technology suggest that the composition of our nuclear forces and our strategy for their employment may be different in the twenty-first century. The time is right for a fundamental rethinking of our expectations and requirements for these unique weapons.

Nuclear weapons are one component of an integrated defence strategy that includes diplomacy and conventional forces. The principal role of nuclear weapons was and continues to be that of deterring any potential adversaries from an attack on America or our vital interests.

This role is expected to continue for as long as nuclear weapons hold the appellation of ýÿsupreme" instruments of military force. However, this does not mean that their role in military planning will not change at all.

Changes in the geopolitical environment and the inexorable advance of military technology here and abroad suggest that the position of nuclear weapons in national security policy will evolve with time.

Given the unique destructive power of nuclear weapons, it is essential that this evolution be planned, to the extent possible, with due consideration of the integration of strategic nuclear forces into a consistent and comprehensive policy for national security.

Even with the dramatic changes that have occurred in the world during the past decade, nuclear warplanning today is similar in many respects to what it was during the Cold War. The Single Integrated Operational Plan (SIOP) is focused on a massive counterattack strategy that aims to eliminate the ability of an adversary to inflict further damage to American interests.

Nuclear weapons provide an assured retaliatory capability to convince any adversary that aggression or coercion would be met with a response that would be certain, overwhelming, and devastating.

It is often, but not universally, thought that nuclear weapons would be used only in extremis, when the nation is in the gravest danger. While there has been some discussion of "single weapon" strikes against isolated targets, such as sites of weapons of mass destruction, most of the attention in nuclear strategy has been and is directed toward large-scale engagements. This may not be true in the future.

The advance of conventional weapons technology may result in the ability of conventional weapons to perform some of the missions currently assigned to nuclear weapons.

For example, take the case of a road mobile ballistic missile. If one knows the location of such a target and if one can place a conventional weapon on that target with meter-scale accuracy, then it can be destroyed without a nuclear weapon.

On the other hand, if one does not know the location of the target to within many kilometers then even a nuclear weapon may not destroy it. The key parameters required for target destruction are intelligence and precision delivery, not the explosive force of the weapon. However, even if a weapon is precisely delivered to the correct target point, countermeasures as simple as steel netting, boulder fields, or decoys complicate reliance on conventional weapons with limited radii of destruction.

The role of nuclear weaponry as the ultimate deterrent to aggression and the ultimate destructive force in combat will likely lead to the retention of at least some nuclear forces for decades to come. However, the composition of our nuclear arsenal may undergo significant modification to respond to changing conditions, changing military needs, and changes in our confidence in our ability to maintain credible nuclear forces without nuclear testing or large-scale weapons production.

Options for precision delivery of nuclear weapons may reduce the requirement for high yield. Lower yield weapons could be produced as modifications of existing weapons designs, or they could employ more rugged and simpler designs that might be developed and maintained with high confidence without nuclear testing and with a smaller nuclear weapons complex than we envision is required to maintain our current nuclear forces.

To the role that nuclear weapons might play in the twenty-first century, starting about 2020. A twenty-year horizon was chosen because over this time scale it is possible to make reasonable projections of technology and some assumptions about the probable threat situation. It takes about twenty years for substantially new weapons technologies to be developed and fielded into dependable military systems.

Since this is true for other countries as well as the United States, one can project the development of potential adversarial capabilities to some degree.

Of course, changes in governments could occur quickly compared to this time scale, but the technology that would be employed against the United States would proceed more slowly. This chapter focuses on state-to-state defence and does not explicitly consider terrorism or the rapid evolution of entirely new state threats. It is unlikely that an emergent power would be able to develop the technology necessary to confront the United States on a time scale faster than two decades without some obvious indicators that would enable our technological or diplomatic response.

Why is this an important issue now? Current plans call for the deployment of the "next generation" of strategic forces in about 2020, including replacements for intercontinental ballistic missiles (ICBMs), the Ohio-class ballistic missile submarine, and perhaps even the venerable B52 bomber. This strategic modernization will be expensive, and it is not too soon to begin the debate over what kinds of strategic forces are needed to meet future needs.

It takes at least a decade to deploy a new technology, and if research and development are required, additional time may be needed. For such a key component of national defence, it is not sufficient to merely demonstrate that new systems work. There must be sufficient time to shake out the inevitable problems associated with new systems so as to make them dependable beyond reasonable doubt of our own government and the governments of potential adversaries.

Time must also be allowed for the negotiation of treaties or other international agreements that support the new force structure and that preclude the marginalization of our forces by either a massive breakout or any other action that would reduce the effectiveness of our forces.

Finally, the twentieth century repeatedly demonstrated that sweeping geopolitical changes occur on a short time scale compared to our ability to respond with new technologies or doctrines. It is imperative to consider the widest range of potential options before a crisis develops and to maintain a sufficiently robust research and development base to enable a response at that time.

The development of naval air power during the 1930s is a prime example of the need to evaluate the role of new technologies well before any anticipated engagement. The development of radar and ballistic missiles during the 1940s is an example of technologies developed during a conflict using preexisting foundations of research and technology. Some investment in thinking about future strategic forces now could reap significant dividends in the future.

Planning for future strategic defence is a highly complex affair that requires the consideration of many possible contingencies. This chapter is not intended to be a complete analysis of such a complex topic. Rather, its purpose is to stimulate thinking about changes in the international environment and technology that might be expected to influence the makeup of our strategic warfighting capability.

In order to set the stage, I first present a brief overview of the geopolitical situation that might reasonably be expected to influence defence strategy in 2020. The weapons technology might be available to the United States and other countries. Some force structures, including weapons and supporting infrastructure, that might satisfy future defence needs. The chapter concludes with a summary and suggestions for further work.

THE INTERNATIONAL SITUATION IN THE TWENTY-FIRST CENTURY

Before one can rationally future defence needs, it is necessary to know what one is defending against. The past decade has demonstrated the difficulty and danger of predicting the geopolitical future, but there are some forecasts that can be made with reasonable confidence.

Strategic Threats to U.S. National Security in the Twenty-First Century

Future national security threats to the United States might be divided into three major categories: major power conflicts, especially those involving Russia and China; regional conflicts, including potential nuclear states such as Iran, Iraq, or North Korea; and conflicts involving terrorist groups and other nonstate organizations.

Only the first two major categories will be considered here, since it is arguable whether there is any role for strategic nuclear forces in dealing with terrorism and substate threats. However, strategic conflicts can be sparked by terrorist acts, as was the case in the First World War and other conflicts.

Russia — During the past 200 years European Russia has sustained a series of catastrophes including the invasion of Napoleon, the Crimean War, the First World War, the Revolution, the Second World War, and now the transition from a communist state to something else.

In each case the country recovered within a generation. Even after the Second World War, when the country was essentially in ruins, it came back to launch Sputnik within twelve years. While one cannot predict what will happen in a country so volatile as Russia, it is not unreasonable to assume that it will endeavour to return to a conventional military power while continuing to rely on a significant nuclear capability. It is clear from Russia's investment in conventional military technology that it wishes to reassert its status in this area and to continue a lucrative business in the international arms trade.

China – China's international aims are in development, but their long stated intention to "reunify" Taiwan into the mainland and their territorial moves in the South China Sea indicate that they plan to play a broader role on the international stage. China has a small nuclear arsenal but one capable of inflicting unacceptable damage on American territory and interests. It is unclear at present what, if any, impact alleged Chinese nuclear espionage will have on the modernization of its nuclear arsenal. However, it is worth noting that China has several nuclear weapons systems in the advanced development stage including a new cruise missile, which presumably can carry a nuclear warhead, and new land-launched and sea-launched ballistic missiles. Road mobile nuclear capable missiles add a degree of survivability to China's limited nuclear arsenal. The desire to develop an operational ballistic missile submarine is another suggestion that China is concerned about the survivability of its nuclear forces and perhaps is a comment on its future goals of power projection outside of the immediate Pacific area.

Other Countries ýÿ The nuclear tests of India and Pakistan again demonstrate that countries will act in their own perceived national interests, sometimes in direct opposition to the wishes of the United States or to previous treaty commitments or arrangements. Continued tensions in South Asia, including Sino-Indian tensions, bear close monitoring, but they may not directly involve the United States. The Middle East will continue to be a problem area due to the misalignment of ethnic, cultural, and national borders. The prospects for Arab or Islamic unification do not appear imminent at present, but historically this unification has relied on a charismatic leader, whose advent is difficult to predict. Continued problems in the Balkans and elsewhere in the world may tax American and allied conventional capabilities, but such conflicts are not expected to assume a nuclear dimension in the foreseeable future. North Korea is presumed to have at least some nuclear capability and has demonstrated remarkable progress in ballistic missile technology, despite its perilous economic condition. Japan and South Korea look upon North Korea's nuclear ambitions with concern and could pursue their own nuclear programs if they felt uncertainty in the American nuclear umbrella. Similar concerns could apply to Taiwan in light of recent statements made by the People's Republic of China.

Nuclear engagement scenarios are not necessarily binary. Third countries may feel compelled to intervene in disputes between nuclear states or in conflicts involving weapons of mass destruction that could spill over into their territory or interests. For example, China may feel a need to act in a nuclear exchange between India and Pakistan. Similarly, Israel may feel a need to act in a major conflict of its neighbours that involved weapons of mass destruction.

5

Biological and Chemical Terrorism

Terrorist incidents in the United States and elsewhere involving bacterial pathogens (3), nerve gas (1), and a lethal plant toxin (i.e., ricin) (4), have demonstrated that the United States is vulnerable to biological and chemical threats as well as explosives. Recipes for preparing "homemade" agents are readily available (5), and reports of arsenals of military bioweapons (2) raise the possibility that terrorists might have access to highly dangerous agents, which have been engineered for mass dissemination as small-particle aerosols. Such agents as the variola virus, the causative agent of smallpox, are highly contagious and often fatal. Responding to large-scale outbreaks caused by these agents will require the rapid mobilization of public health workers, emergency responders, and private health-care providers. Large-scale outbreaks will also require rapid procurement and distribution of large quantities of drugs and vaccines, which must be available quickly.

TERRORIST ATTACKS

In the past, most planning for emergency response to terrorism has been concerned with overt attacks (e.g., bombings). Chemical terrorism acts are likely to be overt because the effects of chemical agents absorbed through inhalation or by absorption through the skin or mucous membranes are usually immediate and obvious. Such attacks elicit immediate response from police, fire, and EMS personnel.

In contrast, attacks with biological agents are more likely to be covert. They present different challenges and require an additional dimension of emergency planning that involves the public health infrastructure. Covert dissemination of a biological agent in a public place will not have an immediate impact because of the delay between exposure and onset of illness (i.e., the incubation period). Consequently, the first casualties of a covert attack probably will be identified by physicians or other primary health-care providers. For example, in the event of a covert release of the contagious variola virus, patients will appear in doctors' offices, clinics, and emergency rooms during the first or second week, complaining of fever, back pain, headache, nausea, and other symptoms of what initially might appear to be an ordinary viral infection.

As the disease progresses, these persons will develop the papular rash characteristic of early-stage smallpox, a rash that physicians might not recognize immediately. By the time the rash becomes pustular and patients begin to die, the terrorists would be far away and the disease disseminated through the population by person-to-person contact. Only a short window of opportunity will exist between the time the first cases are identified and a second wave of the population becomes ill. During that brief period, public health officials will need to determine that an attack has occurred, identify the organism, and prevent more casualties through prevention strategies (e.g., mass vaccination or prophylactic treatment). As person-to-person contact continues, successive waves of transmission could carry infection to other worldwide localities. These issues might also be relevant for other person-to-person transmissible etiologic agents (e.g., plague or certain viral hemorrhagic fevers).

Certain chemical agents can also be delivered covertly through contaminated food or water. In 1999, the vulnerability of the food supply was illustrated in Belgium, when chickens were unintentionally exposed to dioxin-contaminated fat used to make animal feed (6). Because the contamination was not discovered for months, the dioxin, a cancer-causing chemical that does not cause immediate symptoms in humans, was probably present in chicken meat and eggs sold in Europe during early 1999. This incident underscores the need for prompt diagnoses of unusual or suspicious health problems in animals as well as humans, a lesson that was also demonstrated by the recent outbreak of mosquitoborne West Nile virus in birds and humans in New York City in 1999. The dioxin episode also demonstrates how a covert act of foodborne biological or chemical terrorism could affect commerce and human or animal health.

Focusing Preparedness Activities

Early detection of and response to biological or chemical terrorism are crucial. Without special preparation at the local and state levels, a large-scale attack with variola virus, aerosolized anthrax spores, a nerve gas, or a foodborne biological or chemical agent could overwhelm the local and perhaps national public health infrastructure. Large numbers of patients, including both infected persons and the "worried well," would seek medical attention, with a corresponding need for medical supplies, diagnostic tests, and hospital beds. Emergency responders, health-care workers, and public health officials could be at special risk, and everyday life would be disrupted as a result of widespread fear of contagion.

Preparedness for terrorist-caused outbreaks and injuries is an essential component of the U.S. public health surveillance and response system, which is designed to protect the population against any unusual public health event (e.g., influenza pandemics, contaminated municipal water supplies, or intentional dissemination of Yersinia pestis, the causative agent of plague). The epidemiologic skills, surveillance methods, diagnostic techniques, and physical resources required to detect and investigate unusual or unknown diseases, as well as syndromes or injuries caused by chemical accidents, are similar to those needed to identify and respond to an attack with a biological or chemical agent.

However, public health agencies must prepare also for the special features a terrorist attack probably would have (e.g., mass casualties or the use of rare agents. Terrorists might use combinations of these agents, attack in more than one location simultaneously, use new agents, or use organisms that are not on the critical list (e.g., common, drug-resistant, or genetically engineered pathogens). Lists of critical biological and chemical agents will need to be modified as new information becomes available. In addition, each state and locality will need to adapt the lists to local conditions and preparedness needs by using the criteria provided in CDC's strategic plan.

Potential biological and chemical agents are numerous, and the public health infrastructure must be equipped to quickly resolve crises that would arise from a biological or chemical attack. However, to best protect the public, the preparedness efforts must be focused on agents that might have the greatest impact on U.S. health and security, especially agents that are highly contagious or that can be engineered for widespread dissemination via small-particle aerosols. Preparing the nation to address these dangers is a major challenge to U.S. public health systems and health-care providers.

Early detection requires increased biological and chemical terrorism awareness among front-line health-care providers because they are in the best position to report suspicious illnesses and injuries.

Also, early detection will require improved communication systems between those providers and public health officials. In addition, state and local health-care agencies must have enhanced capacity to investigate unusual events and unexplained illnesses, and diagnostic laboratories must be equipped to identify biological and chemical agents that rarely are seen in the United States.

Fundamental to these efforts is comprehensive, integrated training designed to ensure core competency in public health preparedness and the highest levels of scientific expertise among local, state, and federal partners.

KEY FOCUS AREAS

CDC's strategic plan is based on the following five focus areas, with each area integrating training and research:

- preparedness and prevention;
- detection and surveillance;
- diagnosis and characterization of biological and chemical agents;
- response; and
- communication.

Preparedness and Prevention

Detection, diagnosis, and mitigation of illness and injury caused by biological and chemical terrorism is a complex process that involves numerous partners and activities. Meeting this challenge will require special emergency preparedness in all cities and states. CDC will provide public health guidelines, support, and technical assistance to local and state public health agencies as they develop coordinated preparedness plans and response protocols. CDC also will provide self-assessment tools for terrorism preparedness, including performance standards, attack simulations, and other exercises. In addition, CDC will encourage and support applied research to develop innovative tools and strategies to prevent or mitigate illness and injury caused by biological and chemical terrorism.

Detection and Surveillance

Early detection is essential for ensuring a prompt response to a biological or chemical attack, including the provision of prophylactic medicines, chemical antidotes, or vaccines. CDC will integrate surveillance for illness and injury resulting from biological and chemical terrorism into the U.S. disease surveillance systems, while developing new mechanisms for detecting, evaluating, and reporting suspicious events that might represent covert terrorist acts.

As part of this effort, CDC and state and local health agencies will form partnerships with front-line medical personnel in hospital emergency departments, hospital care facilities, poison control centers, and other offices to enhance detection and reporting of unexplained injuries and illnesses as part of routine surveillance mechanisms for biological and chemical terrorism.

Characterization of Biological and Chemical Agents

CDC and its partners will create a multilevel laboratory response network for bioterrorism (LRNB). That network will link clinical labs to public health agencies in all states, districts, territories, and selected cities and counties and to state-of-the-art facilities that can analyze biological agents. As part of this effort, CDC will transfer diagnostic technology to state health laboratories and others who will perform initial testing. CDC will also create an in-house rapid-response and advanced technology (RRAT) laboratory.

This laboratory will provide around-the-clock diagnostic confirmatory and reference support for terrorism response teams. This network will include the regional chemical laboratories for diagnosing human exposure to chemical agents and provide links with other departments (e.g., the U.S. Environmental Protection Agency, which is responsible for environmental sampling).

Response

A comprehensive public health response to a biological or chemical terrorist event involves epidemiologic investigation, medical treatment and prophylaxis for affected persons, and the initiation of disease prevention or environmental decontamination measures.

CDC will assist state and local health agencies in developing resources and expertise for investigating unusual events and unexplained illnesses.

In the event of a confirmed terrorist attack, CDC will coordinate with other federal agencies in accord with Presidential Decision Directive (PDD) 39. PDD 39 designates the Federal Bureau of Investigation as the lead agency for the crisis plan and charges the Federal Emergency Management Agency with ensuring that the federal response management is adequate to respond to the consequences of terrorism.

If requested by a state health agency, CDC will deploy response teams to investigate unexplained or suspicious illnesses or unusual etiologic agents and provide on-site consultation regarding medical management and disease control. To ensure the availability, procurement, and delivery of medical supplies, devices, and equipment that might be needed to respond to terrorist-caused illness or injury, CDC will maintain a national pharmaceutical stockpile.

Communication Systems

U.S. preparedness to mitigate the public health consequences of biological and chemical terrorism depends on the coordinated activities of well-trained health-care and public health personnel throughout the United States who have access to up-to-the minute emergency information.

Effective communication with the public through the news media will also be essential to limit terrorists' ability to induce public panic and disrupt daily life. During the next 5 years, CDC will work with state and local health agencies to develop a) a state-of-the-art communication system that will support disease surveillance; b) rapid notification and information exchange regarding disease outbreaks that are possibly related to bioterrorism; c) dissemination of diagnostic results and emergency health information; and d) coordination of emergency response activities. Through this network and similar mechanisms, CDC will provide terrorism-related training to epidemiologists and laboratorians, emergency responders, emergency department personnel and other front-line health-care providers, and health and safety personnel.

Partnerships and Implementation

Implementation of the objectives outlined in CDC's strategic plan will be coordinated through CDC's Bioterrorism Preparedness and Response Program. Program personnel are charged with (a) helping build local and state preparedness, (b) developing U.S. expertise regarding potential threat agents, and (c) coordinating response activities during actual bioterrorist events. Program staff have established priorities for 20002002 regarding the focus areas. Implementation will require collaboration with state and local public health agencies, as well as with other persons and groups, including

- public health organizations,
- medical research centers,
- health-care providers and their networks,
- professional societies,
- medical examiners,
- emergency response units and responder organizations,
- safety and medical equipment manufacturers,
- the U.S. Office of Emergency Preparedness and other Department of Health and Human Services agencies,
- other federal agencies, and
- international organizations.

Recommendations

Implementing CDC's strategic preparedness and response plan by 2004 will ensure the following outcomes:

- U.S. public health agencies and health-care providers will be prepared to mitigate illness and injuries that result from acts of biological and chemical terrorism.
- Public health surveillance for infectious diseases and injuries---including events that might indicate terrorist activity---will be timely and complete, and reporting of suspected terrorist events will be integrated with the evolving, comprehensive networks of the national public health surveillance system.
- The national laboratory response network for bioterrorism will be extended to include facilities in all 50 states. The network will include CDC's environmental health laboratory for chemical terrorism and four regional facilities.
- State and federal public health departments will be equipped with state-of-the-art tools for rapid epidemiological investigation and control of suspected or confirmed acts of biological or chemical terrorism, and a designated stock of terrorism-related medical supplies will be available through a national pharmaceutical stockpile.

- A cadre of well-trained health-care and public health workers will be available in every state. Their terrorism-related activities will be coordinated through a rapid and efficient communication system that links U.S. public health agencies and their partners.

Recent threats and use of biological and chemical agents against civilians have exposed U.S. vulnerability and highlighted the need to enhance our capacity to detect and control terrorist acts. The U.S. must be protected from an extensive range of critical biological and chemical agents, including some that have been developed and stockpiled for military use. Even without threat of war, investment in national defense ensures preparedness and acts as a deterrent against hostile acts. Similarly, investment in the public health system provides the best civil defense against bioterrorism.

Tools developed in response to terrorist threats serve a dual purpose. They help detect rare or unusual disease outbreaks and respond to health emergencies, including naturally occurring outbreaks or industrial injuries that might resemble terrorist events in their unpredictability and ability to cause mass casualties (e.g., a pandemic influenza outbreak or a large-scale chemical spill). Terrorism-preparedness activities described in CDC's plan, including the development of a public health communication infrastructure, a multilevel network of diagnostic laboratories, and an integrated disease surveillance system, will improve our ability to investigate rapidly and control public health threats that emerge in the twenty first century.

Public Health Agency

- Because the initial detection of a covert biological or chemical attack will probably occur at the local level, disease surveillance systems at state and local health agencies must be capable of detecting unusual patterns of disease or injury, including those caused by unusual or unknown threat agents.
- Because the initial response to a covert biological or chemical attack will probably be made at the local level, epidemiologists at state and local health agencies must

have expertise and resources for responding to reports of clusters of rare, unusual, or unexplained illnesses.

Biological Attacks

Steps in Preparing for Biological Attacks

- Enhance epidemiologic capacity to detect and respond to biological attacks.
- Supply diagnostic reagents to state and local public health agencies.
- Establish communication programs to ensure delivery of accurate information.
- Enhance bioterrorism-related education and training for health-care professionals.
- Prepare educational materials that will inform and reassure the public during and after a biological attack.
- Stockpile appropriate vaccines and drugs.
- Establish molecular surveillance for microbial strains, including unusual or drug-resistant strains.
- Support the development of diagnostic tests.
- Encourage research on antiviral drugs and vaccines.

Critical Biological Agents

Category A: The U.S. public health system and primary health-care providers must be prepared to address varied biological agents, including pathogens that are rarely seen in the United States. High-priority agents include organisms that pose a risk to national security because they

- can be easily disseminated or transmitted person-to-person;
- cause high mortality, with potential for major public health impact;
- might cause public panic and social disruption; and
- require special action for public health preparedness.

Category A agents include:

- variola major (smallpox);
- Bacillus anthracis (anthrax);

- Yersinia pestis (plague);
- Clostridium botulinum toxin (botulism);
- Francisella tularensis (tularaemia);
- filoviruses,
  - o Ebola hemorrhagic fever,
  - o Marburg hemorrhagic fever; and
- arenaviruses,
  - o Lassa (Lassa fever),
  - o Junin (Argentine hemorrhagic fever) and related viruses.

Category B : Second highest priority agents include those that

- are moderately easy to disseminate;
- cause moderate morbidity and low mortality; and
- require specific enhancements of CDC's diagnostic capacity and enhanced disease surveillance.

Category B agents include :

- Coxiella burnetti (Q fever);
- Brucella species (brucellosis);
- Burkholderia mallei (glanders);
- alphaviruses,
  - o Venezuelan encephalomyelitis,
  - o eastern and western equine encephalomyelitis;
- ricin toxin from Ricinus communis (castor beans);
- epsilon toxin of Clostridium perfringens; and
- Staphylococcus enterotoxin B.

A subset of List B agents includes pathogens that are food- or waterborne.

These pathogens include but are not limited to:

- Salmonella species,
- Shigella dysenteriae,
- Escherichia coli O157:H7,
- Vibrio cholerae, and
- Cryptosporidium parvum.

Category C : Third highest priority agents include emerging pathogens that could be engineered for mass dissemination in the future because of

- availability;
- ease of production and dissemination; and
- potential for high morbidity and mortality and major health impact.

Category C agents include :

- Nipah virus,
- hantaviruses,
- tickborne hemorrhagic fever viruses,
- tickborne encephalitis viruses,
- yellow fever, and
- multidrug-resistant tuberculosis.

Preparedness for List C agents requires ongoing research to improve disease detection, diagnosis, treatment, and prevention.

Knowing in advance which newly emergent pathogens might be employed by terrorists is not possible; therefore, linking bioterrorism preparedness efforts with ongoing disease surveillance and outbreak response activities as defined in CDC's emerging infectious disease strategy is imperative.*

Chemical Attacks

Steps in Preparing for Chemical Attacks :

- Enhance epidemiologic capacity for detecting and responding to chemical attacks.
- Enhance awareness of chemical terrorism among emergency medical service personnel, police officers, firefighters, physicians, and nurses.
- Stockpile chemical antidotes.
- Develop and provide bioassays for detection and diagnosis of chemical injuries.
- Prepare educational materials to inform the public during and after a chemical attack

Chemical Agents

Chemical agents that might be used by terrorists range from warfare agents to toxic chemicals commonly used in industry. Criteria for determining priority chemical agents include :

- chemical agents already known to be used as weaponry;
- availability of chemical agents to potential terrorists;
- chemical agents likely to cause major morbidity or mortality;
- potential of agents for causing public panic and social disruption; and
- agents that require special action for public health preparedness.

Categories of chemical agents include :

- nerve agents,
  - o tabun (ethyl N,N-dimethylphosphoramidocyanidate),
  - o sarin (isopropyl methylphosphanofluoridate),
  - o soman (pinacolyl methyl phosphonofluoridate),
  - o GF (cyclohexylmethylphosphonofluoridate),
  - o VX (o-ethyl-[S]-[2-diisopropylaminoethyl]-methylphosphonothiolate);
- blood agents,
  - o hydrogen cyanide,
  - o cyanogen chloride;
- blister agents,
  - o lewisite (an aliphatic arsenic compound, 2-chlorovinyldichloroarsine),
  - o nitrogen and sulfur mustards,
  - o phosgene oxime;
- heavy metals,
  - o arsenic,
  - o lead,
  - o mercury;
- Volatile toxins,
  - o benzene,

  - o chloroform,
  - o trihalomethanes;
- pulmonary agents,
  - o phosgene,
  - o chlorine,
  - o vinyl chloride;
- incapacitating agents,
  - o BZ (3-quinuclidinyl benzilate);
  - pesticides, persistent and nonpersistent;
  - dioxins, furans, and polychlorinated biphenyls (PCBs);
  - explosive nitro compounds and oxidizers,
  - o ammonium nitrate combined with fuel oil;
- flammable industrial gases and liquids,
  - o gasoline,
  - o propane;
- poison industrial gases, liquids, and solids,
  - o cyanides,
  - o nitriles; and
- corrosive industrial acids and bases,
  - o nitric acid,
  - o sulfuric acid.

Because of the hundreds of new chemicals introduced internationally each month, treating exposed persons by clinical syndrome rather than by specific agent is more useful for public health planning and emergency medical response purposes.

Public health agencies and first responders might render the most aggressive, timely, and clinically relevant treatment possible by using treatment modalities based on syndromic categories (e.g., burns and trauma, cardiorespiratory failure, neurologic damage, and shock). These activities must be linked with authorities responsible for environmental sampling and decontamination.

Preparedness and Prevention

- Maintain a public health preparedness and response cooperative agreement that provides support to state health agencies who are working with local agencies in developing coordinated bioterrorism plans and protocols.

- Establish a national public health distance-learning system that provides biological and chemical terrorism preparedness training to health-care workers and to state and local public health workers.
- Disseminate public health guidelines and performance standards on biological and chemical terrorism preparedness planning for use by state and local health agencies.

Detection and Surveillance

- Strengthen state and local surveillance systems for illness and injury resulting from pathogens and chemical substances that are on CDC's critical agents list.
- Develop new algorithms and statistical methods for searching medical databases on a real-time basis for evidence of suspicious events.
- Establish criteria for investigating and evaluating suspicious clusters of human or animal disease or injury and triggers for notifying law enforcement of suspected acts of biological or chemical terrorism.

Biological and Chemical Agents

- Establish a multilevel laboratory response network for bioterrorism that links public health agencies to advanced capacity facilities for the identification and reporting of critical biological agents.
- Establish regional chemical terrorism laboratories that will provide diagnostic capacity during terrorist attacks involving chemical agents.
- Establish a rapid-response and advanced technology laboratory within CDC to provide around-the-clock diagnostic support to bioterrorism response teams and expedite molecular characterization of critical biological agents.

Response

- Assist state and local health agencies in organizing response capacities to rapidly deploy in the event of an overt attack or a suspicious outbreak that might be the result of a covert attack.
- Ensure that procedures are in place for rapid mobilization of CDC terrorism response teams that will provide on-site assistance to local health workers, security agents, and law enforcement officers.
- Establish a national pharmaceutical stockpile to provide medical supplies in the event of a terrorist attack that involves biological or chemical agents.
- Establish a national electronic infrastructure to improve exchange of emergency health information among local, state, and federal health agencies.
- Implement an emergency communication plan that ensures rapid dissemination of health information to the public during actual, threatened, or suspected acts of biological or chemical terrorism.
- Create a website that disseminates bioterrorism preparedness and training information, as well as other bioterrorism-related emergency information, to public health and health-care workers and the public.

EXPOSURE VECTORS FOR CHEMICAL AND BIOLOGICAL WEAPONS

Exposure to chemical and biological weapons can occur through several potential vectors. Airborne releases of agents have remained the primary concern, because very large populations can be exposed by this route. Potential mechanisms of exposure include crop-dusting airplanes, tainted letters, and release into confined spaces (eg, subway tunnels, office buildings, theaters). Although contamination of the water supply is also a potential vector for exposure, there are very few chemical or biological agents that are both water-stable and resistant to water-purification techniques. Finally, the contamination of food that is either unprocessed (eg, uncultivated grain) or processed (eg, a consumer product) is considered a potential means of exposure to chemical or biological weapons.

Specific Vulnerabilities in Children

After events of chemical or biological terrorism, children have a greater risk of both exposure and harm, the result of key developmental and physiologic vulnerabilities.

For each of the vectors of exposure to biological or chemical weapons (air, water, or food), children possess a significantly greater likelihood of exposure because of their intake patterns. Children inhale considerably more air on a per-weight basis than adults (400 vs 140 mL/kg per minute, respectively). Consequently, for any concentration of airborne toxin, a child will inhale more of the substance on a per-weight basis than an adult. Also, substances that are heavier than air have their highest concentration near the ground, closer to the breathing zone of the child.

Because children have less-keratinized, more-permeable skin and/or a proportionately greater body-surface area, they have both greater exposure and a greater likelihood of systemic toxicity to agents that fall on their skin. Children have fluid and food intakes that differ significantly from adults. For example, children ingest approximately 100 mL/kg per day of water, compared with the 40 to 60 mL/kg per day that adults ingest. Children drink more milk than adults, placing them at risk of exposure to agents that can enter the milk supply through contamination of the grass on which cows feed; in the Chernobyl radiation disaster, cows grazed in contaminated pastures, resulting in excess radioactivity in their milk. Children drinking this milk sustained significant exposure to radioisotopes, including iodine and strontium. Finally, children not only eat more food on a per-kilogram basis but also have diets that are distinctly different from adults (eg, greater consumption of fruits).

Once exposed to a chemical or biological agent, children have numerous physiologic vulnerabilities that could lead to a greater risk of harm. These vulnerabilities include undeveloped self-preservation skills that make them less able to flee danger; an immature immune system that makes them less able to contain infection (eg, plague); less fluid reserve, which can result in a greater risk of severe dehydration after exposure to agents that produce excess gastrointestinal fluid loss; and a greater risk of anxiety reactions and posttraumatic stress disorder after witnessing or being victim to a terrorist act.

PUBLIC HEALTH PREPAREDNESS

The All-Hazards Approach

Over the last 5 years, a massive public health effort to improve response capability to future acts of biological terrorism has appeared. Such efforts have included antibiotic stockpiling, resurrection of smallpox immunization, and an unprecedented level of added support to state and local public health departments. Similarly, to respond to a possible chemical attack, extensive resources have been provided to public health authorities and first responders (fire, police, and emergency medical services) to create systems that will provide effective mitigation efforts. The initiation of these response campaigns revealed large-scale weaknesses in state and local public health infrastructure. Moreover, it became evident that intense effort was being directed toward events that might never occur rather than public health threats of much greater likelihood (eg, the appearance of an emerging infection or an unintentional hazardous chemical release). Finally, it became clear that a fragmented and reactive public health–response plan is more expensive and inefficient than a single, comprehensive plan. As a result, disaster-response agencies and public health authorities have increasingly embraced the concept of the "all-hazards approach." Representing a dramatic paradigm shift in the preparation for chemical and biological terrorism, the all-hazards approach is designed to augment public health infrastructure, using an integrated model of disaster response.

Creation of all-hazards response systems has led to significant enhancements in public health–response capabilities. For example, the same protocol created to respond to the appearance of smallpox can be easily modified to contain an outbreak of severe acute respiratory syndrome (SARS). Similarly, an effective public health–

response protocol for a sarin release would be equally effective for a hazardous-materials ("HAZMAT") release in the community.

Syndromic Surveillance

Overt acts of chemical and biological terrorism such as the sarin release in Tokyo present the challenge of rapidly identifying the agent and mobilizing the proper interventions. However, acts of chemical and biological terrorism may also be covert. Examples include the release of anthrax in 2001 and contamination of ground beef with nicotine in 2002. Covert incidents pose a significantly greater public health challenge and are more likely to induce widespread fear than overt events. Mechanisms for early recognition of a covert chemical or biological event, therefore, are necessary to contain the incident and minimize its impact.

Syndromic surveillance, a specialized type of outbreak detection, is a term used to describe mechanisms for monitoring health indices or events that reflect the early stages of an infection or disease of public health importance in an effort to minimize consequences. Syndromic surveillance is considered an important means of identifying public health emergencies in their initial stages. Syndromic surveillance techniques can be clinician based or automated. Many syndromic surveillance systems are emergency department based. In addition, most state and local health departments are pursuing automatic electronic laboratory disease reporting.

The traditional mechanism of syndromic surveillance has been the clinician who recognizes unusual patterns of disease and reports them to public health authorities. The "astute clinician" principle places all health care professionals (including physicians, nurses, emergency medical technicians, epidemiologists, and health educators) in the role of sentinels for the appearance of disease clusters or other clinical abnormalities.

The pivotal role of physicians and other health care professionals in syndromic surveillance, particularly for acts of terrorism, has led the CDC and other agencies to educate clinicians about chemical and biological weapons release and the diseases they produce. Clinical cues, case definitions, and syndromes for chemical weapons exposure have been published, along with numerous resources to expand clinicians' ability to recognize covert terrorist incidents.

Over the last few years, there has also been a rapid increase in the development of real-time, automated syndromic surveillance tools. A rapidly proliferating area, such automated decision support uses software to identify sentinel events such as an unusual amount of work or school absenteeism, changes in consumer purchase of over-the-counter products (eg, cough syrups or antipyretics), and changes in the chief-complaint profile among those who visit primary care physicians or emergency departments. For example, the CDC has developed the Early Aberration Reporting System as a software tool available to clinicians and health departments around the nation.

New Governmental Roles in Emergency Preparedness

Although emergency-preparedness legislation existed before 2001, passage of additional rules between 2002 and 2005 resulted in massive efforts by the federal government to improve public health readiness across the nation. Over the last 4 years, appropriations from federal to state public health agencies have been substantial. The Department of Homeland Security was established as a new member of the federal cabinet. Several departments within the Department of Health and Human Services have undergone extensive change, such as the CDC, Food and Drug Administration, and National Institutes of Health, all of which have reorganized their practice, regulatory, and research priorities to include chemical and biological terrorism, along with other public health threats; in 2002, the CDC established the Office of Terrorism Preparedness and Emergency Response.

At state and local levels, planning for chemical and biological terrorism is now coordinated by multiple agencies, including departments of health, emergency-management agencies, poison control centers, and law enforcement authorities. The Strategic National Stockpile (SNS) has become one of the most important initiatives in mass-casualty disaster response. Designed to respond to disasters that overwhelm local resources, the SNS includes such capabilities as the delivery of medications and supplies to areas of need within 12 hours of the request. SNS supplies include a pediatric formulary and materials for compounding tablets and capsules into liquid formulations.

BIOLOGICAL TERRORISM AND ITS IMPACT ON CHILDREN

Definition

Apart from the natural transnational movement of the pathogenic organisms, their potential use as weapons of biological warfare and bio-terrorism has become far more important now than ever before. Utilization of organisms causing smallpox and anthrax by such terrorist groups can cause greater harm and panic. Biological agents are living organisms or their toxic products that can kill or incapacitate people, livestock, and plants. Bio-terrorism can be defined as the use of biological agents to cause death, disability or damage mainly to human beings. Thus, bio-terrorism is a method of terrorist activity to prevail mass panic and slow mass casualties.

The three basic groups of biological agents, which could be used as weapons, are bacteria, viruses, and toxins. Most biological agents are difficult to grow and maintain. Many break down quickly when exposed to sunlight and other environmental factors, while others, such as anthrax spores, are very long lived. Biological agents can be dispersed by spraying them into the air, by infecting animals that carry the disease to humans, and by contaminating food and water. Potentially, hundreds of human pathogens could be used as weapons; however, public health authorities have identified only a few as having the potential to cause mass casualties leading to civil disruptions.

Causes and Method of Delivery

There are number of causes why biological weapons are potentially more powerful agents to mass casualties leading to civil disruptions. To attract widespread attention and to harm a selected target, these outfits can utilize possibly any biological material, which fulfils some of the criteria of bio-weapons.

- Biological agents can be disseminated with readily available technology. Common agricultural spray devices can be adopted to disseminate biological pathogens of the proper particle size to cause infection in human population over great distances.
- The perpetrators can use natural weather conditions, such as wind and temperature inversions as well as existing building infrastructures (e.g. ventilation system) or air movement related to transportation (e.g. subway cars passing through tunnels) to disseminate these agents and thus to infect or intoxicate a large number of people.
- The expense of producing biological weapons is far less than that of other weapon systems. The methods of biological agent dissemination and delivery techniques include:
- Aerosols-biological agents are dispersed into the air, forming a fine mist that may drift for miles. Inhaling the agent may cause epidemic diseases in human beings or animals.
- Animals-some diseases are spread by insects and animals, such as fleas, mice, flies, mosquitoes, and livestock.
- Food and water contamination-some pathogenic organisms and toxins may persist in food and water supplies. Most microbes can be killed, and toxins deactivated, by cooking food and boiling water. Most microbes are killed by boiling water for one minute, but some require longer. Follow official instructions.
- Person-to-person-spread of a few infectious agents is also possible.

Humans have been the source of infection for smallpox, plague, and the Lassa viruses.

Types

There are three categories of biological agents potential enough to cause mass casualties. However, those in category A have the greatest potential for fear and disruption and most significant public health impacts. The list of these biological agents with a very brief description about them is given below.

- The disease anthrax is caused by the gram-positive, non-motile Bacillus anthracis. Anthrax has been a scourge of cattle and other herbivores for centuries. During the industrial revolution, the inhalation form was first recognized as an occupational pulmonary disease in workers in the wool industries of Europe. Anthrax makes an ideal biological weapon. The inhalation form of disease is highly lethal. The spores can maintain virulence for decades and they can be milled to the ideal particle size for optimum infection of the human respiratory tract. Different clinical forms of the disease are observed, depending on the route of exposure. Inhalational anthrax presents with non-specific symptoms that cannot be distinguished from many more common diseases based on early clinical manifestations or routine laboratory tests. Therefore, despite aggressive medical care sometimes develop rapidly progressive disease and dye.
- If used as a biological weapon, smallpox represents a serious threat to civilian population because of its case fatality rate of 30% or more among unvaccinated persons and the absence of specific therapy. Smallpox has long been considered as the most devastating of all infectious diseases and today its potential for devastation is far greater than at any previous time. Smallpox virus is a member of genus Orthopoxvirus, and it is closely related to the viruses causing cowpox, vaccinia and monkey pox. It is one of the largest DNA viruses known, and it has a bricklike appearance on electron microscopy. Transmission of this virus can occur in several different ways: generally by droplets, occasionally by aerosol, by direct contact with secretions or lesions from a patient, and rarely by formites contacted with the infection virus from a patient. Transmission risk increases if the index patient is coughing or sneezing or if he or she has hemorrhagic disease. Typically, the virus enters the respiratory mucosa and then

travels to regional lymph nodes where it replicates. The incubation period from infection to onset of rash ranges from 7 to 17 days, averaging 12 to 14 days. Smallpox scabs remain infectious until they fall off, whereas chickenpox is no longer infectious once the lesions are crusted.

- The mere mention of the word plague conjures up many images because has already demonstrated a historical potential to kill millions of people across the globe. It is a disease that results from infection by non-motile, gram-negative coccobacillus Yersinia pestis. When stained, its bipolar appearance is often described as resembling a safety pin. Pestis has two important properties that differentiate it from B. anthracis-person-to-person transmissibility and a lack of spore production. Following the bite of an infected flea, plague bacilli are carried via the lymphatic to the regional lymph nodes where they multiply exponentially. This is only weapon besides smallpox, which can cause devastation beyond those persons who are initially infected. With modern air travel, containing an out break of plague could be challenging. A vaccine for plague does exist; however, it is no longer being produced, and it does not demonstrate efficacy against infection by aerosol.
- Botulism or Botulinum toxins are deadly. A toxin is any toxic substance that can be produced in an animal, plant, or microbe. The toxins produce serious disease in human beings. Many natural toxins can be produced by chemical synthesis or can be expressed artificially. Toxins are natural and non-volatile and generally do not penetrate intact skin, which happens in case of chemical weapons. There are different types of toxins and they are immunologically distinct, meaning that antibodies developed against one do not cross-react against others. Those that most commonly cause human disease are types A, B, and E. Humans can be intoxicated either by oral means, inhalation, or wound infection. Mass casualties can be produced through contamination of food source or by aerosol dissemination. The incubation period of botulism can range

from as short as 24 to 36 hours to several days from the time of inhalation.

- Tularemia is caused by Francisella tularensis, which is a gram-negative, non-motile coccobacillus. Tularemia is a zoonotic disease acquired in a natural setting by humans through skin or mucous membrane contact with the body fluids or tissues of infected animals or from being beaten by infected deerflies, mosquitoes, or ticks. It can remain viable for weeks in the environment or in animal carcasses and for years if frozen. Unlike anthrax, which requires thousands of spores to infect someone, tularemia can cause illness with as few as 10 to 50 organisms. After an incubation period of 2 to 10 days, pneumonia symptoms develop associated with weight loss and nonproductive cough. The drug of choice for treatment is streptomycin with other aminoglycosides.

THE BIOLOGICAL WEAPONS CONVENTION

Since ancient times, the use in war of poison and pathogenic agents has been considered a treacherous practice. It was condemned by international declarations and treaties, notably by the 1907 Hague Convention (IV) respecting the laws and customs of war on land. Efforts to strengthen this prohibition resulted in the conclusion, in 1925, of the Geneva Protocol which banned the use of asphyxiating, poisonous or other gases, usually referred to as chemical weapons, as well as the use of bacteriological methods of warfare. The latter are now understood to include not only bacteria, but also other biological agents, such as viruses or rickettsiae which were unknown at the time the Geneva Protocol was signed. (On 1 January 1997, 1 32 States were party to this Protocol.) However, the Geneva Protocol did not prohibit the development, production and stockpiling of chemical and biological weapons. Attempts to achieve a complete ban were made in the 1930s in the framework of the League of Nations, but with no success.

Shortly after World War II, the United Nations called for the elimination of all weapons "adaptable to mass destruction".

Biological and chemical weapons were included in this category of arms along with atomic and radiological weapons. Debates on their prohibition took place in the 1950s and 1960s in the context of proposals for general disarmament but, again, the debate remained inconclusive.

As a separate issue, the prohibition of chemical and biological weapons appeared on the agenda of the Eighteen-Nation Committee on Disarmament in 1968. One year later, the United Nations published an influential report on the problems of chemical and biological warfare, and the question received special attention at the UN General Assembly. The UN report concluded that certain chemical and biological weapons cannot be confined in their effects in space and time and might have grave and irreversible consequences for man and nature. This would apply to both the attacking and the attacked nations. A report by the World Health Organization (WHO) on the health aspects of chemical and biological weapons, issued in 1970, stated that these weapons pose a special threat to civilians, and that the effects of their use are subject to a high degree of uncertainty and unpredictability.

Although simultaneous prohibition of chemical and biological weapons had been considered for many years as both desirable and necessary, towards the end of the 1960s it became clear that such a prohibition was not achievable. In the Eighteen-Nation Committee on Disarmament, where the issue was under discussion, the United Kingdom and a few other Western countries ado pted the view that biological weapons should be banned first. The Socialist and many neutral and non-aligned States were opposed to a separate treatment of these weapons, but finally accepted the Western approach. A factor which facilitated this development was the unilateral renunciation of biological weapons by the United States, announced on 25 November 1969, and the decision by the US government to destroy its stockpile of these weapons, irrespective of a possible future international agreement. On 14 February 1970, the United States also formally renounced the production, stockpiling and use of toxins for war purposes. It stated that military programmes for biological agents and toxins would be confined to research and development for defensive purposes. Subsequent negotiations on a global prohibition of biological weapons led to an international agreement. On 16 December 1971, the text of the convention worked out by the Conference of the Committee on Disarmament (CCD), the successor of the Eighteen-Nation Committee on Disarmament, was commended by the UN General Assembly.

A CRITICAL ANALYSIS OF THE BW CONVENTION

On 10 April 1972, the Convention on the Prohibition of the Development, Production and Stockpiling of Bacteriological (Biological) and Toxin Weapons and on their Destruction was opened for signature. It entered into force on 26 March 1975, after the deposit of the instruments of ratification by 22 signatory governments, including the governments of the Soviet Union, the United Kingdom and the United States, designated as depositaries. By 1 January 1997, the BW Convention had been joined by 140 States, including all the permanent members of the United Nations Security Council.

Scope of the Obligations

The BW Convention prohibits the development, production, stockpiling or acquisition by other means, or retention of microbial or other biological agents or toxins, as well as of weapons, equipment or means of delivery designed to use such agents or toxins for hostile purposes or in armed conflict (Article I).

The Convention has not defined the prohibited items nor the targets to which the prohibitions relate. There exists, however, an authoritative definition of biological agents formulated by the WHO. In its 1970 report, mentioned above, the WHO described biological agents as those that depend for their effects on multiplication within the target organism and are intended for use in war to cause disease or death in man, animals or plants; they may be transmissible or non-transmissible. Toxins are poisonous products of organisms; unlike biological agents, they are inanimate and not capable of reproducing themselves. The Convention applies to all natural or artificially created toxins, "whatever their origin or method of production" (Article I). It thus covers toxins produced biologically, as well as those produced by chemical synthesis. Since toxins are chemicals by nature, their inclusion in the BW Convention was a step towards the projected ban on chemical weapons.

Since the signing of the Convention, there have been no disputes among the parties regarding the definition of biological agents or toxins, but the lack of definition of "weapons, equipment or means of delivery" led to a controversy. In ratifying the BW Convention, Switzerland reserved the right to decide for itself which items fall within the definition of weapons, equipment or means of delivery designed to use biological agents or toxins. The United States entered an objection to this reservation, claiming that it would not be appropriate for States to reserve unilaterally the right to take s uch decisions. In its opinion, the prohibited items are those the design of which indicates that they could have no other use than that specified in the Convention, or that they were intended to be capable of the use specified. There are, however, few weapons, equipment or means of delivery which would meet such criteria.

Under the BW Convention, the prohibition to develop, produce, stockpile or otherwise acquire or retain biological agents and toxins is not absolute. It applies only to types and to quantities that have no justification for prophylactic, protective or other peaceful purposes. Retention, production or acquisition by other means of certain quantities of biological agents and toxins may thus continue, and there may be testing in laboratories and even in the field. According to the clarification given in the course of the negotiations, the term "prophylactic" encompasses medical activities, such as diagnosis, therapy and immunization, whereas the term "protective" covers the development of protective masks and clothing, air and water filtration systems, detection and warning devices, and decontamination equipment, and must not be interpreted as permitting possession of biological agents and toxins for defence, retaliation or deterrence. The term "other peaceful purposes" has remained unclear. One can assume that it includes scientific experimentation.

There are no provisions in the BW Convention restricting biological research activities. One reason for this omission may be that research aimed at developing agents for civilian purposes is difficult to distinguish from research serving military purposes, whether defensive or offensive. Moreover, in the biological field it is difficult to draw a dividing line between research and development; a country can develop warfare agents in research facilities. Once developed, these agents can be rapidly produced in significant quantities. This circumstance and the express authorization to e ngage in production (for peaceful purposes) of biological agents and toxins that may be used in warfare create a risk that the provisions of the Convention will be circumvented. The stipulation that any development, production, stockpiling or retention of biological agents or toxins must be justified does not carry sufficient weight. There are no agreed standards or criteria for the quantities of agents or toxins that may be needed by different States for the different purposes recognized by the Convention. The parties are not even obliged to declare the types and amounts of agents or toxins they possess and the use they make of them. The system of material accountancy that is useful in the verification of certain measures of arms control is not practicable in the case of biological or toxin agents. It is thus not evident how much of a given prohibited substance stocked by a given country would constitute a violation of the Convention. The secrecy surrounding biological research activities and, in particular, the maintenance of defensive preparations, which at certain stages may be indistinguishable from offensive preparations, could generate suspicions leading to allegations of breaches.

The Convention prohibits the transfer of agents, toxins, weapons, equipment or means of delivery, specified above, to "any recipient whatsoever", that is, to any State or group of States or international organizations, as well as sub-national groups or individuals. The provision of assistance, encouragement or inducement to acquire the banned weapons is likewise forbidden (Article III). These non-proliferation clauses appear hard to reconcile with the commitment of the parties to engage in the "fullest possible" exchange of biological agents and toxins, and of equipment for the processing, use or production of such agents and toxins for peaceful ends (Article X). For all such materials and technologies, as well as expertise, are dual-use and as such widespread. To reduce the risk of misuse, an informal forum of industrialized countries, known as the Australia Group (after the country which took the initiative to convene it), decided to apply certain restrictions on transfers of items relevant to the BW Convention. Many nations consider the control arrangements adopted by the Group as complementary to the BW Convention, because an export may be precluded if there is particular concern about its potential diversion for weapon purposes. Other nations consider these arrangements to be discriminatory, because they chiefly affect the developing world. The latter would like to see the Australia Group disbanded and have all export restrictions that might be agreed among all parties incorporated in a legally binding verification document.

Parties to the BW Convention have undertaken to cooperate in the further development and application of scientific discoveries in the field of biology for the prevention of diseases or for other peaceful purposes (Article X). However, since the Convention is essentially a disarmament treaty, it can hardly serve as an effective instrument for such cooperation. The participants in the latest BW Convention Review Conference acknowledged the existence of an increasing gap between the developed and developing countries in the field of biotechnology, genetic engineering, microbiology and other related areas.

The most remarkable feature of the BW Convention is the disarmament obligation of the parties: to destroy or divert to peaceful purposes all agents, toxins, weapons equipment and means of delivery (Article II). The BW Convention was the first treaty providing for the abolition of an entire category of arms. The envisaged destruction or diversion was to take place not later than nine months after entry into force of the Convention, it being understood that for States acceding to the Convention after its entry into force the destruction or diversion was to be completed upon accession. All the necessary safety precautions are to be observed during the destruction operations to protect "populations" (that is, not only the population of the country carrying out these operations) as well as the environment in general.

The United States was the only State to announce that its stockpile of biological and toxin agents and all associated munitions had been destroyed, except for small quantities for laboratory defensive research purposes. It also made it known that former biological warfare facilities had been converted to medical research centres. No other State has made such an announcement. The United Kingdom said that it had no stocks of biological weapons. The Soviet Union stated that it did not possess any biological agents or toxins, weapons, equipment or means of delivery, as prohibited by the Convention, but this statement turned out to be untrue.

RELATIONSHIP WITH THE 1925 GENEVA PROTOCOL

The BW Convention does not expressly prohibit the use of biological or toxin weapons. It only states that the obligations assumed under the 1925 Geneva Protocol, which prohibits such use, r remain valid (Article VIII). However, adherents to the BW Convention are not necessarily parties to the Geneva Protocol. Moreover, the Convention stipulates that nothing in its provisions shall be interpreted as in any way limiting or detracting from the obligations assumed by States under the Geneva Protocol.

This implies that the reservations to the Protocol, which form part of the obligations contracted by the parties, continue to exist. Insofar as the reservations concern the right to employ the banned weapons against non-parties or in retaliation against a party violating the Protocol, they are incompatible with the obligation of the parties to the Convention never "in any circumstances" to acquire biological weapons (Article I).

They also contradict the parties' expressed determination to exclude "completely" the possibility of biological agents and toxins being used as weapons (ninth preambular paragraph). It is for this reason that, in acceding to the BW Convention in 1984, China declared that the absence of an explicit prohibition on the use of biological weapons was a defect which should be corrected "at an appropriate time". Indeed, over the years, a number of States have withdrawn their reservations to the Geneva Protocol, either with regard either to biological weapons alone, or to both biological and chemical weapons. They have thereby recognized that since the retention and production of biological weapons are banned, so must, by implication, be their use, because use presupposes possession.

Nonetheless, in 1996, Iran proposed that the Convention (its title and Article I) be amended so as to make the ban on use explicit rather than implicit. An amendment submitted by a party enters into force for each State accepting it upon its acceptance by a majority of the parties (Article XI). However, the Iranian proposal is opposed by many States which fear the risks of having other provisions of the Convention opened up for renegotiation as well. Some are apprehensive that States not accepting the Iranian-proposed amendment would appear to condone the use of biological weapons under certain circumstances, and since use would be possible only after breaking the BW Convention, the absolute character of the Convention prohibitions would be called into question. What seems less objectionable than an amendment is a solemn declaration of understanding by all parties that the use of microbial or other biological agents or toxins in any way that is not consistent with prophylactic, protective or other peaceful purposes, would be a violation of the Convention.

Verification of Compliance

No specific measures are set forth in the BW Convention to verify compliance with the obligation not to develop, produce, stockpile or otherwise acquire or retain biological agents or toxins for "hostile purposes". Indeed, hostile intentions, like any other intentions, cannot be verified. As mentioned above, the parties are not obliged to declare biological agents or toxins used in non-prohibited activities. Nor are they obliged to declare all laboratories engaged in research and development of substances that could be used as agents of warfare. This is a serious lacuna, because advances in biotechnology have made it possible to produce large quantities of potent toxic substances by a small number of people, in a short period of time, and in facilities which are difficult to identify. Such substances may be stored in inconspicuous repositories and eventually "weaponized", that is, filled into missiles, bombs or spray systems. Consequently, a violator could relatively easily break out from the Convention. What is even more incongruous, States joining the Convention are not required to declare the possession or non-possession of the banned weapons. Nor are States, which may have declared such possession, obligated to prove that they have destroyed the weapons or diverted them to peaceful purposes. The opening-up by the United States of some of its biological facilities for public inspection and international visitors, following the destruction of its stocks, was a voluntary act.

National technical means of verification cannot be relied upon to verify in other countries the non-development and non-production of biological agents and toxins for hostile purposes, and there are at present no international means to perform such tasks. Illegal possession of the banned weapons could be demonstrated indirectly through investigations which the UN Secretary-General is authorized to carry out in response to reports that may be brought to his attention on the possible use of chemical and biological or toxin weapons entailing a violation of the Geneva Protocol or of any other applicable rule of international treaty or customary law. However, such investigations, which may be initiated by UN member States (but not by individuals or non-governmental organizations), could also prove inconclusive, because the diseases allegedly caused by biological weapons might be similar to those occurring naturally, and because it might be difficult for the investigators to determine the identity of the aggressor.

Each party is obliged to take measures, in accordance with its constitutional processes, to prohibit and prevent the activities banned by the Convention from taking place within its territory and under its jurisdiction or control anywhere (Article IV). The term "measures" applies to legislative, administrative or regulatory measures, whereas the term "under its jurisdiction or control" (also used in Article II referred to above) extends the bans to non-self-governing territories administered by States parties, and to territories under military occupation. "Anywhere" implies that even transnational corporations operating in the territories of non-parties to the Convention are covered by the prohibitions if they remain under the jurisdiction or control of the parties. Not all parties, however, have taken the steps required to ensure domestic compliance with the Convention. This is all the more regrettable in that biological agents appear to be becoming attractive, for terrorist purposes, to players other than States According to reliable reports, the Aum Shinrikyo sect, which released nerve gas in a Tokyo subway train, had also been working on the development of biological weapons and in 1995, shortly before the arrest of its leader, was close to completing this programme.

On the international level, the parties have undertaken to consult one another and to cooperate in solving problems relating to the objective or the application of the provisions of the Convention. Such consultation and cooperation may also take place "through appropriate international procedures within the framework of the United Nations and in accordance with its Charter" (Article V). Since the Convention does not explain what "appropriate international procedures" amount to, the participants in the BW Review Conferences agreed that such procedures should include the right of any party to request that a "consultative meeting", open to all parties, be convened promptly at expert level.

The parties have the right to lodge with the UN Security Council complaints regarding breaches of the Convention. They have undertaken to cooperate in carrying out any investigation which the Security Council may initiate on the basis of the complaint received, and they are entitled to be informed of the results of such investigation. Each complaint must contain "all possible evidence" confirming its validity (Article VI). However, only a few States have the means to collect such evidence. Others may not be in a position to do so, and could not always count on obtaining relevant information from foreign sources, even from their allies. There is thus a possibility that, for political or other reasons (for example, unwillingness to disclose the nature or the source of the evidence), certain powers will deliberately overlook transgressions committed by some States to the detriment of others. A State which suspects a violation, but lacks reliable information and therefore does not possess sufficient evidence, may have its request for consideration rejected by the Security Council. Even if the Security Council agreed to discuss a charge which did not satisfy the above requirement, there would always be a danger that the case would not receive proper examination. For the Council is not entitled (or equipped) by the UN Charter to check compliance with arms control agreements; nor is it empowered to take action against violators of such agreements. Only when the Council finds that the situation created by the violation can lead to international friction may it recommend, under Chapter VI of the UN Charter, "appropriate procedures or methods of adjustment" to the State or States concerned. This may not always be the case.

In 1992, the President of the UN Security Council stated, on behalf of its members, that proliferation of weapons of mass destruction, which include biological weapons, would constitute a "threat to international peace and security", and that appropriate action would be taken to prevent it. That action could include the application of coercive measures under Chapter VII of the UN Charter. However, the statement of the President of the Security Council has no binding legal effect. Even if it were transformed into a formal decision of the Council to have such effect, it would not necessarily enable the Council to act in all pertinent instances. The power of veto possessed by the permanent members of the Council can always be used to protect violators of treaties, especially when the violator happens to be a great power. A suggestion, put forward during the BW negotiations, that the Security Council's permanent members should waive their right of veto at least with regard to resolutions concerning investigations of complaints, was not accepted This is why proposals have been repeatedly made that a representative body of States parties — rather than the United Nations — should deal with investigations of alleged breaches of the BW Convention. If, in 1982, the UN General Assembly requested the UN Secretary-General to investigate alleged violations of the ban on use of chemical and biological weapons, it did so primarily because the ban, as embodied in the 1925 Geneva Protocol, is widely considered to form part of international customary law to be observed by all States, parties and non-parties to relevant treaties alike.

The circumstance that the fact-finding stage of the complaints procedure is not clearly separated from the stage of legal/political consideration and judgment is a serious shortcoming of the BW Convention. It makes it difficult to ascertain a violation. Moreover, a State under suspicion of having violated its obligations has no international impartial mechanism to turn to in order to free itself from that suspicion. Ill-considered allegations can therefore be made with impunity.

In the case of an established violation, parties would have to provide or support assistance, in accordance with the UN Charter, to a party which so requested, if the Security Council decided that this party had been exposed to danger as a result of the violation (Article VII). It appears from the negotiating history that assistance was meant primarily as action of a medical or other humanitarian or relief nature. In the understanding of at least the United Kingdom and the United States, it would be for each party to decide whether it could or was prepared to supply the requested aid. In other words, assistance would be optional, not obligatory: it could be refused without incurring the charge of non-compliance.

The Convention provided for a review conference of the parties to be convened five years after its entry into force (Article XII). Later, the parties decided to meet at least every five years; these Conferences review the operation of the Convention, taking into account the relevant scientific and technological developments.

ALLEGATIONS OF NON-COMPLIANCE

Several allegations of non-compliance with the BW Convention have been made since the Convention entered into force. Those which received most attention were the "Sverdlovsk" and "Yellow Rain" cases.

The Sverdlovsk Case

In March 1980, the United States accused the Soviet Union of maintaining an offensive biological weapons programme which included production, weaponization and stockpiling of biological warfare agents. The accusation was based on the suspected airborne release of anthrax spores from a Soviet biological facility, which caused an outbreak of anthrax in the city of Sverdlovsk in April and May 1979. The Soviet Union confirmed that there had been an outbreak of anthrax in the Sverdlovsk region, but attributed this occurrence to the sale of anthrax-contaminated meat in violation of veterinary regulations. It provided little additional information. The issue was the subject of bilateral US/Soviet consultations, and various groups of scientists met to evaluate the Soviet account of the incident, but the US government maintained its accusation. In 1992, the Russian authorities admitted that a breach of the BW Convention had been committed. They undertook, under a decree issued by the President of the Russian Federation, to open secret military research centres to international inspection and convert them to civilian use.

The "Yellow Rain" Case

In 1981, the US government accused the Soviet Union of being involved in the production, transfer and use of trichothecene mycotoxins in Laos, Kampuchea and Afghanistan in violation of both the 1925 Geneva Protocol and the BW Convention. The allegation was categorically rejected by the Soviet Union. US charges were based on reports by alleged victims and eye-witnesses who stated that since the autumn of 1978 enemy aircraft had been spraying a toxic yellow material (hence the name of the case). Chemical analyses of samples of the yellow material and medical checks of the affected persons were conducted to substantiate the case. However, as the investigations proceeded, with the involvement of laboratories in different countries and a careful scrutiny of the eye-witnesses' reports, the reliability of the evidence was increasingly questioned. Some authoritative scientists found that the yellow substance consisted to a large extent of excrements of wild honeybees, and extensive analytical efforts in several laboratories failed to confirm the initial positive reports of trichothecenes.

Assessment

As compared to other arms control agreements, the negotiations for the BW Convention — conducted separately from those on chemical weapons with which they had been associated for decades

— encountered few obstacles and were concluded relatively quickly, in a common taboo on use. The reasons were as follows.

Biological weapons are unpredictable in their effects and of limited value in combat. Since cheating under a BW Convention could not yield significant military advantages to the cheating party, a ban on biological weapons without verification of compliance was considered by the negotiators to be free of serious security risks. By contrast, chemical weapons are predictable, capable of producing immediate effects and, consequently, useful incombat. Banning their possession without elaborate and intrusive methods of verification was, therefore, deemed impossible. Most states which joined the BW Convention did so on condition that the complete prohibition of biological weapons would be recognized as a step towards a complete prohibition of chemical weapons (Preamble and Article XI).

The aim of the BW Convention was not so much to remove an immediate peril, as to eliminate the possibility that scientific and technological advances, modifying the conditions of production, storage or use of biological weapons, would make these weapons militarily attractive. Indeed, progress in biotechnology is making it increasingly possible to "improve" upon known biological agents. Normally harmless organisms which do not cause diseases can be modified so as to become highly toxic and produce diseases for which there is no known treatment. But the Convention is comprehensive enough to cover all relevant scientific and technological developments, including biological agents and toxins that could result from genetic engineering processes.

The disclosure by the UN Special Commission of an extensive biological weapons programme in Iraq, as well as reports that certain other nations, too, have or are seeking to acquire a biological weapon capability, indicate that the threat of biological warfare remains real. Since the BW Convention has no instruments to check compliance, there is a need for verification machinery to deter would-be violators. Negotiations for a verification protocol, or another legally binding document strengthening the Convention with measures of control, have been going on in an ad hoc group of States, open to all parties, since January 1995. So far, however, agreement has proved elusive. Until it is reached, parties to the Convention are expected to implement the confidence-building measures they have agreed at their Review Conferences. The most important among them are measures enhancing the transparency of activities involving biological agents and toxins. They include exchanges of information on facilities and research programmes relevant to the Convention, on vaccine production, and on significant and unusual outbreaks of diseases.

Eventually, to make possible a differentiation between treaty-prohibited and treaty-permitted activities, the objects of the prohibitions will have to be more clearly defined, and the criteria necessary to assess compliance will have to be unambiguously established. Moreover, apart from short-notice visits to declared sites, on-site inspections of undeclared sites will have to be accepted without reservation by all parties. It is, of course, understood that sensitive commercial proprietary information and national security information, not directly related to the BW Convention, must be reliably protected. A special organization will be needed to oversee the implementation of the parties' obligations.

PREPAREDNESS FOR CHEMICAL AND BIOLOGICAL TERRORISM

School and Child Care Centre Preparedness

Children spend most of their waking hours in school or child care centers, away from their parents and guardians. Despite the fact that the majority of most children's day is spent in the care of the school system, efforts to create a blueprint that assists schools in developing comprehensive disaster-response protocols have been weak. School districts remain highly variable in the extent of their preparation for public health emergencies of any type, including chemical and biological terrorism.

Ideally, every school should produce its own response protocols rather than following a one-size-fits-all disaster plan that fails to take into account the school's physical plant, student size and characteristics, the presence of children with special needs, school nurse availability, and proximity to certain areas such as industries, rail yards, or highways. All schools, in conjunction with local public health officials, should develop comprehensive evacuation and sheltering-in plans. Because local school bus fleets can typically evacuate only a fraction of children at one time, a means of mobilizing additional transport vehicles should be developed.

Hospital Preparedness

Hospital protocols for pediatric victims of chemical or biological terrorism must be established in both pediatric and nonpediatric hospitals. These disaster protocols require an integrated response from the emergency department, ICU, operating rooms, and other key clinical areas within the hospital. Response needs include an adequate number of pediatric supplies, and a staff trained in the care of ill children will be needed to minimize morbidity and mortality. All hospitals should have disaster protocols for pediatric patients, including mobilization of child life specialists, volunteers, and others who can provide comfort and distraction to children, particularly if those children are not yet united with their parents.

To be fully prepared for chemical or biological terrorism, pediatric and general hospitals must also have an evacuation plan should the hospital environment become uninhabitable. Although protocols for "vertical evacuation" (ie, the removal of patients to other floors within the same building) are well established in hospital-based disaster response, comprehensive plans for complete building evacuation are less well developed. Pediatric hospitals requiring full evacuation may have the additional challenge of transporting pediatric patients to health care facilities with relatively few pediatric resources. Nonetheless, memoranda of agreement with nearby or affiliated institutions are a key part of a comprehensive pediatric hospital disaster plan.

After exposure to a chemical or biological weapon, children may become covered by toxic material that can produce skin injury or be absorbed, producing systemic toxicity. In the case of infectious material, the contamination of skin could be sufficient to represent a threat to health care professionals as well as the victim. When children are covered with unknown but potentially dangerous chemical or infectious material, immediate decontamination is required. Topical decontamination has 2 distinct components: disrobing and showering. To minimize exposure to health care professionals and patients within the health care facility, the child should be disrobed outdoors, before entering the ambulance or building. Disrobing alone accounts for more than 85% of topical decontamination and is an extremely effective means of ending exposure. When possible, the victim should disrobe himself or herself to minimize exposure to others. Health care professionals should not assist in disrobing unless they are wearing appropriate PPE.

Showering complements disrobing by further removing chemicals, microbes, and debris. As with disrobing, showering must occur outdoors; protocols should include strategies for preventing hypothermia in children. Principles of showering include the establishment of 3 management zones in the decontamination staging area (so-called hot, warm, and cold in reference to the site's degree of contamination), use of water that has been warmed to a temperature of 100°F, a water pressure of 60 psi, and, if possible, containment of the wastewater. If the toxic material is oily or firmly adherent to the child's skin, soap or a mild shampoo should be used; solutions such as mild bleach should not be used on children because of the risk of skin injury. If an outdoor shower is not available, the child can be simply disrobed before being brought into the health care facility for care. Decontamination can be a frightening procedure for children, exacerbated by the identity-concealing PPE that clinicians are wearing. Efforts should be made to keep parents nearby; when possible, parents should be used to assist with their child's decontamination.

All health care professionals who assist in decontamination must protect themselves by wearing appropriate PPE. Currently, there are 4 levels of PPE, ranging from level A, which is the highest level of protection, to level D, which consists of simple gown, gloves, and surgical mask. For hospital personnel, level C PPE (a chemical-resistant suit and gloves, with an air-purifying respirator) is considered adequate for hospital-based management of most contaminated victims. Health care facilities should develop plans for rapid access to such equipment. Staff should be appropriately trained.

Community Health Centre Preparedness

Community health centers (CHCs) and local health departments are, in most major metropolitan areas, an important source of "safety-net" health care and social support to a community. In a large-scale terrorist disaster, CHCs could play a pivotal role in supporting the community and nearby hospitals. First, in the event of an infectious outbreak, families will likely go to their CHC for treatment and to obtain information from professionals whom they trust and who are more likely to provide culturally competent care. In addition, after a multiple-casualty incident, hospitals may become too crowded to treat every patient. In such cases, CHCs could potentially be used as alternate care sites, providing care to those with minor injury and assisting in interventions (eg, mass administration of antimicrobial agents). CHCs, therefore, should be included in planning by local public health authorities.

Office Preparedness

The pediatrician should have an important role in the community response to any disaster involving children. First, the pediatrician's office may be the preferred site of care for many victims who are transporting themselves for treatment. Both chemically contaminated children and children with suspected illness from a biological weapon might go directly to the pediatrician's office. Consequently, pediatricians should consider the development of office protocols for disasters, including (1) management of a child who requires decontamination, (2) management of a child with a potentially transmissible infection, and (3) management of a sudden influx of pediatric patients after a large-scale incident. The AAP textbook *Childhood Emergencies in the Office, Hospital, and Community* is a useful resource to assist in office planning for such emergencies. Pediatricians should also consult their state and local health departments, because most have electronic health alert networks.

Surge Capacity

An effective response to large-scale chemical or biological terrorism (ie, an incident with more casualties than routine operations can accommodate) requires the creation of surge-capacity protocols. Federal, state, and local public health authorities are essential in assisting health facilities during crises of large magnitude. Nonetheless, both pediatric and nonpediatric hospitals should consider how a large-scale event would affect their facility. Plans for such an event might include (1) the creation of additional bed spaces through cohorting, (2) mechanisms for the rapid discharge of inpatients to increase capacity, (3) an inventory of all sites in the hospital where critical care can be provided, (4) establishment of a site, ideally out of the hospital, for patient triage, (5) identification of care sites for those whose injuries are minor, (6) mechanisms for labeling and tracking patients, particularly children who arrive without personal identification, and (7) plans for maintaining hospital security by preventing the entry of contaminated victims and other unauthorized individuals. For nonpediatric hospitals, surge-capacity plans for a mass-casualty chemical or biological incident involving children should also include mechanisms for mobilizing health care professionals with pediatric expertise. Disaster medical assistance teams (DMATs), supported by the US Public Health Service, have been created by the National Disaster Medical System to provide assistance to regions after a large-scale disaster. However, among the 27 DMATs in the United States, only 2 are dedicated pediatric DMATs, significantly limiting the federal response capability to a pediatric mass-casualty incident. The Metropolitan Medical Response System, another federal effort designed to create regional "medical strike teams," has no clearly established pediatric capability or standards.

Mental Health

The mental health consequences of terrorism are extensive and, in many cases, enduring. Children have a disproportionate risk of developing emotional and behavioral sequelae; investigations after the September 11th attacks found that as many as 25% of children developed acute anxiety followed by posttraumatic stress disorder. Children can develop a broad range of behavioral problems after a disaster, whether they witness the incident or simply observe their parents' response to an incident (eg, from a television broadcast). Overt manifestations may include emotional lability, insomnia, frequent crying, depression, fear, and "anniversary grief." Alternatively, mental health consequences may also be subtle and elusive (eg, manifesting as multiple somatic complaints).

Parents may similarly become psychological casualties after chemical or biological terrorism. Visual replay of events on television may contribute to the development of long-term behavioral disturbances. As with children, the parent may have overt or subtle signs of distress. Adults typically display loss of appetite, insomnia, depression, hopelessness, and acute anxiety.

Finally, health care professionals who care for victims of chemical or biological terrorism can develop mental health consequences. There is an extensive body of literature indicating that health care professionals can become extremely depressed, developing posttraumatic stress disorder after caring for victims. To reduce the risk of this occupational hazard, the concept of critical incident stress debriefing (CISD) was created many years ago.

In principle, a prompt debriefing session can be therapeutic by permitting staff to verbalize their feelings and anxieties about what they have experienced. CISD has become a common part of postevent disaster management. Recently, however, questions about the efficacy of CISD in reducing mental health sequelae among health care professionals have been raised.

There are increasing concerns that the process of debriefing forces health care professionals to relive events, undoing internal resolution that is already underway. In addition, the process of group debriefing may carry the risk of having health care professionals hear about disturbing events that they themselves did not witness, creating anxiety and depression that was not present initially. Although this issue remains controversial, there is consensus that efforts should be made to identify health care professionals who are suffering psychological sequelae from their involvement in responding to an act of chemical or biological terrorism.

Individual/Family Preparedness

Large-scale disasters, whether they are natural (eg, hurricanes or floods), unintentional (eg, hazardous-materials release), or intentional (ie, terrorist), can occur at any time. All families, particularly families with children, should have a disaster plan. Such plans should include communication in the event of cellular phone failure, a reunification plan if disaster occurs when family members are not together, and emergency provisions in the home. Multiple resources are available to assist families in home disaster planning.

CIVIL CHEMICAL AND BIOLOGICAL WARFARE ATTACK

Following the attacks in New York in September 2001, the spectre of urban attack by terrorists using chemical and biological warfare (CBW) agents again raised its head and led to a wave of speculation and near panic on both sides of the Atlantic Ocean. Newspaper articles about 'weapons of mass destruction' abounded, and emergency and hospital medical services made provisions for the management of large numbers of casualties. In the United States, mass ingestion of prophylactic antibiotics began and gas masks were purchased in large numbers. Television pictures of emergency personnel clad in protective suits (many of them totally inappropriate for the real degree of risk) were widely transmitted and for several weeks the public awaited a world-wide chemical/biological Armageddon.

In the event, the reality was confined to the distribution of anthrax spores through the US postal system, which fortunately claimed only a few lives. Nevertheless this attack, coming after the use of a military organophosphate nerve agent by terrorists in Japan in 1995, demonstrated that urban chemical and biological attack was possible and posed a problem for emergency and hospital medical services around the world. The risk of deliberate urban release of chemical and biological agents persists and is not new. From the point of view of casualty management, it is important that the momentum generated by the events of last autumn should be sustained. The appearance in this issue of a review concerning the implications of chemical and biological agents for anaesthesia and intensive care is therefore very appropriate. Many clinical specialities may be involved in the management of CBW casualties, but that of anaesthesia and intensive care has a critical role to play since the speciality, more than most others, has the academic background in physiology, applied pharmacology and pathophysiology, and is able to understand the injuries provoked by CBW agents. More importantly, it is able to respond with immediate and continuing life support. It is therefore essential that anaesthetists should be closely involved in the management of CBW casualties and should be properly informed about the risks and the special handling procedures required.

Most busy anaesthetists do not have ready access to information about CBW agents. White has produced a useful, comprehensive document detailing a wide range of chemicals, toxins and organisms that have been proven or suspected to be agents of warfare, and more recently of urban terrorist attack. Two points about the extensive range of hazards presented in the review are particularly important.

First, despite widespread public and political belief, biological and chemical agents are not strictly weapons of mass destruction but weapons of mass injury, a point recognized by a number of clinical experts including an ex-Soviet source. In this respect, they may lead to mass fatalities where medical resources are limited or non-existent, but with properly organized and equipped medical services the picture may be quite different. Unlike nuclear weapons, biological and chemical agents do not cause mass destruction of material and physical trauma. Biological and chemical agents should therefore be viewed in their own pathophysiological context. The persistence of the Nuclear, Biological and Chemical (NBC) classification owes more to diplomatic manipulation and the balance of military power than medical reality. White has appropriately classified CBW agents as weapons of mass injury rather than destruction, which is a more realistic term for anaesthetists used to the business of supporting life in difficult circumstances. This does not alter the fact that, untreated, CBW agents may lead to substantial loss of life. However, advanced life support and guidelines for longer term treatment do exist, and can radically alter the clinical picture.

Secondly, it is important to realize that not all the hazards listed in the review are equally likely to be used by terrorists. A few have been identified and used, such as sarin and anthrax. Most, however, are still confined to the area of speculation (sometimes backed by intelligence information). The existence of a hazard does not necessarily imply a threat, a term which implies a means of delivery and intention on the part of the assailant, apart from possession of a hazard. In terms of planning and training, it is more realistic and less nihilistic to build from experience of chemical hazards that have or could be used by terrorists, backed by experience gained from industrial toxic release. Knowledge of the management of naturally occurring epidemics is equally valuable for the management of a deliberately induced epidemic (a biological weapon attack). For those clinicians who feel they have a lack of experience in such cases, it is worth noting that considerable clinical analogous experience exists, which can be used in the management of unfamiliar pathology. For anaesthetists in particular, the essential life support procedures involved are very familiar from more conventional areas of practice.

CBW Attack as a Special Case

In civil life, populations are at constant risk from accidental exposure to toxic substances, as they are from naturally occurring epidemics. These are the natural equivalents of the intentional toxic release and epidemics that constitute CBW. Accidental civil toxic releases are managed according to the United Nations-controlled, hazardous materials control system (HAZMAT), which provides detailed information to emergency services about the properties and management of toxic substances at their place of use or while they are in transit. HAZMAT databases provide information for protection and decontamination, and clinical management protocols. The system is designed to manage accidental releases but provides a valuable framework for the management of casualties from deliberate releases. The difference between accidental and deliberate (terrorist) releases is that the identity of the toxic agent may not be known with certainty in the case of the latter, and so measures must be put into place that cover the worst case scenario of the agent being highly toxic, persistent and transmissible. Most HAZMAT incidents involve small numbers of casualties with varying degrees of exposure. Some of these may have the effects of both toxic and conventional trauma, for example after an explosion, such as that which occurred at a chemical factory in Toulouse, France in September 2001. The notion of mass casualties may not always therefore be appropriate, although both chemical and biological accidental releases have occurred in the past, giving rise to large numbers of injured and dead.

Much information exists about the management of HAZMAT incidents and the author has made good use of the internet sources that are now available. HAZMAT is a valuable model and all anaesthetists involved in disaster management should be aware of the stages in the overall management of a HAZMAT incident, and of the risks related to the toxicity, latency of action, persistency and transmissibility of the agents involved. These four characteristics are common to both chemical and biological agents, and determine the degree of risk as well as the appropriate reponse. *Toxicity* is a familiar concept in anaesthesia, and toxic effects appear with a specific *latency*, which is important for the use of agents in deliberate release. In general, chemical agents and toxins have short periods of latency before specific signs and symptoms appear.

In contrast, classical biological warfare agents have extended latency periods (usually familiar as incubation periods) before the effects of the induced disease begin to appear. *Persistency* relates to the ability of a toxic agent to remain in the environment into which it had been released and is a function of the physico-chemical properties of the agent. For chemical agents, the persistency may be variable but for most biological warfare agents, with the exception of spore-forming agents such as anthrax, persistency is usually very short. However, *transmissibility* may take place as a result of the physical contamination of the victim due to a persistent chemical agent or as a result of infection in the case of an airborne agent. Transmissibility is therefore a potential menace in the case of biological warfare agents because of infection down the casualty management line.

What are the Hazards likely to be Faced?

Many known chemical agents (e.g. chlorine, phosgene and hydrogen cyanide) are readily available industrially and their properties are listed in standard sources and databases, which are cited in the review in this issue. Others, such as organophosphates, are familiar as pesticides but are also used by the military as nerve agents that may be synthesized in improvised laboratories. Certain biological warfare agents are recognized as being a more likely threat than others, given the difficulty of delivery and the sensitivity of the agents to meteorological conditions. Thus, anthrax is now an established threat that is more important than the rare viral haemorrhagic fevers, which are the domain of specialist physicians. It is important that biological attack should be viewed as a special case of an epidemic.

Medical Management of Casualties

Following CBW attack, anaesthetists may be involved at several points, and are thus in danger of primary and secondary exposure. In some countries, anaesthetists form part of the primary emergency response and are familiar with the dangers of toxic exposure and the need for protection and decontamination. Anaesthetists may also be involved in management in the emergency room, operating theatre management and the intensive care unit.

In France, special plans were put in place for the management of terrorist toxic release following the Japanese sarin attacks in 1995, which have been recently modified as Plan Biotox. The plans provide special mobile medical response teams (with training and protective suits) as well as protected medical teams to receive casualties who escape the HAZMAT cordon. Anaesthetists are involved at both these points and must have a good understanding of the importance of casualty decontamination. In the hospital, anaesthetists must be aware of the effects of certain toxic agents on the conduct of general anaesthesia for the management of accompanying physical trauma. There are effects on the status of the patient before an operation and on the anaesthetic agents themselves. A good example is the effects of exposure to organophosphate anticholinesterases on the action of neuromuscular blocking agents, which is covered by White.

Many toxic hazards have long latency effects, which lead to the necessary management of patients in the ICU. Long-term ventilation may be required for neuromuscular problems, toxic pulmonary oedema and associated adult respiratory distress syndrome. Mass toxic casualties will place a heavy burden upon emergency and intensive care services as a result of the short and longer term actions of toxic agents.

Attacks using bacterial and viral biological agents essentially pose the problem of epidemic infection, although intensivists are required for the management of the resulting complications, including multiple organ failure. There is a long latency in most cases, but there may be ultra-short and intermediate latency effects if a bacterial toxin is used as a toxic agent.

Management of Specific Pathophysiology

Toxic agents may attack all somatic systems, but the respiratory system is the most vulnerable in the short and intermediate term, leading to fatality in some cases if resuscitation is not started early and continued. There are many pathophysiological processes leading to respiratory failure after toxic injury, affecting both the airway, and the control and mechanics of breathing. There may be, as in the case of organophosphates, failure of the respiratory centres and paralysis of the muscles of breathing through neuromuscular blockade. The review covers this in some detail. The more water-soluble toxic agents, such as chlorine, cause irritation and the production of secretions in the nasopharynx with laryngeal spasm. There may be blockage of the main airways with bronchial and bronchiolar constriction. Finally, many toxic substances act at the level of the alveoli causing toxic pulmonary oedema. Both the central and peripheral nervous systems may be affected as in the case of sarin poisoning, where the respiratory centres are depressed and there is a depolarizing neuromuscular block. The airways may be affected at both the upper and lower levels with cough and laryngeal spasm, production of secretions and vomitus, bronchospasm, bronchiolitis and toxic pulmonary oedema.

Many substances produce ciliary paralysis, which compounds the bronchial problem. Clinically, the combined effects are to produce increased airway resistance and reduced compliance. This leads to a failure of alveolar ventilation, a rise in end-tidal carbon dioxide, hypoxia and cardiac arrest.

Anaesthetists—a Voice to be Heard

Anaesthetists clearly have a vital role to play in the management of CBW casualties, but in many countries their involvement with planning and provision of care has been relatively limited, particularly in the prehospital and emergency room areas. Many of the special government CBW advisers are from the public health, toxicology and pathology specialities. They do not have first hand experience of the emergency and intensive care life support measures required to break the link between mass injury and mass loss of life. It is important for anaesthetic professional bodies to take an interest in the subject and explain the role anaesthetists have to play in the management of chemical agent injury. For the general public, most of whom are still unaware that anaesthetists are medical practitioners, this may be something of a revelation.

Training and close integration of anaesthetists into toxic emergency response teams is essential, but training by exercise is notoriously difficult for busy clinicians who have more than enough real problems to deal with. Nevertheless, it is vital that anaesthetists understand the real risks from CBW and the HAZMAT procedures to avoid becoming the next casualty. Above all, the speciality must give out a clear and positive message about the real dangers of CBW, and the appropriate planning and life support procedures that should form the medical response. This will not only serve to provide some comfort to a frightened general public, but will provide much needed focus for the rational management of casualties from a CBW attack. Attack on a nuclear power plant or spent fuel facility

In 2002, the United Kingdom (UK) had in operation 31 nuclear reactors in 13 NPPs. Of these reactors, 30 are gas-cooled and graphite-modified types: 16 of these are the Magnox reactors operated by British Nuclear Fuels Limited (BNFL); while 14 are Advanced Gas-cooled Reactors (AGRs) owned by the private nuclear power generator British Energy. The last reactor to enter service was a Pressure Water Reactor (PWR) completed in 1995, owned by British Energy. NPPs in most countries are protected by containment vessels several feet thick and are equipped with redundant safety systems. Armed guards and other security systems also protect them. In order to cause a core meltdown and disperse a substantial amount of the NPP's radioactive material into the atmosphere, attackers would have to defeat the plant's security systems and destroy or disable its multiple safety systems simultaneously. Yet NPPs are capable of withstanding a commando-style raid by only a small group of lightly armed insurgents. A heavily armed group might therefore be able to overwhelm a NPP's security systems, especially with insider knowledge of the security.

Besides a commando-style raid, other methods of attack exist. These might involve hijacked airplanes, a maritime vessel with crew-served weapons on-board (surface-to-surface missiles, for example), or a truck packed with explosives. In fact, a large truck bomb detonated outside the protected area of a NPP could cause sufficient damage to critical safety systems and lead to a core meltdown. By far the most potentially devastating radiological release would come from sabotage to a NPP or spent fuel facility: both of these facilities contain huge concentrations of highly radioactive material and would generate the nuclear or chemical energy needed for wide dispersal of the radioactive material.

International security standards differ, however. The Three Mile Island NPP facility in the USA was designed to withstand the impact of a Boeing 707, although it might be vulnerable to a full speed, direct hit from larger commercial airliners, such as a 767. But the UK's NPPs were never constructed with such an attack in mind. The fact that 30 out of 31 of the UK's reactors are graphite-moderated types is also a cause for concern because when graphite is used as a moderator it burns easily. In 1986, the fire in the graphite-type Chernobyl reactor lasted for over a week and released radioactivity over 1,000 metres into the atmosphere, spreading it over a large area. If an airliner crashed into a UK graphite reactor, a similar long lasting fire with long-distance fallout is possible. Bellona recommends improved security at the UK's NPPs, including better containment for reactors to withstand the crash impact from an airliner or from a high-yield conventional explosive detonated offsite. Security improvements at the Magnox reactors could prove uneconomical, as they are due to close by 2010.

NPPs burn uranium fuel in their cores, which produce highly radioactive and physically hot spent fuel rods: rods are removed from the reactor and those from the Magnox and AGR stations are plunged into onsite cooling ponds for a short period of time before being transferred to containers (flasks) and sent to Sellafield for reprocessing – a method of handling spent nuclear fuel. Rods from the PWR station are initially stored in onsite water-filled storage pools. BNFL operates two reprocessing plants at Sellafield, Magnox B205 and Thermal Oxide Reprocessing Plant (THORP). B205 operates according to the Plutonium Uranium Extraction method and reprocesses fuel from British Magnox reactors. THORP was designed to separate plutonium for use in 'breeder' reactors, but now reprocesses spent nuclear fuel (SNF) from British AGRs as well as imported SNF. Other than Sellafield, there are only two other major reprocessing plants in operation worldwide: Cap de la Hague in France and Mayak in Russia.

The Sellafield plant houses 21 steel tanks in above ground concrete cells that contain high level radioactive waste in the form of self heating, acidic liquid. This radioactive waste has to be constantly cooled and stirred to prevent a chain reaction, which is achieved by continuously being cooled and agitated to prevent the stored waste from boiling and causing a radiological release. The tanks contain 2,400kg of caesium-137, a radioactive material responsible for offsite radiation exposure from Chernobyl, although the amount released from Chernobyl was approximately 27kg. It is estimated that if an airliner crashed into one of the key structures at Sellafield, it would release into the atmosphere 44 times the radioactivity of the 1986 Chernobyl accident.

If the cooling system were sabotaged, or if terrorist attack on the facility were successful, it would release liquid waste into the Irish Sea, along with strontium-90, caesium-137 and technetium-99, which has a half-life of 213, 000 years.

Such radioactive substances would contaminate fisheries and travel north from Cumbria, heavily contaminating fisheries in western Scotland. Anywhere downwind of Sellafield during the release would be rendered uninhabitable for generations, and people caught in the fallout would have a higher chance of contracting cancer. Depending on the wind direction, cities such as Dublin, Edinburgh, Leeds and Newcastle would be well within fallout range.

Indeed, in a report to the House of Commons Defence Committee on 9 January 2002, Dr Gordon Thompson, executive director of the Institute for Research and Security Studies in Cambridge, Massachusetts, suggested that an attack on the B205 facility could release 100 times the radioactivity produced by the Chernobyl accident, which would make the north of England uninhabitable for generations.

Moreover, a report by the Nuclear Installations Inspectorate on 2 July 2002 reported that two sets of tanks housing medium-level radioactive waste at Sellafield were so old and in such a dangerous condition that they pose an unacceptable risk.

BNFL has been warned that neither the structural integrity of the tanks, nor the building containing them, could be guaranteed beyond ten years. While BNFL has already surrounded the tanks with a steel building and commissioned specialist machinery to empty the tanks, the condition of the tanks require the building of new tanks or another solution for processing the waste. Bellona advocates the need for crash-proof tanks to contain the medium and high-level radioactive waste stored at Sellafield. The liquid waste should be immobilised as soon as possible and disposed of geologically.

Storage Transports

In 1996, BNFL opened the Sellafield MOX Plant (SMP) for the production of mixed oxide (MOX) fuel, receiving its licence for production in October 2001. The only use for the plutonium that THORP and B205 have produced is to mix it with uranium oxide and fabricate MOX fuel for use in light water reactors. While the UK has the facilities to produce MOX fuel, it does not use MOX fuel. And given the cost of conversion, British NPP operators have no plans to convert their plants to burn MOX fuel. BNFL, having already built a MOX fuel manufacturing plant, has been forced to look overseas for customers in countries including Germany, Switzerland and Japan. The transportation of nuclear materials, such as fresh MOX fuel and SNF for reprocessing, means that there will be an ever increasing traffic in nuclear materials by air, land and sea. Shipments of SNF and fresh MOX fuel might be vulnerable to terrorist attack and could be used to create a radiological explosion or to gain the material to fabricate a radiological dispersal device such as a "dirty bomb".

No nuclear freight is allowed to travel through the Channel Tunnel. Previously, SNF for reprocessing sent to Sellafield was shipped into Dover Docks by train-ferry before travelling on by rail. The ferry has now been withdrawn from service and all flasks go by sea to Barrow-in-Furness, and then by train to Sellafield. Flasks are made of steel and are lead-lined in order to contain the intense heat and radioactivity of the spent fuel rods and are carried on special low-loading freight wagons. While the flasks are designed to meet International Atomic Energy Agency safety standards, a successful terrorist attack might cause either a high-speed derailment or collision, which could release the radioactive contents.

BNFL operates seven vessels for the transport of MOX fuel. Two of these vessels are armed with 30mm cannons. Armed officers from the UK Atomic Energy Authority (UKAEA) Constabulary, which provide security for civil nuclear sites and for the transport of nuclear material within the UK, are on guard against boarders. Should the Constabulary be overpowered, would-be attackers would than have to crack open the vessels' reinforced hatch covers and unload the rods without the aid of deck cranes. Yet BNFL's vessels only have a top speed of 13 knots and are not as maneuverable or well-defended as a military or coastguard escort vessel. *Jane's* maritime specialists suggest that the vessels are capable of repelling a light attack and should be protected by at least one well-armed frigate. And while MOX fuel flasks can resist temperatures of 800C for up to 30 minutes, fires on ships can burn for 24 hours at a temperature of 1,000C.

MOX fuel is plutonium and uranium blended and held in ceramic form, so it is possible to undertake the chemical separation of plutonium from fresh MOX fuel. While it is debatable whether or not this could be used to fabricate a crude nuclear device, the material could be used to make a dirty bomb capable of scattering plutonium dust in the wind: just one speck of plutonium breathed into the lungs is enough to cause cancer, so the population near any blast involving radioactive material would have to be evacuated immediately. Given the security threats of transporting fresh and spent MOX fuel, including the risk of accidents at land and sea and nuclear material proliferation, as well as the additional costs of increasing security, Bellona calls for a ban to be placed on the international transport of MOX fuel.

PROTECTION DURING CHEMICAL EMERGENCIES

In case of a suspected or proven release of unknown chemicals or CW agents, the important elements of emergency response are: (i) detection and identification of the agent, (ii) physical and medical protection against the agent and (iii) decontamination.

Detection

The rapid identification and qualitative and quantitative determination of the unknown agent is necessary for the selection of adequate protective measures (protective masks and clothing as well as medical treatment), the mapping of contamination area and decontamination procedures. For onsite verification, especially involving CW agents, several handheld detection devices are available, including Three Colour Detector (TCD) paper, Residual Vapor Detection (RVD) Kit, Water Poison Detection Kit (WPDK) and chemical agent monitors. These devices have several limitations, such as low specificity and inability to detect all CW agents. Definitive identification of an agent can be carried out onsite in a mobile analytical laboratory or in an off-site laboratory, and this will generally take many hours.

Clinical symptoms and signs in exposed individuals may be the most useful indicators of the likely agent. This is followed by an on-the-spot analysis with detection paper (TCD). The paper, impregnated with reagents, reacts with the liquid CW agents to produce three distinct colors.

The paper sticks to any surface and the colour change occurs within 30 s, mustard agent turns it red, G-nerve agent turns it yellow and V-nerve agent turns it green. The disadvantage is that it may give false-positive results with many other substances.

The RVD kit is a portable, disposable CW agent detector kit that can detect CW vapors in air with a high specificity. The detection tubes are made of glass with break-off tips and are filled with impregnated chemicals on silica.

A definite volume of air is sucked by pump strokes. Colour change of the silica indicates the presence of a particular agent. Detection tubes are available for individual agents. Blister and nerve agents, phosgene, cyanogens chloride and hydrogen cyanide in the atmosphere can be detected by this kit. Similarly, poisonous substances present in water sources can be detected with the help of WPDK. This kit contains different reagents marked with numbers, test procedures for known CW agents and results based on simple colour change for detection.

Many instruments are available for point detection of CW agents. These are mainly based on three principles: ion mobility spectrometers (IMS), gas chromatograph (GCs) and surface acoustic wave sensors (SAWS).

Hand-held chemical agent monitors, based on the principle of ion-mobility spectrometry (IMS), are the most common devices used for the detection of CW agents, particularly blister and nerve agents. The GID-3 (Smiths) is a British IMS for onsite detection of common CW agents. The GID-2A is another version for fixed locations designed for unattended operation and continuous monitoring. The hand-held improved chemical agent monitor (ICAM) is a portable IMS device. The M8A1 is another IMS-based automatic CW alarm detector used during the 1991 Gulf war and it is replaced with the Automatic Chemical Agent Alarm (ACADA), which is a high-resolution IMS. ACADA can detect agents in a few seconds and can clean itself for fresh detection within 1 min. The other variants of IMS are RAID (Bruker's) and M-90 (Environics).

Handheld CW agent detectors, viz. AP2C (France) or CHASE (Israel) based on the flame photometry principle, is also frequently used. It can detect chemiluminescent reactions of sulfur or phosphorus-containing organic compounds in a hydrogen/air flame.

Surface Acoustic Wave Sensors (SAWS) work in the same manner as do Quartz Crystal Microbalances (QCMs), but at higher frequencies and greater sensitivities. The Joint Chemical Agent Detector (JCAD) employs an SAW-based technology. The JCAD is a handheld, lightweight CW detector and it combines with an electrochemical cell.

Portable gas chromatograph is used for automatic real-time continuous agent monitoring. In this, air is used as carrier gas and air sample is drawn through a pre-concentrator loop filled with an adsorbent material. A photoionization detector (PID) is used to detect the agents. The entire cycle from sample collection to detection takes about 5–10 min.

Gas chromatograph coupled with mass detector (GCMS) fitted on a vehicle can be used for unambiguous detection of most of the organic compounds, including CW agents, at very low concentrations. However, this hyphenated technique is complex, requires a skilled operator, is difficult to maintain and does not provide much advantage in comparison with off-site analysis, especially when chemical incident occurs at remote site when the mobile lab cannot approach easily. The commercially available portable GCMS-based instruments include HAPSITE (Inficon's), EM series (Bruker's), MM1 or MM2. No suitable onsite detection equipment or methods for the detection of psychomimetic agents are available except GCMS.

In addition to the above electrochemical-based detectors for nerve agents (NAD), standoff detection instruments (M21, RAPID) are also available. The M21 remote sensing chemical agent alarm (RSCAAL) is based on a passive infrared detector and is capable of detecting nerve and blister agents in the vapor phase from a distance of up to 5,000 m. Instruments based on other techniques, such as molecularly imprinted polymer (MIP) sensors, biosensors, surface plasmon resonance (SPR), conductive polymer sensors, etc. are under development stage.

All the detection methods have susceptibility to interferences or false-positive results. The best way is to use two types of detectors working on different principles to obtain accurate data.

Protection

The main twin aspects of physical protection are the creation of an artificial barrier between the toxic agent and the individuals and the provision of "breathable air." The barrier has to provide protection against liquids, aerosols or gases. The breathable air is accomplished by two ways: directly connected to a source (oxygen or pure air cylinder) or detoxification of contaminated air by passing through a canister. However, the use of a respirator can cause physiological discomforts such as breathing resistance, heat stress and vision and communication problems, resulting in the loss of efficiency.

The canister contains a "high-efficiency particulate aerosol (HEPA) filter media" for the aerosol retention and the gaseous contaminants from air are removed by the impregnated carbon through adsorption, catalytic decomposition and chemisorption processes.

Thus, full-face protective masks provide good protection for both the respiratory tract and the eyes. The face mask should have a good field of vision and speech transmission preferably with a microphone. These respiratory protective masks in different sizes are required to suit different face sizes. In case of body protection, liquid-impermeable full protective gears should be used for highly contaminated areas whereas toxic vapor-impermeable/air-permeable protective suits can be used. The impermeable suit is made up of nylon fabric coated outside with neoprene and another side with butyl rubber.

The permeable protective clothing consists of three layers: the upper layer is oil, water and fire retardant nylon fabric, the middle layer is a carbon-coated non-woven fabric and the third layer is a simple cotton fabric layer.

The protection gloves consist of an outer butyl rubber glove for chemical protection and an inner cotton glove for the absorption of perspiration water. Similar to gloves, overboots made up of butyl rubber are worn over the already used shoes to protect the footwear against contamination. The term "Personal Protective Equipment" (PPE) is used to denote complete protective gears i.e. face mask, suits, gloves and boots.

Collective protection to a group of people in vehicles or shelters is provided by providing purified air by filtration of contaminated air through large filters. The advantage of this is that individuals inside the protected area are not required to wear masks separately.

There are four levels of personal protection for dealing with hazardous substances.

These are described as levels A, B, C and D for chemical protective clothing in combination with different types of respiratory protection. Level A protection should be worn when the highest level of respiratory, skin, eye and mucous membrane protection is needed. This protection consists of a fully encapsulated, vapor-tight, chemical-resistant suit, boots and gloves together with a self-contained breathing apparatus (SCBA).

Level B protection should be selected when the highest level of respiratory protection is needed, but a lesser degree of skin and eye protection is required. This equipment consists of a chemical-resistant suit, chemical-resistant boots and gloves and SCBA.

Level C protection should be selected when the types of airborne substance are known, concentration is measured, criteria for using air-purifying respirators are met and skin or eye exposures are unlikely. This PPE consists of a chemical-resistant suit, full-face mask with air-purifying canister-equipped respirator and chemical-resistant boots and gloves. Level D protection provides no respiratory protection and minimal skin protection and should not be worn on any site when respiratory or skin hazards exist.

A recent review brings out NBC protective clothing, their types, various clothing materials used, their evaluation procedures, washing methodologies and decontamination methods as well as the futuristic trends, such as detection and decontamination-integrated NBC protective clothing based on electrospun nanofiber technology and molecularly imprinted polymer technology.

Decontamination

Decontamination is the conversion of toxic chemicals into harmless products either by destruction or by detoxification. Decontamination is a complex process involving processes involving highly toxic chemicals with diverse properties, adverse conditions and a wide variety of subjects to be treated, e.g. human skin and eyes, equipment with metal/wooden/plastic surface, field, etc. In terms of CW agents, decontamination can be defined as reduction or removal of chemical agents. This may be accomplished by physically removing the agents or by chemically neutralizing them. Decontamination is most effective when conducted within 1 min of exposure, but this is practically rarely possible.

Physical decontamination is easy and acts universally, but is not as effective as chemical decontamination.

It involves mainly adsorption of the toxic chemical on adsorbents such as Fuller's earth, kaolin, talc, activated carbon, etc., or removal of agents by spraying simple water or soap water under pressure. In emergency situations, the adsorbent may even be flour, saw dust or soil. There are many dry formulations containing Fuller's earth, such as PDK-1, PDK-2, M-291 kit that are available for decontamination of skin and equipment. The main disadvantage of the physical method is that the adsorbent or water used for decontamination should be detoxified later and disposed off carefully. Water spray should not be used in case of head or skin contaminated with mustards as it will spread to other body surfaces.

Chemical decontamination converts the toxic CW agents into innocuous products that can be handled safely. The chemical reactions that are generally applied in chemical decontamination methods are either nucleophilic reactions or oxidations. A commonly used skin decontaminant is the 0.5% hypochlorite solution or household bleach. Alkali (sodium or potassium hydroxide) dissolved in methanol or ethanol detoxifies most of the CW agents, but should not be used in decontaminating skin other than in extreme emergencies. Chloramines are effective against mustards and V-agents but are ineffective against G-agents. Sodium carbonate solution renders G-type nerve agents harmless, but with V-agents, it produces a toxic product.

Many ready-to-use effective chemical formulations have been developed and are commercially available. For example, DS2 is a universal decontamination solution for equipment and field use. This is investigated in depth and is available under different names. It is a composition of sodium hydroxide (2%), ethylene glycol monomethylether (28%) and diethylenetriamine (70%). The active ingredient in this formulation is ethylene glycol monomethylether, which acts as a nucleophile and hydrolyses the CW agents into non-toxic products. It is a clear, amber-colored solution and is used in the portable decontamination apparatus. DS2 reacts with GB and HD to effectively reduce their hazards within 5 min. Within 30 min contact time, DS2 neutralizes all known toxic chemical agents. It can damage paints as well as plastics, rubber and leather materials.

The American decontamination kit called M258A1 and M280 contain the active ingredients ethanol (72%), phenol (10%), NaOH (5%), ammonia (0.2%) and water (12%). Similarly, the German emulsion C8 is composed of tetrachloroethylene (15%), water (76%), anionic surfactant (1%) and calcium hypochlorite (8%). It is non-corrosive and can penetrate into paint to dissolve and react with the imbedded agent without damaging the paint.

The microemulsion-based (multi-purpose chemical, biological decontaminant) MCBD system contains water (60%), tetrachloroethylene (7%), n-cetyl trimethyl ammonium chloride (28%) and traces of cosurfactant, $(n\text{-Bu})_4$ NOH. To this microemulsion, Fichlor (4%), sodium 2-nitro-4-iodoxybenzoate (0.1%) and sodium borate are added for reactions with the agents.

The MCBD system was designed to be superior to the C8 system because it is a more stable emulsion at a lower pH of 10, contains less tetrachloroethylene and is partially catalytic.

The variables that determine the effectiveness of decontamination are contamination time, temperature, contamination density and decontamination medium, nature of agent and nature of decontaminants. The requirements of an ideal decontaminant or decontamination formulation are rapid in action, efficiency, harmless to humans, non-corrosive, stability in long-term storage and washable with water. There is a great deal of recent discussion and re-evaluation of decontamination agents and strategies and, therefore, careful consideration of the most current recommendation is important. Decontamination must be performed on all victims and responders before they cross into the clean area.

CWC

On April 29, 1997, the world's first multilateral disarmament Treaty "Chemical Weapons Convention" entered into force. The CWC text has a preamble, 24 articles and three annexes, namely an annex on chemicals, an annex on verification and a confidentiality annex.

The main objective of the CWC is to prohibit development, production, acquisition, retention, stockpiling transfer and use of chemical weapons. It mandated the Organisation for the Prohibition of Chemical Weapons (OPCW), with its headquarters at The Hague, the Netherlands, to eliminate the scourge of chemical weapons forever. It requires every country signatory to this Convention to destroy existing CW stockpiles and chemical weapons production facilities under its jurisdiction.

The most unique feature of the Treaty is its comprehensiveness and a strict inspection and verification regime. In addition, each State Party undertakes to provide protection and assistance through the Organisation if chemical weapons have been used against a State Party or if a State Party is threatened by such weapons. The CWC also provides for international cooperation among States Parties in the pursuit of chemistry for peaceful purposes. As on date, 188 countries are signatories to the convention. OPCW inspectors also verify the consistency of industrial chemical declarations and, together with State Parties, monitor the non-diversion of chemicals for activities prohibited under this convention.

It has been estimated that more than 100,000 compounds are controlled under the CWC, although, in practical terms, the actual number of CW agents, precursors and degradation products that are contained in the OPCW database is in thousands. The OPCW Central Analytical Database is a compilation maintained by the OPCW laboratory, and it contains analytical data of the chemicals that fall under the CWC.

6

Nuclear Proliferation and the Potential Threat of Nuclear Terrorism

For many centuries, security strategies have been based on boundaries: the strategic placement of cities and borders to take advantage of natural barriers; defences that relied on walls, trenches and armadas; and the use of ethnic and religious groupings or other categories to distinguish friend from foe. In the 20th Century, the advent of airplanes, submarines, ballistic missiles and weapons of mass destruction began to undermine this approach to security – by making borders increasingly porous, and by enabling the remote delivery of destruction on a scale previously not envisioned. But the forcing factor – the change that has altered the international security landscape so drastically that it has compelled a fundamental reevaluation of security strategies – is, in fact, globalization. The global community has become interdependent, with the constant movement of people, ideas and goods. Many aspects of modern life – global warming, Internet communication, the global marketplace, and yes, the rise in international terrorism – point to the fact that the human race has walked through a door that cannot be re-entered. Our approaches to national and international security must be in keeping with this reality.

Today, our focus is on nuclear proliferation and the potential threat of nuclear terrorism in Asia and the Pacific – and I am pleased at the opportunity to share with you my perspectives on the challenges we face, and how the IAEA is working to strengthen nuclear security and the nuclear non-proliferation regime. But I would emphasize at the outset that, while much of our work must begin locally and regionally, we must not forget to think globally, because ultimately the existence of a nuclear threat anywhere is a threat everywhere, and as a global community, we will win or lose this battle together.

NUCLEAR PROLIFERATION AND NUCLEAR VERIFICATION

Turning first to the threat of nuclear weapons proliferation: the *Treaty on the Non-Proliferation of Nuclear Weapons (NPT)* remains the global anchor for nuclear non-proliferation and nuclear disarmament. Despite flaws in the system, implementation of the NPT continues to provide important security benefits — by providing assurance that, in the great majority of non-nuclear-weapon States, nuclear energy is not being misused for weapon purposes. Although the NPT is sometimes perceived as a project of the industrialized world, its benefits extend across any geopolitical divide. Still, it is clear that the events of the past few years have placed the NPT and the regime supporting it under unprecedented stress, exposing some of its limitations and pointing to areas that need to be adjusted. A number of conspicuous lessons and insights can be gained from the recent experience of the IAEA in verifying undeclared nuclear programmes in Iraq, Iran, Libya and North Korea.

Perhaps the most important lesson is that verification and diplomacy, used in conjunction, can be effective. The Iraq experience demonstrated that the nuclear inspection process — while requiring time and patience — can be effective even when the country under inspection is providing less than active cooperation. When international inspectors are provided adequate authority, aided by all available information, backed by a credible compliance mechanism, and supported by international consensus, the verification system works. The report recently issued by the Iraq Survey Group confirmed the conclusions the IAEA was providing to the United Nations Security Council before the war, when we said we had found no evidence to suggest that Iraq had reconstituted any element of its former nuclear weapon programme — a conclusion that clearly came as a relief to all concerned.

Looking more broadly at recent IAEA experience in other countries, it is clear that, for nuclear verification to be successful, IAEA inspectors must have adequate authority. The "any time, any place" authority granted by the Security Council in the case of Iraq was extraordinary, and it is not likely that countries would voluntarily grant the IAEA such blanket rights of inspection.

Nonetheless, within the NPT framework, adequate authority can be achieved in those countries that accept the so-called "additional protocol" as a supplement to their NPT safeguards agreement. The additional protocol provides the Agency with significant additional authority with regard to both information and physical access. As illustrated by the IAEA's experience in Iraq before the first Gulf War, without the authority provided by the protocol, our ability to verify nuclear activities is mostly limited to the nuclear material already declared — with little authority to verify the absence of undeclared, or clandestine, nuclear material or activities. By contrast, our recent efforts in Iran and elsewhere have made clear how much can be uncovered when the protocol is applied. Perhaps the most disturbing lesson to emerge from our work in Iran and Libya is the existence of an extensive illicit market for the supply of nuclear items, which clearly thrived on demand. The relative ease with which a multinational illicit network could be set up and operated demonstrates clearly the inadequacy of the present export control system. The fact that so many companies and individuals could be involved (more than two dozen, by last count) — and that, in most cases, this could occur apparently without the knowledge of their own governments — points to the shortcomings of national systems for oversight of sensitive equipment and technology. It also points to the limitations of existing international cooperation on export controls, which relies on informal arrangements, does not include many countries with growing industrial capacity, and does not include sufficient sharing of export information with the IAEA.

Clearly, it is time to change our assumptions regarding the inaccessibility of nuclear technology. In a modern society characterized by electronic information exchange, interlinked financial systems, and global trade, the control of access to nuclear weapons technology has grown increasingly difficult. The technical barriers to mastering the essential steps of uranium enrichment — and to designing weapons — have eroded over time. Much of the hardware in question is 'dual use', and the sheer diversity of technology has made it much more difficult to control or even track procurement and sales.

The only reasonable conclusion is that the control of technology is not, in itself, a sufficient barrier against further proliferation. For an increasing number of countries with a highly developed industrial infrastructure — and in some cases access to high enriched uranium or plutonium — the international community must rely primarily on a continuing sense of security as the basis for the adherence of these countries to their non-proliferation commitments. And security perceptions can rapidly change. This leads to the important conclusion that ways and means should be found to better control the sensitive parts of the fuel cycle — namely, the production of enriched uranium and the reprocessing of plutonium.

The concept of multilateral control or oversight over proliferation sensitive parts of the nuclear fuel cycle has been the subject of many studies and initiatives over the years. Recent non-proliferation and security challenges make it important and appropriate that we revisit this subject. Several months ago, I appointed a group of senior experts to look into various options for multilateral control. I also asked the group to look into how to guarantee the supply of reactor technology and fuel, and the possibility of setting up an international scheme for the management and disposal of spent nuclear fuel. The group plans to submit a report next March, before the NPT Review Conference, on the results of its study.

The evolution of the North Korean situation over the past 18 months also carries an important lesson — that is, that the international community cannot afford not to act in a timely manner in cases of non-compliance, and before available options are narrowed. Beginning in the mid-1980s, the Democratic People's

Republic of Korea (DPRK) took seven years to fulfil its obligations under the NPT to conclude a safeguards agreement with the Agency. In 1992, shortly after this agreement was concluded and the IAEA began inspections, we sounded the alarm that the DPRK had not reported its total production of plutonium. From that time forward, the DPRK has been in continuous non-compliance with its NPT obligations, and has not allowed the IAEA to fully verify its nuclear programme. At the end of 2002, the DPRK capped that non-compliance by ordering IAEA inspectors out of the country, dismantling the monitoring cameras, breaking IAEA seals and, a few weeks later, declaring its withdrawal from the NPT.

Naturally, all of these actions were promptly reported by the Agency to the Security Council — but with little to no response. This lack of timely action may have complicated finding a solution, and may have conveyed the message that breaking the non-proliferation norms with impunity is a doable proposition — or, worse, that acquiring a nuclear deterrent will bring with it a special treatment.

The final lesson, an insight that has been demonstrated repeatedly, is that insecurity breeds proliferation. It is instructive that nearly all nuclear proliferation concerns arise in regions of longstanding tension. In other words, nuclear proliferation is a symptom, and the patient cannot ultimately be cured as long as we leave unaddressed the underlying causes of insecurity and instability — such as chronic disputes, the persistent lack of good governance and basic freedoms, the growing divide between rich and poor, and newly perceived schisms based on ethnic or religious differences.

It is in this context that I have begun to stress not only the value but also the limitations of the IAEA's role. While the Agency can use verification effectively to bring to closure questions of compliance with legal and technical requirements, the long term value of these efforts can only be realized to the extent that they are reinforced by all other components of the non-proliferation regime, and followed by the necessary political dialogue among concerned States to address underlying issues of insecurity, and to build confidence and trust. I should note that verification, supported by diplomacy, has been an important part of the efforts so far in Iran and Libya, and in that sense I can only hope that the continuation of the six-party talks on the DPRK nuclear programme will yield results that will include, inter alia, full IAEA verification.

Focus of Future Efforts

Looking to the future, it is clear that the imperatives that first led to the development of the IAEA's nuclear security plan have not diminished. We are now beginning a major review of our nuclear security activities. The main elements of a revised plan of activities are already emerging. One aspect of the new plan is to complete the international infrastructure of legal instruments, as well as relevant recommendations and guidelines.

One such legal instrument is the *Convention on Physical Protection of Nuclear Material (CPPNM).* For a number of years, work has been progressing on a draft amendment to the CPPNM that would expand its scope and strengthen existing provisions.

In July, at the request of the Government of Austria and 24 co-sponsoring States, I circulated proposed amendments to the *CPPNM* to all States Parties. The aim of these amendments, as proposed, is to extend the scope of the Convention to cover nuclear material used for peaceful purposes not only in international transport and storage, but also in domestic transport, storage and use, as well as the protection of nuclear material and facilities used for peaceful purposes from sabotage.

While consultations are ongoing to resolve a few outstanding issues, it is my hope that we can convene a diplomatic conference early next year to amend the *Convention* and expand its scope.

A second aspect of the new plan will be to accelerate a shift in emphasis from evaluation to action.

While we will continue to deliver advisory and needs assessment services, the work of the past three years have given us a much better understanding of Member State needs, and we will be working with States to give more emphasis to security upgrades and technical assistance.

A third point of focus will be to enhance the sustainability and self-reliance of nuclear security programmes in Member States. This will include helping States establish the needed regulatory frameworks, assisting in the implementation of international guidelines, and addressing continued training needs. For example, major security enhancements are expected as we assist States in implementing the revised Code of Conduct on source safety and security. More than 60 States have already begun working towards implementation of the Code. The Agency is also developing Integrated Nuclear Security Support Plans with individual Member States, as frameworks for helping to address their nuclear security needs over the longer term.

The Importance of Regional Efforts

It is clear that the benefits of IAEA assistance — and the reach of our limited resources — can be maximized by coordinating our activities with other international and regional organizations and through the use of regional partnerships. The Australian Government has established a regional project on the Security of Radioactive Sources, and the IAEA hopes to contribute to the success of that project, using funds designated by the US Department of Energy for assistance in establishing Regional Radiological Security Partnerships. Australia, the IAEA, and the USA, together with other States in the region — notably, Indonesia, Malaysia, Thailand and Vietnam — are already in the process of developing a work plan.

COOPERATIVE THREAT REDUCTION

Congress enacted the Nunn-Lugar Cooperative Threat Reduction (CTR) program in 1991, addressing, in Senator Lugar's words, "the dominant international proliferation danger: the massive nuclear, chemical and biological weapons infrastructure of the former Soviet Union."6 The CTR program had four key objectives:

- Destroy nuclear, chemical, and other weapons of mass destruction;
- Transport, store, disable, and safeguard these weapons in connection with their destruction;

- Establish verifiable safeguards against the proliferation of these weapons, their components, and weapons-usable materials; and
- Prevent the diversion of scientific expertise that could contribute to weapons programs in other nations.

According to Senator Lugar, the CTR program to date has separated 6,564 Russian nuclear warheads from their missiles and stored fissile material from those weapons. Over 30,000 tactical nuclear weapons have been stored, and non-weapons employment provided for thousands of Russian nuclear scientists.

CTR programs have evolved and expanded over time, adjusting to Russian, NIS, and U.S. priorities, as well as to changing perceptions about which threats posed the greatest risk. The programs have also bowed to bureaucratic intransigence and practical considerations upon occasion. In one notable incident, the Department of Energy provided blankets to facility guards, because DoE officials discovered that they were leaving their posts to collect wood to build fires. As the economy worsened in Russia in the mid-1990s, CTR projects were developed to provide alternative employment and sources of income for unpaid or out-of-work WMD scientists. At the same time, more frequent reports of theft of nuclear material highlighted the need to allocate CTR resources to material protection, control and accounting (MPCA) measures for nuclear material, consolidation of nuclear weapons and material; and secure transportation. The United States developed a practical approach: "quick-fixes," like bars on windows, blast-proof doors, fences, followed by a second stage that included more sophisticated security measures like sensors, cameras, and personnel access measures.

CTR as Precedent

The Cooperative Threat Reduction Program, at its inception, was a novel approach to a novel problem. The idea that two former adversaries could cooperate on such sensitive matters as nuclear weapons and material security was radical, but so too was the prospect of Russia's WMD infrastructure unraveling. Although some of the kinds of assistance and measures undertaken in the

CTR program are clearly applicable to India and Pakistan, the circumstances that have led to the development of a similar nuclear terrorist threat are quite different. Among the many factors that have made CTR successful, one of the key factors was a basic level of agreement about the threat and a willingness to cooperate. Russia had already agreed to strategic nuclear reductions under START I — the only question was how to implement those reductions quickly and who would pay for them. The fact that Soviet nuclear weapons had been targeted at the United States for so many years presented a compelling reason for the United States to help.

Obviously, there is no similar agreement between India and Pakistan or with the United States. Moreover, India has long maintained that it will disarm when the other nuclear weapon states reduce their stockpiles to a similar level. Thus, destruction and dismantlement activities are not now applicable. CTR chain of custody programs applied to the weapons and material that were taken out of service and thus did not raise questions about enhancing safety, security and control over Russia's active nuclear weapons stockpile. Doing similar things for India and Pakistan might be desirable from a security standpoint, but questionable politically.

Establishing verifiable safeguards against the proliferation of existing nuclear weapons, components, and materials is the most applicable of all the CTR objectives for India and Pakistan. However, the situation of Pakistan and India is different from that in Russia and offers one major complication: threat reduction measures aimed at an outside/terrorist threat may conflict with nuclear deterrence. For example, making materials and weapons safe from theft or espionage may logically lead to consolidating material and weapons at as few sites as possible.

However, that consolidation could increase one's vulnerability to a preemptive strike by an adversary. In the case of Russia and the NIS, the risk of a preemptive strike did not weigh into calculations of risk; any obstacles to consolidation have been primarily those of cost and effort in constructing adequate facilities (like the Mayak plutonium storage facility). For India and Pakistan, however, the fear of a preemptive strike is prominent. Rumors of an Indian or even Israeli preemptive attack on Pakistani nuclear weapons capabilities have erupted in Pakistan predictably during crises. The last objective — that of preventing diversion of scientific expertise — is also applicable to India and Pakistan.

However, the underlying causes for concern are different, and therefore may call for different solutions. In the Russian case, the lack of financial security has been a documented incentive for scientists to offer their services abroad; in Pakistan, the incentive is more likely to be associated with sympathy for terrorist aims. "Brain drain" projects in the NIS have been predicated on the assumption that there are more scientists than can be paid or are needed, but there are no indications that Pakistani and Indian scientists are superfluous to their nuclear weapons programs. Both India and Pakistan are probably interested in retaining their nuclear experts. Although it has been politically acceptable to fund former WMD scientists in Russia and the NIS to do non-weapons-related work, it might be politically unacceptable to fund current WMD scientists in India and Pakistan at higher levels simply to keep them "in the program." Brain-drain projects in India and Pakistan, if such projects were implemented, would likely focus on personnel reliability testing and psychological profiling.

CTR's Critics

Some arguments against expanding CTR challenge its effectiveness. Opponents have suggested that assisting Russia has simply created opportunities for the Russians to spend their money in other defence-related areas. Some supporters, in contrast, argue that CTR has not done enough quickly enough. Those that argue that CTR has not done enough have suggested that the programs have focused misguidedly on nuclear weapons rather than nuclear material security, wherein the greatest threat lies.

Some analysts believe that any assistance at all sends the wrong message to India and Pakistan (e.g., acceptance of their possession of nuclear weapons), that assistance could be misused or misappropriated and that, in the end, U.S. assistance may wind up improving Indian and Pakistani nuclear capabilities in ways we had not foreseen. Proponents of the CTR program in the NIS have argued that the program was implemented with a key principle — that cooperation would serve the objective of enhancing physical security and protection of nuclear assets and not enhance any operational capabilities. Some argue that this principle, particularly since India and Pakistan have not joined the NPT and are *de jure* non-nuclear-weapons states (NNWS), must also be adhered to in the case of any assistance to those states.

NONPROLIFERATION CONTEXT

Until North Korea's February 2005 declaration of a nuclear weapons capability, India and Pakistan were the only states outside the Treaty on the Nonproliferation of Nuclear Weapons (NPT) to declare, openly, their nuclear weapons status. When India and Pakistan tested nuclear weapons in 1998, a curious dilemma emerged for the international community — was it possible to acknowledge a nuclear weapons capability without conferring nuclear weapons status? Several months after the test, then Deputy Secretary of State Strobe Talbott stated in *Foreign Affairs* that the United States "cannot concede, even by implication, that India and Pakistan have by their tests established themselves as nuclear-weapons states... To relent would break faith with those states that have forsworn a capability they could have acquired. Moreover, it might inadvertently provide an incentive for other countries to blast their way into the ranks of the nuclear-weapons states." The international community so far has sidestepped questions of nuclear weapons status, but some have suggested that India and Pakistan have become a model for new nuclear weapon states.

On the question of nuclear assistance to non-nuclear weapon states, however, consensus in the international community is strong, well-established, and embodied in the NPT. Before the Nuclear Nonproliferation Treaty entered into force in 1970, views on sharing nuclear technology and even nuclear weapons swung wildly between sharing everything and sharing nothing. According to one source, the United States contemplated giving India some nuclear weapons to counter the Chinese nuclear arsenal, shortly after China's first nuclear test in 1964. Nuclear weapon states have voluntarily shared technology among themselves and some have spied on each other. China initially advocated nuclear proliferation as an inevitable and possibly stabilizing factor in world relations (although it joined the NPT in 1992). Nuclear weapon states have also shared technology with those states outside the NPT, the most notable example being China's reported sharing of nuclear weapons blueprints with Pakistan. And, reportedly, Pakistan shared that design with Libya.

Negotiators of the Nuclear Nonproliferation Treaty (NPT) in the mid-1960s realized that almost any kind of international nuclear assistance is potentially useful to a nuclear weapons program.26 Nuclear weapons — more than biological or chemical weapons, or missiles — require such precision in design and construction that any assistance, from technical information, to hints about solving technical problems (for example, how to shape the fissile core), to equipment or components — can be valuable to an aspiring nuclear weapons state. Therefore, nuclear weapon states, under Article I of the NPT, commit "not to transfer to any recipient whatsoever nuclear weapons or nuclear explosive devices or control over such weapons or devices, directly or indirectly; and not in any way to assist, encourage or induce any non-nuclear weapon state to manufacture or otherwise acquire nuclear weapons or nuclear explosive devices." In contrast to the obligation of the nonnuclear- weapon states under Article II not to receive nuclear weapons or related assistance, this commitment incurred no verification measures. In part, this omission may have rested on the assumption that holders of nuclear weapons technology would not impart the most sophisticated and directly weapons-relevant information to non-nuclear weapons states. Clearly, however, negotiators felt comfortable with focusing verification on the recipient states. All states are obliged under Article III, paragraph 2 of the treaty not to provide source or special fissionable material or equipment to any non-nuclear-weapon state unless the material is subject to IAEA safeguards.

Nuclear safeguards are the primary means "to establish and clarify the peaceful purpose of most international nuclear assistance." Not simply an invention of the NPT, safeguards existed in bilateral arrangements since the earliest nuclear trade as a way of preventing the misuse of material with obvious military applications. Beyond their technical importance in ensuring that states cannot develop nuclear weapons "the quick way," safeguards have become the acid test for a state's nonproliferation-worthiness. U.S. export control laws, arms export control laws and nonproliferation policies have incorporated the distinction between those states with full-scope safeguards (on all material in their state) and those without. Moreover, the international nuclear nonproliferation regime has taken its cues from laws and policies developed by the United States. When, for example, the Nuclear Suppliers' Group adopted full-scope safeguards as a prerequisite for nuclear supply, it was adopting a policy that the United States had implemented a decade earlier. Since the discovery of the Khan network, efforts have accelerated to make the new nonproliferation acid test the adoption of the Additional Protocol.

At the same time, efforts to prevent proliferation have not blinded states to concerns about the safety and security of proliferant states' nuclear weapons. To some observers, however, proposals to provide security and safety measures seem to be tainted by a certain hubris — that is, nuclear weapon states have considered themselves to be responsible with their nuclear weapons, whereas lesser industrialized states could not be as responsible. Until China's nuclear test, the only nuclear weapon states were those with large, industrial economies. To some extent, global concern about terrorism might lessen sensitivities about whether or not India or Pakistan "need" help. Nonetheless, repeated Pakistani officials' statements to the press about the security of their arsenal appear to reflect a"hands-off" attitude, implying that Pakistan is quite able to protect and secure its own weapons. India, for its part, has remained silent on the subject. More importantly, however, the sensitivity surrounding nuclear weapons is such that even between the closest of allies — for example, the United States and the United Kingdom — proposals to share permissive action links (PALs, which only allow authorized parties to arm the warhead) reportedly have been met with disinterest.

SOUTH ASIA AND THE MIDDLE EAST: PROLIFERATION LINKS

While an analysis of proliferation in the Middle East is outside the scope of this study, it is necessary to highlight existing and potential links between the Middle East and South Asia, apart from the A.Q. Khan network mentioned above. Khan's network provided significant know-how to Iran in the late eighties and early nineties (including centrifuge technology), though the full extent of these transfers has still not been confirmed. While nuclear links between Iran and Pakistan have ended for now, Islamabad's nuclear connection to the Middle East remains, such as through possible collaboration with Saudi Arabia.

From the South Asian proliferation perspective, the close ties between Saudi Arabia and the development of Pakistan's nuclear program is a crucial development. News reports as well as official U.S. government analyses have claimed that Riyadh provided considerable financing for Pakistan's nuclear and missile program in the past, but some reports now suggest a more proactive role by Saudi Arabia-in terms of nuclear energy development itself. This is in line with the announcement in November 2006 by six Arab states-Saudi Arabia, Morocco, Egypt, Algeria, Tunisia, and the United Arab Emirates-that they would develop civilian nuclear programs. Earlier, in 2005, Saudi Arabia applied for and was granted exemption from nuclear inspections through the IAEA's 'small quantities protocol.' Before that, a widely quoted 2003 report in The Guardian stated that Riyadh was considering three nuclear options: (a) building a nuclear deterrent, (b) allying with a nuclear power, or (c) working toward a nuclear weapon free zone in the Middle East. Recent developments suggest that a combination of the first two options might be adopted given that it is highly unlikely that Iran and Israel relinquish their nuclear programs in the near future.

This is where Pakistan's role could be significant. German news reports stated in early 2006 that Pakistani scientists assisted Saudi efforts to develop a nuclear program and that this was done under the guise of pilgrimages to Saudi Arabia between 2003 and 2005. Several high-ranking Saudi royals as well as government officials are among the few non-Pakistanis who have toured Islamabad's nuclear facilities. These include defence minister Prince Sultan (now also crown prince) who visited the Kahuta uranium enrichment facility in 1999, and a son of the current Saudi ruler, King Abdullah, who attended a test of the nuclear-capable 950-mile range Ghauri missile in 1999. These developments suggest that if Riyadh decides to acquire nuclear weapons, the spotlight could be on Pakistan as one of the sources. A factor that could prompt Saudi Arabia to pursue nuclear weapons would be if Tehran unambiguously builds it own nuclear weapon, prompting Israel to shed the opacity over its arsenal.

While disincentives for Pakistan to go along this route are considerable (most notably, U.S. opposition), there are also incentives for Islamabad to aid the Saudis in their quest-cheap oil from Saudi Arabia, and a favorable endorsement for the Musharraf regime (or a successor regime) from powerful conservative Sunni religious and political groups within Pakistan. A 2003 news report quoted an anonymous Pakistani official who claimed that Riyadh and Islamabad had concluded a secret agreement under which Pakistan would receive subsidized oil in exchange for transferring nuclear technology. In 2004, Iranian government sources also claimed that they had information that confirmed this agreement, but there was no further corroboration of this from other sources. Therefore, even if there is no immediate possibility of such a transfer, Saudi Arabia could pursue this with Pakistan in the future to hedge against nuclear developments in the Middle East.

A key incentive for Pakistan could also be to use Saudi Arabia for strategic depth purposes. Islamabad's traditional geographic buffer against Indian military campaigns was Afghanistan, but that was lost after the fall of the Taliban in 2001. Ostensibly, Pakistan requires strategic depth to protect its forces (conventional and nuclear) from an armored offensive by the Indian military, which could cut off the country similar to the 1971 war. Saudi Arabia could provide a base for stationing Pakistani nuclear devices that would be safe from the reach of Indian missiles and give Islamabad a semblance of second-strike capability. This idea of looking towards the Middle East for strategic depth is not new.

In the 1990s, former Prime Minister Benazir Bhutto, skeptical of the reliance on Afghanistan, recommended Iran as a more useful ally for purposes of strategic depth.

Apart from the Pakistan-Saudi Arabia link, concerns have also been expressed (especially in the U.S. Congress) over India's ties to Iran, at a time when the IAEA and western powers led by the United States are working toward controlling Tehran's uranium enrichment program. These concerns have arisen during the broader debate in Washington on the nuclear agreement with India. In particular, attention has focused on India's long-standing political and diplomatic relationship with Iran as well as the imposition of sanctions on two private Indian companies suspected of transferring chemicals meant for rocket fuel as well as chemical weapons. The Indian government claimed that both companies (Balaji Amines Ltd. & Prachi Poly Products) were doing legitimate business with Iranian firms. Balaji Amines insisted that they had been supplying products used for manufacturing life-saving drugs such as ampicillin and other antibiotics, but nevertheless, New Delhi ordered the company to stop all trade with Iran.

Both India and Pakistan have attempted to ensure that they are in compliance with the latest international regulations against Tehran's nuclear program. In February 2007, Pakistan froze assets of several individuals and other entities connected to Tehran's nuclear and missile projects in accordance with UN Security Council resolution 1737. In the same month, New Delhi banned exports of equipment and technologies to Iran that could be used in nuclear and missile development projects.

The Iran nuclear issue has been an important point of discussion in context of the Indo-U.S. nuclear agreement. The Hyde Act, passed by the U.S. Congress in December 2006, endorses nuclear cooperation between India and the United States, but it also states that New Delhi should assist the international community in clamping down on Iran's nuclear program. Furthermore, in May 2007, a group of U.S. senators sent a joint letter to Indian Prime Minister Manmohan Singh articulating their dissatisfaction over India's military ties with Iran, especially a 'joint defence working group' between the two countries. Nuclear ties between India and the United States are not limited to nuclear trade between the two, but also extends to discussions over restricting proliferation elsewhere.

Prime Minister Manmohan Singh has stated in the past that New Delhi does not favour another nuclear power in the neighborhood, and India voted against Iran at the IAEA in September 2005 and February 2006. However, two factors have restrained the Indian government from opposing Iran's nuclear weapons program more forcefully. First, the scramble for energy resources has made the Iran-Pakistan-India (IPI) natural gas pipeline a crucial economic issue for India. Stern Indian opposition to Iran's nuclear program would jeopardize the proposed IPI pipeline from Iran to India. The pipeline is considered to be of crucial importance to India in order to sustain high economic growth rates in the coming years. Thus, economic imperatives, specifically the need for energy sources, are an important factor in nonproliferation positions of countries such as India and China. In this context, New Delhi has reiterated that the construction of the pipeline will proceed in spite of pressures from Washington to cancel the project.

Second, for New Delhi, another variable is satisfying domestic political constituencies that are skeptical of the nuclear overtures from Washington that come at the cost of long-standing ties with Tehran. Since the Congress Party-led coalition government depends on parliamentary support from Communist parties, the government is obliged to periodically hold positions on contentious issues such as the Iranian nuclear program. The Manmohan Singh government has stated that it would be guided by India's national interest on the Iran nuclear issue, but this does not clarify to what extent India would be willing to go along with the United States on this issue. Some recent reports have also stated that New Delhi could play a more formal role in mediating the growing tensions over Iran's nuclear program in conjunction with the UN Security Council. However, it is unclear what form this would take.

In sum, nuclear issues in South Asia cannot be examined in isolation from developments elsewhere. Historically close political ties have existed between the South Asian subcontinent and the

Middle East, and therefore, regional rivalries and bilateral relations play an important role in shaping decisions that impact broader nuclear issues, including horizontal proliferation.

Indo-U.S. Nuclear Cooperation

Since July 2005, when the U.S. and Indian governments unveiled their nuclear cooperation agreement, a debate has risen over its impact on the global nonproliferation regime. This agreement will allow India to acquire nuclear technology and materials from the United States and other suppliers. In return, New Delhi will designate which of its nuclear facilities are for civilian use and which are for military use. The former list would be opened up for international inspections. Prior to implementation, New Delhi will have to conclude a safeguards agreement with the IAEA, while the Nuclear Suppliers Group (NSG) will have to effect changes in its rules to enable nuclear cooperation between its member states and India.

The Hyde Act passed by the U.S. Congress in December 2006, authorized the Bush administration to bring into place a nuclear cooperation mechanism with India, after concluding a bilateral agreement under Section 123 of the U.S. Atomic Energy Act. Negotiations on the '123' agreement began in early 2007, but as of early June, talks were stalled on a few contentious issues. The disagreement is over five main items; (i) the right to reprocess spent fuel, (ii) the conversion of a voluntary moratorium on nuclear testing into a legal commitment by India, (iii) the assured supply of fuel by the United States, (iv) the return of all equipment to the United States if India conducts a nuclear test, and (v) the level of inspections of Indian facilities.

The nuclear deal reflects an influential view in India that the nonproliferation regime embodied in the NPT is defective. According to Indian Prime Minister Manmohan Singh, the regime is ineffective and that the international community should introduce measures that restrict nuclear proliferation more effectively without suppressing peaceful uses of nuclear energy. At the same time, the contention is that India is a responsible nuclear state that has adhered to the guidelines of nonproliferation (without legally being part of the NPT regime) through strict export controls and denying nuclear assistance to other states, unlike the record of some nuclear weapon states.

A basic feature of this agreement is that by acquiring uranium from foreign sources (to free up domestic supplies) and by placing a set of nuclear facilities on the military list, India can increase its fissile material production for weaponization purposes. However, a different line of analysis examines the implications of increased uranium supplies in the context of India's fledgling nuclear submarine project. This perspective views that rather than increasing nuclear warhead production, New Delhi would use the expansion of its uranium supplies and enrichment capability to fuel its nuclear submarine project, a key element of India's desire to achieve a secure second strike capability under its credible minimum deterrence doctrine.

There are two separate lines of criticism of the deal; the first focuses on the nonproliferation objective, and the second on India's strategic needs. The first perspective is that the agreement will weaken the global nonproliferation regime by condoning India's nuclear weapons program. The argument is that by introducing India-specific changes to global as well as domestic U.S. nonproliferation laws, it will be more difficult to prevent nuclear transfers involving other countries such as China-Pakistan and Russia-Iran. A further objection is that even with 14 reactors under safeguards, 8 others will remain on the military list, free to manufacture plutonium for several nuclear weapons annually. Additionally, critics have stated that the agreement so far does not commit India to eschew nuclear testing formally, or to end fissile material production.

The second criticism comes most notably, from members of the nuclear scientific community in India, who contend that elements of the agreement would in effect cap India's nuclear program and constrain its thorium-based three stage nuclear project. They argue that while New Delhi has maintained a unilateral moratorium on nuclear testing, it does not want such a clause legalized in a bilateral treaty. The argument here is that India might have to reconsider its moratorium in the event that

China or Pakistan conducts a nuclear test. In addition, India's scientific community and government have insisted that it be explicitly granted the right to reprocess spent fuel for the three stage nuclear project that exploits the ample thorium reserves in the country (about 30% of the global supply). The Indian government wants to retain reprocessing rights as part of an advanced nuclear fuel cycle. This would involve recycling uranium oxide fuel while the consequent plutonium would be used with thorium in fast breeder reactors. However, some Indian scientific experts have stated that even if reprocessing rights and technology are not granted under the 123 agreement, it is likely that the initial reactors bought by New Delhi will come from Russia and France, rather than the United States. It is entirely possible that trade with these two countries, especially Russia, will involve reprocessing rights and sale of reactors and fuel. On the other hand, Indian analysts criticize the reported objective of the U.S. government of insuring that India's nuclear trade with other supplier states has equally rigorous conditions attached. Finally, Indian analysts have faulted the U.S. position of not allowing assurances of fuel supplies and of prohibiting India from stockpiling nuclear fuel.

Thus, the nuclear agreement between India and the United States has been criticized on the grounds of its potential impact on the global nonproliferation regime as well as its impact on India's strategic nuclear program. It must also be noted that since the bilateral 123 agreement between India and the United States is still under negotiation, it is too early to assume the eventual direction of the nuclear agreement framework. Even if the two countries conclude the 123 agreement satisfactorily (for both sides), India still must obtain approval for nuclear trade from the NSG and has to negotiate a safeguards agreement with the IAEA.

The China Issue

Several rationales have been offered as justification for the nuclear agreement (such as economics, strategic alliance, and nonproliferation benefits), but perhaps the most intriguing is one has been left largely unstated by the two governments-that of balancing China. Both India and the United States are concerned about the future direction of Chinese foreign and security policy.

For the United States, aiding India through nuclear cooperation as well as a strategic partnership, Washington would be able to balance China more effectively in the region. In the process it would divert China from its main security issue-Taiwan. For India, the agreement is a significant diplomatic and strategic addition to its capabilities vis-à-vis China, with both the possible increase in fissile material production and a strengthened strategic partnership with the United States.

One argument supportive of the Indo-U.S. agreement stresses that China has built up Pakistan as a counter to India for several decades, a policy that involved transfers of nuclear and missile technology. It must also be noted that more than a year before the Indo-U.S. nuclear agreement was first announced in July 2005, there were reports in March 2004 that China was planning to provide Islamabad with a nuclear reactor. The implication is that that the Beijing-Islamabad nuclear partnership might have continued in any case. Nevertheless, it is important to consider the current pattern of nuclear cooperation between China and Pakistan in the light of the Indo-U.S. deal. Regardless of the pros and cons of the deal, it can be used by Beijing to lay the grounds for legitimizing continued nuclear collaboration with Pakistan. A sign of this has been China's argument that any changes in the NSG rules should be criteria-based rather than country specific.

In December 2005, China began construction of the 300 MW second phase of the Chashma Nuclear Power Plant (contracted in May 2004), subsequent to the commissioning of the first phase in September 2000. Parallel to the Indo-U.S. deal, China and Pakistan also reportedly agreed to a nuclear cooperation arrangement under which as many as six nuclear reactors of at least 600 MW capacity would be provided to Islamabad. As of now, no other details are available so it is not clear what kind of safeguards will be installed, though some sources have stated that this initiative is being opposed by the NSG.

Reports of a possible Beijing-Islamabad nuclear agreement gained ground ahead of Chinese President Hu Jintao's visit to Pakistan in November 2006. However, no such deal was announced during the visit, leading to a conclusion that Beijing is possibly waiting to see the final shape of the Indo-U.S. agreement to gauge its impact on China. However, one influential Pakistani analyst stated that the lack of a public nuclear cooperation agreement between Beijing and Islamabad does not mean that such an arrangement will not come about; China can supply Pakistan with the required nuclear technology at a more politically convenient time.

Pakistan's desire for a stronger and more public nuclear relationship with China is in part because Islamabad failed to obtain a similar arrangement with the United States. Some Pakistani commentators have in fact argued that their country needs nuclear cooperation with the United States (and other suppliers, for that matter) more than India because the gap between existing energy supplies and future energy requirements is far more serious for Pakistan that it is for India. A senior Pakistani official connected to the nuclear program, stated in October 2006 that Washington's nuclear policy should be guided by a "criteria-based" approach rather than one geared toward a single country. However, U.S. government officials have stated that they have no intention of considering a similar agreement with Pakistan. It is likely that this refusal has much to do with the activities of the A.Q. Khan network as well as Islamabad's reluctance to allow a full interrogation of Khan by U.S. experts that would shed light on some unanswered questions related to the network.

Islamabad has cited the fact that Washington declined to offer Pakistan a nuclear cooperation agreement as a motivation for increased self-reliance on nuclear energy, through indigenous fuel manufacturing capabilities. In this context, government officials in Pakistan stated in April 2007 that the country would set up an installation for fuel testing for use in nuclear plants in a quest for "complete technological capability." As highlighted previously, Pakistan's overall agenda is to redress the perceived widening of the nuclear imbalance with India. Nevertheless, Pakistani experts have admitted that Islamabad's quest for increased nuclear capability is a result of the tacit rivalry between Beijing and New Delhi and the latter's desire to catch up with China. Apart from the impending nuclear technology transfers from Beijing, recent reports have also stated that the Musharraf regime has commenced construction of a 1,000 MW heavy water reactor that will potentially produce adequate plutonium for as many as 50 warheads per year. In addition, Islamabad is setting up a commercial scale nuclear reprocessing plant to allow production of weapons grade plutonium. Such activities would enable Islamabad to stockpile as much fissile material as possible before a future FMCT comes into force.

These developments suggest that Islamabad is attempting to diversify its nuclear weapons program through plutonium, as opposed to its traditional reliance on uranium as fissile material. Plutonium allows for more compact weapons and provides increased flexibility for the arsenal. For Islamabad, this is critical for developing a second strike capability against India. However, some Indian scientific experts have stated that even with the new Pakistani reactor, India will still be able to maintain an insurmountable lead in fissile material production through unsafeguarded reactors under the nuclear agreement.

Chinese support is key to Pakistan's quest for some strategic benefits vis-à-vis India, especially if the U.S.-India nuclear agreement reaches the implementation stage. In a possible attempt to reduce Chinese opposition to the nuclear deal with Washington, New Delhi has committed itself, in principle, to civilian nuclear cooperation with Beijing, a declaration announced during President Hu's visit to New Delhi in November 2006. This could be viewed as an incentive from Beijing to dissuade India from a potential anti-China partnership with Washington. Nuclear trade between India and China is not necessarily an empty proposal; it has a precedent. In 1995, India acquired low enriched uranium from China for the Tarapur nuclear reactors. The official Chinese position is opposition to any NSG amendments that would adversely effect the non-proliferation regime, and that they would consider viable arrangements at the NSG, and not bilaterally. Beijing's response reiterates its view that any exceptions should not be India-specific and should include other states.

Interestingly, Indian Foreign Minister Pranab Mukherjee stated in November 2006 that New Delhi does not have any problem with a similar nuclear agreement between Pakistan and China. If this attitude is indeed the Indian government's position, the implication could be that New Delhi is confident that the benefits it will accrue from the agreement with the United States far outweigh the possible increase in nuclear cooperation between China and Pakistan.

Commercial Issues

The Indo-U.S. nuclear agreement also demonstrates that changes in the nuclear supplier regimes will not be restricted only to bilateral nuclear trade between the United States and India. Nuclear energy firms from several countries other than India are already lining up to negotiate commercial nuclear deals with India. NSG member states such as Australia are considering approval of changes in the group's rules to permit nuclear cooperation with New Delhi. Even though Australia (a major uranium producer) has not yet agreed to revoke the prohibition of supply to India, Australian companies such as BHP Billiton are anticipating lucrative sales. Other important members of the NSG have also supported civilian nuclear cooperation with India, within the appropriate IAEA safeguards framework. French and Canadian companies have also contacted the Nuclear Power Corporation of India (one of the main government nuclear energy entities), in connection with the supply of light-water nuclear power related equipment.

Thus, nuclear energy companies are important players in the future of this agreement as well as the broader nonproliferation regime. Firms such as General Electric and Bechtel have lobbied the Bush administration in favour of the agreement. Besides deals in the nuclear energy sector, the expectation is also that such cooperation will facilitate contracts in the conventional military sector, especially with respect to the impending deal for 126 fighter aircraft for the Indian Air Force, a deal worth about $9 billion. Aerospace giants such as Lockheed Martin and Boeing are among the contenders for the contract. Therefore, the implication is that the incentives go well beyond the nuclear energy sector.

Finally, it is instructive to consider the scenario if the nuclear agreement between India and the United States is scrapped, either because of insurmountable differences over the 123 agreement or later in the implementation stage. In India, several members of the influential atomic energy scientific community have expressed reservations over the agreement as have the communist parties and the opposition Bharatiya Janata Party (BJP). In the United States as well, there has been considerable opposition from nonproliferation experts as well as sections of the political establishment. It is not certain if the reservations expressed by the Indian government towards certain clauses of the December 2006 Hyde Act will be rectified in New Delhi's favour in the bilateral 123 agreement, which again has to be approved by the U.S. Congress. Given these complicating factors, the implications of scrapping the agreement are immense; affecting broader bilateral ties between India and the United States, the nonproliferation regime in general, and the global nuclear energy market.

REDUCING THE THREAT OF NUCLEAR TERRORISM

Paradoxically, with the end of the Cold War – a time in history where large parts of the Northern Hemisphere could have been be annihilated in a less-than-an-hour nuclear exchange – today's nuclear security picture is as unclear as ever. Well-established nuclear weapon states still hold sizeable nuclear arsenals, juvenile nuclear weapon possessors are boosting their stockpiles, and a new set of states have revealed disturbing nuclear ambitions and a strong appetite for nuclear weapons. Prospects of renewed horizontal – and possibly vertical – state nuclear-weapon proliferation are real. And, as this wasn't enough, some sub-national groups have revealed a definitive interest in nuclear explosives.

The topic of this chapter is the most novel and undefined, and probably least understood, of all contemporary nuclear dangers: the threat of nuclear terrorism. While the effects of such a scenario would be quite limited compared with an all-out nuclear exchange, the intentional use of even a single nuclear weapon in a densely populated area would leave in its wake a massive, unprecedented public health and environmental catastrophe.

Assessing and understanding the risk seems essential. However, the (fortunate) lack of empirical data, limitations in terrorist trend analysis, and the inherent complexities surrounding of the issue of nuclear terrorism render any probabilistic assessments a daring endeavour. Temptations to try to identify the probability of future acts of nuclear terrorism in accurate and absolute terms should thus probably be avoided.

Through a simple stepwise risk assessment methodology, where risk is viewed as a product of probability and consequence, this paper attempts to qualitatively assess the technical aspects of the nuclear terrorism threat, and how this risk best can be reduced. The work of Bunn et al. (2003, 26) on the successive steps towards a successful act of nuclear terrorism will be used as a framework for the analysis. It will be shown that the most efficient way to reduce – and in fact even eliminate – the risk of nuclear terrorism is to initially deny terrorists access to fissile material through optimal protection, control and accounting practices. Not only seem any other countermeasures further down the line to be more costly. The effects tend to be more arbitrary and with less secure outcomes.

Throughout the paper, no attempt will be given to assess the motivational side of nuclear terrorism, to discuss possible nuclear terrorism scenarios beyond the use of crude nuclear explosive devices,[2] or to criticize any of and the current hard-driving political rhetoric surrounding the phenomenon of nuclear terror.

NUCLEAR TERRORISM RISK ASSESSMENTS

As nuclear weapons are of limited or no use for the overwhelming majority of terrorist groups (Rapoport 2001), the probability (P) of nuclear terrorism may generally be regarded as low. At the same time, however, any successfully performed acts of nuclear terrorism would leave devastating consequences (C) in its wake. Nuclear terrorism may therefore be seen as a low-probability/high consequence event. As such, the risk is not zero, and cannot – and should not – be neglected:

R= P x C, = > R '" 0

Accordingly, it has been argued that governments should institute measures to make nuclear terrorist threats less likely to emerge, and should create operational capabilities that can give them a reasonable chance of detecting, defeating and minimizing the consequences of the nuclear terrorist threat (Falkenrath 1998, 58). From a medical point of view, however, the ability of health personnel to provide post-attack prophylaxis is limited. Risk elimination and prevention of nuclear terrorism thus seem key.

Any terrorist with nuclear ambitions will have to follow a specific stepwise path to accomplish the goal of nuclear havoc. The steps will be of both a motivational and a capability-building character. To maximize the chances of preventing a nuclear terrorist attack, each of these successive steps should be systematically assessed.

Step Action

S1 Form a highly capable group with extreme objectives S2 Decide to escalate to the nuclear level of violence S3 Steal nuclear weapons material S4 Acquire nuclear weapons material S5 Smuggle material to safe haven S6. Construct nuclear explosive device S7 Smuggle nuclear explosive device into target country S8 Transport nuclear explosive device to target location S9 Detonate nuclear explosive device.

Each of the steps has to be performed in the order indicated, as each rests upon the previous one. The probability for a successful nuclear terrorist attack may thus be expressed as the product of the probability of all single steps S1,S2, …, S9:

P = P(S1) x P(S2) x….. P(S9) = _ P(S i) i = 1, 9

Steps S1 and S2 are both of a motivational or intentional character, and fall therefore outside the core scope of this paper. Steps S3–S9, however, will all be the subject of further analysis. Each of these (technical) steps are a prerequisite for nuclear terrorist havoc – and each and every one of them depends upon the preceding step. The total probability P may thus be severely limited – even reduced to zero – if one or more of the partial probabilities P(Si) become minuscule or zero.

This is an essential point: The risk of nuclear terrorism could be (drastically) reduced – even eliminated – by installing proper barriers at critical points along the nuclear terrorist pathway. This allows, moreover, for a comparative "cost–benefit" analysis to determine where in the "nuclear terrorism chain" investments are likely to yield the highest gains (in terms of reduced probability of nuclear terrorism).

Stealing Nuclear Weapons Material

The initial step towards a technical nuclear capability is to get hold of sufficient quantities and qualities of fissile material. While most of the fissile material worldwide is duly protected and accounted for, the huge amounts produced during the Cold War could make proper control challenging. As the quantity of weapons-useable material increases, so does the proliferation risk of the material (Dreicer and Rutherford 1996, 30). There have been multiple documented cases of theft of kilogram quantities of weapons-useable material, especially in countries of the former Soviet Union. In February 2002, US intelligence confirmed to Congress that weapons-grade and weapons-useable nuclear materials have been stolen from some institutes in Russia (Collina and Wolfsthal 2002).

During the past decade, unprecedented co-operative work between the USA and Russia has been carried out to secure fissile material. However, much of the challenges remain. Hundreds of metric tons of nuclear material lack improved security systems. As of March 2003 – after a decade of cooperation – the US Department of Energy (DOE) had assisted Russia in protecting about 228 metric tons, or some 38%, of its weapons-useable nuclear material (United States General Accounting Office 2003, 25).

Insider thefts have turned out to be a particular problem. Soviet-era physical security systems were built on a philosophy of "guards, guns and Gulag" (Bunn et al. 2002, 35). Morale in the nuclearweapon complex then was high, and insiders were not really a threat, as personal surveillance was tight and potential buyers of stolen fissile material absent. Post-Soviet experiences have proven otherwise (Koupriyanova 1999).

Acquiring Stolen Nuclear Weapons Material

Fresh fissile material is only mildly radioactive, with a limited level of toxicity in solid form. The material can be held safely in bare hands. It becomes hazardous only if finely divided, dispersed and ingested into the lungs. Due to the extreme density of the material, critical masses of weapons-grade uranium and plutonium occupy only small volumes – about a grapefruit size for uranium and a golfball size for plutonium (Harris 2001, 82). These small volumes and low toxicities could make handling of near-critical amounts of fissile material relatively uncomplicated.

However, no final buyer – only sellers and middlemen – has yet been identified in what seems to be a fairly persistent black market for fissile material. According to the IAEA's Illicit Trafficking Database,5 about 600 illicit trafficking incidents have taken place since 1 January 1993. Of these, some 400 incidents have been confirmed by states. A little less than half of the confirmed cases (175) involve nuclear material, including 18 cases with highly enriched uranium or plutonium (Anzelon 2001). None of the quantities of seized nuclear material was in itself enough to produce a workable nuclear explosive. On the other hand, one successful transfer of high-quality nuclear material could be one too many, and the seizures produce a disturbing picture. The extent to which undetected illicit trafficking has occurred remains unknown.

Smuggling Nuclear Material to a Safe Haven

If the country of origin of the fissile material is different than the planned country of destination for the nuclear explosive device, the material may have to be transferred across several international borders. To customs and other law-enforcement officers this represents an opportunity for intercepting the material. Unfortunately, the low radiation signatures complicate such seizures, as do the need for specialized training and equipment, the number of legitimate border crossings, and – of course, limited opportunities and customs resources to control all travellers and goods.

Every day, more than 15 million cargo containers are moving around at sea or land, or await delivery. Inspectors examine only two percent of the containers, and often only after these have travelled long distances (Economist 2002). Despite comprehensive efforts and extensive international co-operation, only a fraction of the drugs smuggled is stopped, and it seems unlikely that this fraction should be any higher for fissile material. Experiences with the interdiction of drugs and other trafficking suggest that seizures represent as little as 10% – and a maximum of 40% of the gods actually being smuggled (Williams and Woessner 1995, 2).

Constructing Nuclear Explosive Device

After arriving in their safe haven or point of destination with the nuclear material, the terrorists need to assemble the various weapons components. To construct a workable nuclear explosive device any actor – a state or a sub-state group – must follow a series of technical steps (Carnegie Analysis 2001):

(1) develop a design for its nuclear device or obtain such a design from a nuclear weapon state,
(2) produce the fissile material for the core of the device or obtain it from an external source and then shape the fissile material into appropriate nuclear parts,
(3) fabricate, or obtain from outside, the non-nuclear parts of the device, including the high-explosive elements and triggering components that will detonate the nuclear core,
(4) verify the reliability of these various elements individually and as a system, and, finally, assemble all of these elements into a deliverable nuclear armament, commonly referred to as "weaponization".

None of these steps are straightforward. Constructing even a crude nuclear explosive device could thus be a daunting task for terrorists. However, a modest (terrorist) program aiming simply at producing crude nuclear weapons could probably circumvent the need for extensive domestic know-how and resources, and the rapid spread of technological knowledge may boost terrorists' weaponization attempts. The design and production of nuclear weapons today is a far simpler process than it was during the Manhattan Project (Military Critical Technologies 1999). Not only is much of the basic technical information needed to construct a workable nuclear device readily available in the open literature (see e.g. Serber 1992, Barnaby 1996). States and terrorists would have highly differing requirements to their weapons (Bremer Maerli et al. 2003, 731–732). This could make weapons designed to meet the "terrorist nuclear weapon standards" less technically challenging than traditional state nuclear weapons.

Firstly, a state would be at least as concerned with the nuclear device not going off during storage and transportation, as with optimising the yield and detonation of the weapon. While safety requirements are strong for states, such concerns could be given less consideration by terrorists, especially groups with strong affection to martyrdom. Secondly, the reliability concerns may be equivalently low amongst terrorists. While an ignition failure or a fizzle yield would be unfortunate from the viewpoint of terrorists, states must have some assurances that their weapons do function if they are supposed to do – e.g. during a nuclear exchange.

As such, reliable nuclear weapons could be a matter of survivability for a state. Again, this will raise performance requirements and complicate production. Thirdly, any explosion in the lower kiloton range represents an unprecedented terrorist yield, and even failed plutonium explosives may serve as radiological dispersion devices. States on the other hand, want fairly accurate and known yields to predict damages and the number of weapons needed. Similarly should the security of their nuclear devices be an issue for states, and probably not for terrorists.

Fourthly, nuclear weapons for military uses are normally required in fairly large numbers, and they must be delivered by conventional military means (missiles, mortars etc.). This requires large-scale industrial structures, with a (invariable) stock of competent workers. It could, moreover, require indigenous fissile material production capacities, as dependence on (potentially perfidious) external suppliers could negatively impact the future nuclear capacity of the state. To terrorist group, a single supply of high-quality fissile material may be adequate for their (limited) nuclear ambitions.

Smuggling Nuclear Explosive Device into Target Country

After a workable nuclear device has been constructed, it will have to be transferred to the location of planned detonation, a process which could also involve border crossings. Blocking such nuclear smuggling has inter alia been a major part of the US Homeland security measures to better control US borders. In the wake of rumours about Al-Qaeda's alleged progress toward obtaining a nuclear or radiological weapon in Afghanistan, hundreds of new and sophisticated radiation detection sensors were deployed to US borders, overseas facilities and points around Washington DC. The sheer size and weight of the explosive devices could render clandestine transport difficult. The ability of the sensors to detect the devices and the nuclear materials, however, may be limited. After assembly radiation signatures from the fissile material are likely better masked due to the metal casing of the explosive device – making border detection harder and handling easier.

Transporting Nuclear Explosive Device to Location

One of the most important constraining factors for state nuclear weapons is delivery. The weight capacity of delivery vehicle and the space available must be large enough to carry a military nuclear warhead. Development of reliable delivery systems and slender nuclear explosives are technically challenging and expensive, sometimes leaving nuclear bomb planes the only alternative for states. Crude terrorist nuclear weapons, however, will easily fit into a van – and perhaps even an automobile. Other non-military means of delivery could involve trucks, hot-air balloons, or ships. The terrorist means of delivery into or against a country is thus essentially infinite. Clearly, this level of relative mobility and limited size coupled with weak gamma ray radiation (discussed above) could make detection of a crude nuclear device in a busy urban environment extremely challenging (Harris 2001, 83). To avoid transportation altogether, possible perpetrators could assemble the nuclear explosive device in an out-of-the-way downtown residence (Boutwell et al. 2002). If the device is detonated by a timer and remote control, this could provide ample time for getaway.

Detonating Nuclear Explosive Device

The final step will be to detonate the nuclear device – releasing the devastating blasts, heat and radiation. Of course, the device may fail or fizzle – producing a limited yield. Once potential terrorists have the needed material, however, the actual construction of the ignition for the nuclear explosive device may be comparatively easier (Schaper 2002, 19). The ease of which this should happen depends upon the technical sophistication of the weapon, hereunder for instance the use of neutron triggers (Serber 1992, 51).

Compared to having a stolen intact nuclear warhead at hand, terrorists who construct their own crude devices would probably have an easier task detonating the device – knowing the device from scratch and avoiding (potential) difficulties associated with any permissive action links (PALs) to prevent unauthorised use etc. Uranium-based, crude gun-type devices could be an item of particular concern due to the low neutron-background. According to Luis W. Alvarez, a Nobel Laureate in Physics and a prominent nuclear weapon scientist in the Manhattan Project, gravity itself may suffice to set of a nuclear explosion with highly enriched uranium.

ASSESSING THE STEPS AND POSSIBLE COUNTERMEASURES

The number of steps terrorist have to perform on their way towards nuclear havoc offer governments opportunities to install a range of different countermeasures. Initial measures will focus on risk prevention through boosted security at facilities containing fissile material. Later countermeasures emphasises risk responses, e.g. through surveillance and detection of fissile material and/or of potential perpetrators.

Each and one of the steps towards nuclear terrorist havoc will challenge possible perpetrators. The risk of nuclear terrorism would for instance be drastically reduced if the perpetrators had a hard time smuggling the nuclear explosive into the target country (S7). The probability of successfully transferring a crude nuclear device a cross a border would depend highly on the level and sophistication of the (technical) border control and terrorists' own skills. In reality, however, efforts to detect and interdict nuclear smugglers are extremely unlikely to reduce the likelihood anywhere close to zero (Allison 1995, 69).

The detection of fissile material is anything but easy. Assuming – probably far too generously – that customs and others are indeed able to seize 60 to 70% of the nuclear gods, this could still leave one third of the illicit nuclear material outside the hands of law enforcement officials. Experiences from drug trafficking, moreover, suggests that when law enforcement is increased along one route, this tends not to result in less trafficking, but rather a re-routing along new routes that involves less risks for the perpetrators (Williams and Woessner 1995, 3). Since 1994, reported illicit trafficking incidents in Europe have declined. Simultaneously, however, since 1999 there has been a revival in such incidents in the Caucasus, Central Asia, and Turkey (Zaitseva 2002).

Similar considerations could be made for detection of a readily assembled nuclear explosive device inside a country or a city. The radiation emitted from the device is limited and possible hideouts numerous. For any hopes of a successful detection, rescuers need to be fairly close to the object. The possibility of higher neutron backgrounds due to lower enrichment levels and the relatively higher amounts needed for more fissile material in crude nuclear devices than intact nuclear warheads, could increase radiation levels, and thus ease detectability. However, for a hidden crude nuclear explosive device, the shape, material composition, and shielding is unknown – further complicating detection.

Nuclear terrorist risk assessments need, moreover, to take into consideration the differing standards between possible terrorist nuclear explosive devices and state nuclear weapons. While military nuclear weapons must meet an array of requirements before fielded, terrorists' obstacles to constructing a nuclear explosive device may be lower than anticipated. While responsive countermeasures like border-control, intelligence, sting operations, etc. clearly have a role to play in fighting nuclear terrorism, law-enforcement officers and others may thus fight in vain – and against the clock – the closer the potential nuclear terrorist perpetrators are to succeeding. A key factor that, moreover, should affect decisions about nuclear terrorism threat reduction activities is that the nature of the terrorist threat and the targets, weapons, and means of delivery will change over time, often in response to successful countermeasures

(Committee on Science and Technology for Countering Terrorism 2002, 36). Terrorists will adapt to the defences in place and seek the weakest known spots. Reducing vulnerability by protecting particular targets may therefore be neither prudent nor desirable.

Anther option would be detection of suspects and possible perpetrators. This may call for rigours countermeasures including extensive public surveillance. Such surveillance could, however, be at odds with fundamental civil liberties and should be used with care.

Conclusion From an assessment of the various steps on the nuclear terrorism pathway, it seems clear that that the most effective countermeasures are those focusing on the early steps – and in particular those that can prevent fissile material from being stolen in the first place. Highly enriched uranium and plutonium are the essential ingredients of any nuclear device. Possession of a sufficient amount of fissile material establishes a critical step and the primary impediment towards accomplishing a functioning device (Arbman et al. 2002). Denying terrorists access to these materials would thus effectively reduce the risk of nuclear terrorist havoc to zero, independent of other technical capabilities and competence (associated with subsequent steps) that the terrorists might have. As such, it represents the nuclear terrorism chokepoint and probably the most cost-effective way to avoid nuclear terrorism. Denying terrorists fissile material could thus be the be-all and end-all of efforts to prevent nuclear terrorism. Technical barriers should by itself no longer be regarded sufficient to avoid large-scale nuclear havoc.

In sum, only preventive, and not responsive, countermeasures are likely to provide the long-term and sustainable nuclear security solutions that everyone is looking for. Averting acts of nuclear terrorism are likely to be much more cost-efficient than dealing with its consequences. Therefore, the stocks of highly enriched uranium and plutonium should be duly protected – and drastically and urgently reduced.

7

Bioterrorism: Communicating an Effective Response

The DHHS bioterrorism preparedness began in earnest in FY 1999 with more than 155 cooperative grants from the CDC covering all fifty states for some component of laboratory science, surveillance, planning and preparedness, communications and information technology, and training. As we begin to examine lessons learned from the recent anthrax events, we can take stock of these preparedness measures and imagine what might have unfolded if this infrastructure had not been in place.

Tribute should be paid to the many walks of public health, particularly to many present today who worked diligently to provide emergency services during the recent anthrax releases. Within DHHS, many accolades also go to our CDC, the Public Health Service Commissioned Corps, and other agencies within the Department that provided vital services during this act of bioterrorism. I would like to comment briefly on a few of the many lessons learned that will help shape the upcoming bioterrorism program within DHHS during the upcoming year. First, the initial event in Florida and thereafter during the emergency, the issue of communications was arguably one of the most important areas in our public health response. The way in which we generate and communicate information during an emergency is incredibly important to effectively deal with the problem at hand and to reassure the public. It was clear that the media was able to gather information from a wide range of sources. For example, test results, from laboratories that may be initially operating outside of the federal response were moved into the public consciousness and the political arena at a remarkable speed. There was often little distinction made between a false positive, a presumptive positive, and a confirmed positive test result by the media. This greatly complicated the dissemination of processed information by health officials operating at the state and local level.

Clearly, in the future, our bioterrorism preparedness efforts will need to pay more attention to the infrastructure associated with health communications and information dissemination. A few common strategies for example will pay dividends in dealing with such an emergency from the public health perspective. First, having a state or local plan that provides for a single, consistent, authoritative spokesperson will be extremely important in addressing the public. Consideration for prepackaged infectious disease information, local spokespersons to disseminate a clear message, and the ability to rapidly investigate rumors will also be vital to tackling the communications issues associated with a fast developing epidemic response.

With respect to the recent anthrax emergency, it was clear when public health experts took a prominent role in the national news media and began to promote their message, it had a tremendous positive effect in helping the public understand what was being done on their behalf. For example, when state and local public health professionals began talking about the meaning of specific laboratory tests, information about exposure, or the need for medical prophylaxis the media was far more supportive of the response than when conflicting information from different and sometimes dubious sources were communicated. Consequently, it is essential that our public health infrastructure have a strong communications capacity that can be activated during an emergency. This will greatly assist the public health community in providing an informed perspective on science, public health, epidemic control measures, and other pertinent response issues.

A second issue to be learned from the recent anthrax attack is the importance of investing in laboratory infrastructure. It was very reassuring to know that the laboratory staff who confirmed the initial Florida case had been trained by CDC and were using standardized CDC reagents. Through the combined work of the Association of Public Health Laboratories (APHL), American Society of Microbiology (ASM), CDC, DoD, DOE and others, 81 such network laboratories are currently in place across the nation.

From the events associated with the recent anthrax releases, it is clear that a greater investment in linking these laboratories and in ensuring vital surge capacity will be needed in the future. In addition, the distinction between laboratories of the network and other laboratories outside of the network were often unimportant to the media and some response organizations. As a consequence, proper tracking of laboratory samples from various response sites became an important issue. It was clear that expanded laboratory sample tracking and coordination of results information will continue to be very important issues for future preparedness highlighting the importance of developing systems of electronic laboratory reporting. Another aspect of laboratory readiness that was not anticipated in the scope of the current response laboratory network was the need for a large environmental sampling component and some method for redistributing work throughout the network.

A third major lesson learned from recent events is the extreme importance of training front line healthcare providers, including nurses, doctors, clinicians, and infectious disease consultants in disease recognition. It was an alert clinician who initially identified many of these cases and then notified public health and law enforcement officials to trigger an investigation. Increasing our efforts to educate such providers will be extremely important to an ongoing bioterrorism preparedness effort.

A fourth lesson learned is that the public health infrastructure is strategically important to the national security of the United States. Before these events, during discussions that took place in FY 1999, the belief that the public health infrastructure needed to be enhanced in key areas was not widely shared within the interagency emergency response community. However, as the current emergency unfolded, the interagency community as well as the various other sectors of government began to view the public health infrastructure as being strategically important to the national security of the United States. I hope these beliefs will continue to drive an investment into our increasingly important public health infrastructure for some time to come.

Finally, recent events tested the adequacy of our stockpile and our ability to deploy it. The reality of deploying push packages and therapeutic prophylaxis into populations is very different from planning such activities in an office environment. During this response, it was apparent that stockpiling is more than simply a warehouse activity and many of our efforts to ready stocks work very well. Issues to be addressed in the future include, how much of the stockpile should be immediately ready to go, how much stock should be vendor-managed for delayed arrival, what drugs need to included, and how it should be best packaged. This reinforced our notion that stockpiling and the policy that directs its deployment will be an extremely important component of an overall national bioterrorism preparedness program. In conclusion, Winston Churchill, who was involved in the dawn of chemical warfare in WWI and who also served as prime minister of England during WWII when the radiation age appeared, would probably tell us today that our investment in selected public health infrastructure and readiness for epidemics remains one of the best ways to prepare our population for the current threat of bioterrorism.

OVERVIEW

The focus of this session of the workshop was an assessment of known threats. Anthrax is a proven risk and of immediate concern. Smallpox is equally urgent because of its capability for person-to-person transmission and the large number of completely susceptible individuals in the United States and around the world. Presenters discussed details of the bioweapons potential and treatments available for each of these threats along with those of three other "highpriority" potential bioterrorist agents: plague, tularemia, and botulinum toxin. However, these are not the only credible bioterrorist agents out there. For example, the former Soviet Union is known to have weaponized at least thirty biological agents, including several vaccine- or drug-resistant strains.

There are many imaginable bioterrorist scenarios, but if the goal is to induce mass casualties, an aerosol attack is probably most likely. Aerosols exhibit wide-area coverage, and their small particle size allows them to deposit very deeply in the lung tissue which is where many agents, including anthrax, induce maximal damage. A large amount of agent disseminated under good meteorological conditions over a substantially sized city could have considerable downwind reach, resulting in large numbers of casualties. Food-borne bioterrorism, which could encompass a variety of agents, must also be considered an equally likely threat. Agents that cause foodborne illness are easy to obtain from the environment and often have very low-dose requirements. Foodborne pathogens may in fact be the easiest bioterrorism agent to disseminate. In addition to public health risks, there are several important agricultural risks which were mentioned briefly but not discussed in detail during this workshop.

Anthrax

B. anthracis is a very stable organism because of its ability to sporulate. Most naturally occurring anthrax cases are cutaneous and are transmitted from agricultural exposure. The incidence of infection is unknown; most cases occur in underdeveloped countries. Throughout the world, since the late 1930s, attenuated strains have been used as live veterinary spore vaccines and have proven to be highly effective in controlling disease in domesticated animals.

Since the 1950s, one of these strains has been used as a live attenuated strain in humans in countries of the former Soviet Union. The molecular pathogenesis of anthrax, including the exact target of its lethal factor, is largely unknown. However, enough is known that we can begin to predict where second-generation vaccines and various antitoxin modalities might work. Currently, there are three types of preventative or therapeutic countermeasures against anthrax: vaccination, antibiotics, and various adjunctive anti-toxin treatments. In terms of developing new therapeutics, initial immediate efforts should be to evaluate already licensed antibiotics. Longer-term efforts should include identifying protective antigens that are effective against modified strains; developing vaccines that act more quickly and would be more useful in a post-exposure scenario; exploring the combined use of vaccines and antibiotics; and exploring new antitoxin treatments. Critical to all of these efforts is the need for a large-scale central animal testing facility.

Smallpox

Smallpox has several features that make it an attractive bioterrorist agent: it is highly stable; it is infectious by aerosol; it is highly contagious; most clinicians lack experience recognizing the disease; and, because vaccination against smallpox ceased after eradication, most of the world's population is highly susceptible to infection. Even though a smallpox vaccine exists, there are several unresolved bioterrorism- related issues regarding smallpox vaccination:

- It is not clear which health care providers should be immunized preceding any potential outbreak versus immediately following an outbreak.
- The current supply of vaccinia immune globulin is insufficient for treating all of the expected adverse effects associated with vaccinia immunization, should all 300 million doses of cell-cultured vaccinia that are currently being produced be administered.
- The cell-cultured vaccine that is currently being produced is considered only a stop gap measure since it cannot be used in immunocompromised individuals or children.
- It is unclear whether the available vaccine would protect against aerosol exposure of the type and magnitude that would be expected in a bioterrorist event. Although monkey/monkeypox studies have shown that yes, the vaccine does provide adequate protection, it is unclear how applicable these studies are to smallpox in humans.

Currently, most research and development efforts for smallpox therapeutics are focused on antiviral drugs. Thus far, the leading candidate is cidofovir, which has been approved under an IND for treating disseminated vaccinia but has not been approved for treating smallpox. Despite its promise, however, cidofovir is unsuitable for mass casualty use. More effort needs to be directed toward other therapeutics, such as immunomodulators.

Plague

Plague—a deadly and highly contagious disease—was weaponized in the former Soviet Union for aerosol delivery and engineered for antimicrobial resistance and possibly enhanced virulence. In the WHO modeling scenario that was developed in 1970, a 50-kilogram release over a city of five million would cause about 150,000 cases, or 36,000 deaths, in the first wave. A secondary spread would cause a further 500,000 cases, or 100,000 deaths. Plague requires intensive medical and nursing support and isolation for at least the first fortyeight hours, followed by two to three weeks of slow convalescence. The hospitalization and isolation that would be required for this many people in a single city is nearly unimaginable.

Currently in the U.S., there is no available plague vaccine. The live vaccines that are sometimes used in other countries have unacceptable adverse effects. There are, however, a number of laboratories trying to develop a new generation vaccine, as well as new delivery methods. Several different types of antibiotics that can be used to treat plague are included in the national pharmaceutical stockpile. Antibiotic treatment must be instituted early during the course of infection, otherwise death occurs in three to six days.

Tularemia

Tularemia was weaponized as an aerosol both in the U.S. and the former Soviet Union where it was also engineered for vaccine-resistance. In the WHO modeling scenario of 1970, 50 kg over a city of 5 million would incapacitate 250,000 people and cause 19,000 deaths. Tularemia is highly infectious but not contagious. Treatment is similar to that for plague but more extensive, as is the post-prophylaxis to prevent relapses of disease. The tularemia vaccine is a live attenuated vaccine that was previously available as an investigational drug through DoD and is now being investigated by the Joint Vaccine Acquisition Program. However, it does not offer full protection against inhalational transmission, and it takes about fourteen days for protection to develop. The vaccine has been recommended for use in people who work routinely with the organism in the laboratory, but it is unknown whether it would be useful in first responders at high risk for exposure.

Botulinum Toxin

Botulinum toxin has several features that make it an attractive bioweapon, including its extreme potency and lethality; the ease of its production, transport and misuse; and its profound impact on its victims as well as the health care infrastructure. Like tularemia, it has a very diverse mode of transmission: it can spread through foods, beverages or as an aerosol. Botulinum toxin, of which there are seven serotypes, kills by paralytic ability and is one of the most poisonous substances known.

Although an investigational vaccine exists, immunization is really not a viable option for bioweapons defense: the vaccine is still only investigational even after ten years; its components are aging and losing potency; it only protects against toxins A, B, C, D, and E, not serotypes F and G; it is very painful to receive; it requires a booster at one year; and the use of it would deprive the recipient for life of access to medicinal botulinum toxin.

The army has developed an equine antitoxin that provides coverage against all seven toxin serotypes, but the supply is limited and the drug carries the risk of serious allergic reaction. However, equine antitoxin is inexpensive to produce and could be made in large quantities if a specialized facility were available. A human-derived botulinum antitoxin has been developed as an orphan drug but is very difficult to produce in large quantities and is of limited use because it protects against only five serotypes.

DoD is developing a recombinant vaccine which is not expected to become a licensed product, however, for at least another ten years. Researchers are also developing recombinant human antibodies as an alternative therapeutic option. Antibodies have several distinct advantages as bioweapons defense agents: they induce immediate immunity; they can be produced in unlimited quantities; and they are highly potent. In fact, an unlimited supply of human recombinant antitoxin is probably the best defensive measure against botulinum toxin.

ANTHRAX

Anthrax has a long history: apocryphal accounts describe it as the fifth and sixth plagues in Exodus, when dust was cast into Pharaoh's eyes; it was the first disease for which a microbial etiology was determined by Robert Koch; and the anthrax vaccine was one of the first live vaccines, developed by Pasteur and one of the first examples of attenuation of a fully virulent organism for use as a vaccine. Physicians in the latter part of the 19th century, particularly in England, were well aware of the clinical and pathological aspects of anthrax. It is now incumbent upon a new generation of physicians to become intimately familiar with this disease.

There are several characteristics of *B. anthracis* that make it a potentially very lethal bioweapon, most importantly its stability and infectivity as an aerosol and its large footprint after aerosol release. An aerosol release of anthrax could potentially affect millions of individuals. The organism's stability stems from its ability to sporulate. Dormant spores are estimated to have survived in some archaeological sites for hundreds of years. The spores occur in soils worldwide and infect grazing herbivores. After they enter their mammalian host, they germinate into actively replicating vegetative cells. When the mammalian host dies and its carcass is exposed to the air, the bacteria sporulate. It is unknown whether spores go through a germinationreplication- sporulation cycle in the soil, or whether amplification of bacterial numbers occurs only within the host.

Under natural circumstances, humans become infected only via contact with infected animals or contaminated animal products. Anthrax is primarily a developing world disease associated with agricultural exposure causing cutaneous or gastrointestinal infection. However it emerged as "woolsorter's disease" in the industrial world in the latter half of the 19th century. With the rise of the industrial revolution, the large quantities of contaminated animal products being processed in enclosed rooms generated aerosols of anthrax spores which caused the first known cases of inhalational anthrax. Today, inhalational anthrax is extraordinarily rare.

The incidence of all forms of anthrax is unknown because reporting is unreliable. Large anthrax outbreaks tend to occur during breakdowns of the public health structure, for example during war. Ten thousand human cases occurred in Zimbabwe during the 1970's and early 1980's; only eight of these cases were reported to be inhalational anthrax although no autopsies were performed. *B. anthracis* is a large gram-positive, sporeforming, non-hemolytic, nonmotile bacillus. Its known virulence factors include a polyglutamic acid capsule, which is antiphagocytic and without which the organism is attenuated; and the well-known lethal and edema toxins. Like most bacterial pathogens, the virulence determinants are encoded on plasmids. The two toxins are encoded on one plasmid, and the genes responsible for synthesis of the capsule are on a smaller plasmid. It is possible, under specific laboratory conditions, to eliminate the smaller plasmid and produce an unencapsulated, attenuated strain of bacteria that still produces both toxins. Since the late 1930's and early 1940's, the Sterne strain and others similar to it have been used throughout the world as live veterinary spore vaccines that have proven to be highly effective in controlling disease in domesticated animals. Since the 1950's, a similar strain has been used as a live attenuated vaccine for humans in the former Soviet Union. It is also possible to delete the toxin plasmid, resulting in an avirulent organism that produces only capsule. Inhalational anthrax is characterized by lymphadenitis of the tracheobronchial and mediastinal lymph nodes and mediastinitis. On chest x-ray, the lungs are usually clear while there is usually mediastinal widening and often pleural effusions. The incubation period is usually a week or less. The initial symptoms are mild and non-specific and include fatigue, which can be very profound, headache, fever, chills, and sweats. There may or may not be a cough, usually non-productive. Because the disease is centered in the mediastinum, patients sometimes experience a sense of precordial discomfort. Abdominal pain has been prominent in some cases. As the infection progresses, symptoms include the abrupt onset of dyspnea, tachycardia, increased chest pain, and occasionally stridor. Pneumonia may occur but is usually absent. There is a rapid progression to cyanosis, shock, and death.

An early diagnosis is enormously important. The definitive criterion for establishing a diagnosis is isolation of the bacteria from blood, pleural or cerebral spinal fluid, or other tissue. Since there is no other gram-positive bacillus that causes sepsis in healthy individuals, the isolation of a bacillus from the blood should alert every clinical microbiology department to the diagnosis of anthrax. A chest x-ray or CT scan should also show the characteristically enlarged mediastinum. An outbreak would be characterized by large numbers of previously healthy people with these symptoms appearing in emergency rooms and physician offices.

Our knowledge of the gross pathogenesis of this disease is good but, as with many infectious diseases, we know very little about its molecular pathogenesis. The infectious spore enters the body either through a break in the skin, the GI tract, or by the respiratory route. In the skin and GI tract, the spore germinates locally. After entry through the respiratory tract, the spore is transported from the lung via macrophages to the regional lymph nodes. It spreads from node to node producing hemorrhagic necrosis and then extending into the mediastinum. From the lymph it spreads into the systemic circulation. About fifty percent of individuals with inhalational anthrax have evidence of meningitis. Impairment of respiratory function due to interference with lymphatic and vascular outflow associated with mediastinitis and pleural effusions is likely the primary mechanism of death.

The anthrax toxin, which causes edema and cell necrosis, probably contributes to death as well. Although the anthrax toxin is similar to many other bacterial and plant toxins, it is unusual in the sense that the functional domains reside on separate proteins. The individual proteins by themselves are inactive and have no biological function. Only when protective antigen combines with lethal factor does it constitute lethal toxin, and only when it binds with edema factor does it constitute edema toxin. Protective antigen binds to a cellular receptor where a cell surface protease cleaves it, releasing a small 20 kD fragment and exposing a cryptic site on the molecule; it then forms a heptamer and subsequently binds to either edema or lethal factor. This whole complex is then internalized by receptormediated endocytosis into an acidic vesicle. Under conditions of low pH, the complex inserts into the membrane and, like other toxins, the enzymatic toxin components are delivered to the cytosol. Edema factor raises cyclic AMP levels to pharmacological levels, which is clearly responsible for some of its biological effects. The exact target of lethal factor, a zinc protease, remains, to date, unknown. As follows from this model there are several potential targets for antitoxin therapeutics. The recent identification of a motor protein that controls sensitivity, or resistance to lethal toxin, will hopefully lead to additional antitoxin strategies. The current human vaccine is thought to act predominantly by inducing antibodies that block the binding of protective antigen to the cell surface receptor and block the binding of edema and lethal factor to the cell-bound protective antigen although the antibodies may also act on the organism itself. It is unclear whether anthrax pathogenesis involves a cytokine cascade. If so, the recent licensure of activated protein C for use in sepsis could have important ramifications for anti-anthrax therapy. The possible role of cytokines in anthrax warrants further evaluation. The multiple studies that have tested adjunctive treatment for sepsis should be used to guide this effort.

There are many unresolved issues with regards to prophylaxis and treatment. For example, which antibiotics should be used? Do we need adjunctive treatments? What if the *B. anthracis strain* is antibiotic- or vaccine-resistant?

About ten years ago, Russian investigators reportedly produced both multidrugresistant and vaccine-resistant *B. anthracis* strains. In terms of therapy, there are several points to be emphasized. First, it should be remembered that antibiotics affect only the bacillus, not the spore. Thus it is possible that sufficient numbers of ungerminated spores may persist in an exposed individual after completion of a course of antibiotics, only to cause disease upon subsequent germination when antibiotics are no longer present. The conditions which govern the germination of spores *in vivo* remain obscure. Secondly, the notion that inhalational anthrax is invariably fatal once symptoms occur is likely untrue as evidenced by the survival of some of the current cases. Indeed, there is experimental evidence supporting the efficacy of late-stage intensive treatment in non-human primates showing signs of bacteremia or even mediastinitis. Lastly, there are many other antibiotics that show activity *in vitro* that may extend the therapeutic options for prophylaxis and treatment. These need to be evaluated in animal models before consideration for human use. The Department of Health and Human Services, with input from the Department of Defense, is currently focusing on three therapeutic issues: testing licensed antibiotics that could be used to treat anthrax; developing human antibodies against the current vaccine, which has been administered to about 500,000 individuals; and assessing combined vaccine and antibiotic use. Other issues that need to be addressed include: identifying near-term, mid-term, and long-term research goals; identifying new protective antigens that are effective against modified strains; producing vaccines that work more quickly, particularly from the perspective of a post-exposure scenario; and, critical to all of these efforts, developing a large-scale central animal testing facility as evaluation of new treatments in humans will likely be extremely difficult.

MEDICAL COUNTERMEASURES AGAINST THE RE-EMERGENCE OF SMALLPOX VIRUS

The recent bioterrorist attacks involving anthrax have increased awareness that biological agents are truly weapons of mass destruction. Unlike anthrax, the smallpox virus is a contagious disease with fairly high rates of human to human transmission. As such, the use of smallpox as a bioterrorist agent is considered to pose an even greater threat than anthrax.Following publication of the Institute of Medicine report *Assessment of the Future Scientific Needs for Live Variola Virus* in 1999, collaborative research involving the Department of Defense (DoD) and the Department of Health and Human Services (DHHS) was initiated to address the recommendations suggested by the Report. The subject of today's presentation focuses on the recent research and our development of an animal model for Variola (smallpox) virus infection.

The desirability of animal model development is driven by the proposed Food and Drug Administration Animal Efficacy Rule, which was written to facilitate approval of countermeasures for infectious diseases, such as smallpox, which do not occur naturally in human populations. The Rule requires that pathophysiology of the animal model disease be faithful to the human disease course, and that the efficacy study endpoint must be based on reduced morbidity or mortality. Insight into the "toxemia" of human smallpox might be achieved by application of modern tools of virology and immunology to the model infection. Conventional wisdom holds that variola does not produce smallpox-like disease in any species other than humans; however, cynomolgus monkeys infected parenterally with variola strain were reported to develop non-specific, febrile disease. In studies conducted by the DoD in collaboration with the Centers for Disease Control, we tested four variola strains for virulence in monkeys exposed to high infectious doses delivered by aerosol, intravenous, or a combination of routes. Eventually, we identified a virus strain that produced a lethal disease process resembling rapidly progressive, human smallpox. Initially, two variola strains (Yamada and Lee) were used to expose monkeys to aerosolized doses of 108 plaque-forming units (PFU). Results were disappointing, since the disease courses were mild and nondescript. Subsequent studies used different variola strains (Harper & India 7124), higher doses (109 PFU), and included intravenous inoculation, which may be critical.

Three of four monkeys exposed to the Harper strain by a combination of aerosol and intravenous routes died rapidly, three to six days after exposure. Likewise, all four monkeys exposed to the India strain died, although one developed a more protracted disease course and died on day 13. Subsequent inoculation of four monkeys with 109 PFU India 7124 via the intravenous route alone yielded uniform rapid lethality. In subsequent attempts to obtain a more slowly evolving disease course, lower doses produced systemic infections and more protracted disease courses, but no deaths.

Hematologic evaluation of lethally infected primates revealed profound leukocytosis, with WBC > 50,000/mm3 (20% monocytes) in acutely ill animals. Platelet counts dropped to an average of 125,000, consistent with coagulation factor perturbations and fibrin deposition associated with evolving disseminated intravascular coagulation (DIC). Serum chemistry evaluations revealed profound increases in serum creatinine and blood urea nitrogen consistent with kidney lesions as well as elevations in AST and ALT consistent with hepatic damage. Infectious virus at concentrations > 108 PFU/g were retrieved from all visceral tissues obtained from acutely moribund or terminal monkeys at necropsy. This is consistent with the demonstration of viral antigens by immunohistochemistry in association with pathological lesions in these same tissues. Infectious viral burdens in monkey # C-713 (which died on day 13) were lower. Infectious virus was also retrieved from throat swabs of iv-inoculated animals within 48 hours of exposure, before the evolution of skin lesions or fevers. It is probably that these animals are contagious at this early stage of infection; isolation of virus from throat swabs of human smallpox-infected patients was never systematically attempted. Detection of viral genomes in the blood of inoculated monkeys as early as one day after inoculation was achieved using TaqMan PCR. This assay, which requires less than one hour to run, promises to detect infection during the asymptomatic prodrome, when countermeasures such as antiviral drugs are predicted to be most effective.

Additional insight into the pathogenesis of variola in lethally infected primates is being obtained by evaluation of high-density cDNA microarray data, which measures and classifies gene expression in peripheral blood cells obtained sequentially. RNA was prepared from isolated peripheral blood leukocytes, labeled as fluorescent cDNA for microarray analysis, and hybridized to arrays which include >10,000 uniquely named genes. Using a two-color comparative hybridization format, expression patterns were analyzed according to biological themes. Gene expression analysis identified dramatic response patterns that correlated with lethality and gave insight into pathogenesis. Several relevant biological themes included interference with interferon, IL-18, and TNF-alpha, inhibition of interleukin-1 beta and apoptosis. Activation of coagulation cascade factors, and down regulation of immunoglobulin response and cell mediated immunity-related genes were also related to lethality. Microarray evaluations will be extended to include tissue expression patterns, comparisons with other virus infections (especially monkeypox) in primates, and in vitro systems with primary target cells. Potential benefits of host genome-wide expression profiling include early detection of infected individuals, recognition of variant agents and prognostic markers, identification of virulence and disease, novel therapeutic and prophylactic strategies, and determination of early signatures of a protective immune response to vaccination.

Further refinements of this primate model are necessary before it can be exploited to test antiviral drugs or other countermeasures in accordance with the FDA Animal Efficacy Rule. Ideally, a combination of viral strain, dose, and route can be identified which produces a less accelerated disease course, one that more closely reflects the temporal course of human smallpox. The observation that certain strains of variola can produce fulminent disease in monkeys is a breakthrough in the quest for effective countermeasures for smallpox. This outcome is the exact opposite of what was predicted, since until now it was assumed that the host range of variola was restricted to humans.

Evaluation of the model disease course has yielded considerable insight into the nature of the "toxemia" associated with human smallpox. In addition, clinically relevant samples of blood and tissues have been obtained and tested, to validate modern diagnostic strategies such as TaqMan PCR. Using this technique, we have demonstrated the feasibility of obtaining a definitive diagnosis of exposure to smallpox virus during the prodrome. This capability should improve the likelihood of successful intervention using antiviral drugs. The production of these clinical samples is a significant byproduct of animal model development. The samples constitute a national resource for validation of diagnostic strategies based on detection of smallpox viral genomes and antigens now, and in the future.

Further refinement of the primate model for smallpox will include evaluation of the sub lethal, yet severe, infections associated with lower doses of inoculum virus. Objective, quantifiable correlates of disease severity may eventually be substituted for lethality in efficacy evaluations of candidate antiviral drugs and other countermeasures. As model refinement continues, concurrent advances in the identification of useful antiviral drugs are anticipated. These advancements, combined with further enhancements in diagnostic strategies, are reasonable milestones projected for this collaborative DoD/DHHS research program. Effective mitigation of an adversary's most potent biological weapon (smallpox) must be a national priority.

TULAREMIA AND PLAGUE: ASSESSING OUR UNDERSTANDING OF THE THREAT

Yersinia pestis and *Francisella tularensis* are category A critical biological agents that pose a risk to national security because they could be easily disseminated (both agents) or transmitted person-to-person (*Y. pestis*), could cause a high mortality, and require special action for public health preparedness (CDC, 2000). Both agents have been weaponized as aerosols, the expected mode of delivery in a bioterrorist attack (Inglesby et al., 2000; Dennis et al., 2001). Plague holds special concern because of its potential to cause panic, its contagiousness in the pulmonary form, its fulminating clinical course and high fatality, and the possibility that it could be engineered for plasmid-mediated resistance to multiple antimicrobial agents (Galimand et al., 1997). Sepsis with either agent can result in catastrophic physiological consequences of compliment and cytokine cascade (systemic inflammatory response syndrome [SIRS]). Severity of illness is expected to require intensive medical care, including respiratory and other organ support that might readily overwhelm hospital response capacity (Inglesby et al., 2001). Pneumonic plague's contagiousness would require isolation and possible quarantine, which would complicate medical and public health management. A WHO model of the release of 50 kg of *Y. pestis* over a city of 5 million predicts 500,000 cases with 100,000 deaths when both primary and secondary transmission are considered; a similar model for release of *F. tularensis* predicts 250,000 persons incapacitated and 19,000 deaths (WHO, 1997).

Bioterrorism Aphorisms

- Do not assume anything
- Expect the unexpected
- What we know is not much
- Bioterrorism is, among other things, unnatural
- We do not know what we do not know
- We are not ready

Standard, classical microbiological diagnostic tests would be of limited value in a major bioterrorism event, since they are time consuming and labor intensive; unfortunately, newer, rapid testing methods for these agents, such as antigen detection and DNA amplification, are neither standardized nor widely available. Recommendations for antimicrobial treatment of plague or tularemia patients in a bioterrorist attack have been developed for both the mass- and contained- casualty situations (Inglesby et al., 2000; Dennis et al., 2001). The principal recommended antimicrobials are available through the National Pharmaceutical Stockpile. Two of these, gentamicin and ciprofloxacin, are not FDA-approved for treating plague or tularemia. Post-exposure antimicrobial prophylaxis is recommended to protect certain populations in the event of bioterrorist use of either plague or tularemia agents, but it would be difficult to identify populations at risk and administer drugs to them in a timely fashion. In the case of plague, isolation of cases and their close contacts, and quarantine of exposed populations could be difficult to enforce and would likely create fear and chaos (Inglesby et al., 2001).

Historical vaccines for plague and tularemia, based on killed and live attenuated preparations respectively, are currently unavailable in the United States, and a newer generation of vaccines and immunotherapeutics is greatly needed to address pre- and post-exposure prevention of disease. Recombinant protein subunit vaccines (against F1 and V antigens singly, in combination, and as fusion products) have been developed for plague (Titball and Williamson, 2001). One subunit combination product has recently undergone Phase I clinical testing in the U.K. A microencapsulated formulation shows promise for respiratory tract delivery (Eyles et al., 1998). Further, oral administration of a *Salmonella typhimurium* mutant expressing the F1 antigen of *Y. pestis* protects mice against subcutaneous inoculation of a virulent plague strain (Titball et al., 1997). Intraperitoneal administration of monoclonal antibodies to the F1 antigen protects mice against both parenteral and aerosol challenge with human pathogenic *Y. pestis* strains (Anderson et al., 1998). Similar vaccines and recombinants have not yet been developed for use against tularemia, but recent progress in sequencing of the *F. tularensis* genome may lead to identification of candidate immunoprotective proteins (Karlsson et al., 2000).

Recent advances in *Y. pestis* and *F. tularensis* strain typing, using multiplelocus, variable-number tandem repeat analyses are expected to provide rapid tracking of outbreak strains as well as providing a foundation for deciphering global genetic relationships of these organisms that could be useful in the event of a BT attack (Johansson et al., 2000; Klevytska et al., 2001; Farlow et al., 2001). Personal experience gained by participating in CDC responses to bioterrorist use of *Bacillus anthracis* reinforces the need to think freely about potential misuse of *Y. pestis* or *F. tularensis,* to heed lessons learned, and to ensure that preparedness and response needs are met before a critical event occurs.

RESEARCH CONSIDERATIONS FOR BETTER UNDERSTANDING OF BIOLOGICAL THREATS

Because they are our best protection against infectious disease, it is necessary that we continue to develop, approve, and introduce new vaccines against many naturally occurring infectious diseases and against some biological weapons threat agents. Yet the U.S. tends to focus its discussion of bioweapons vaccines and therapeutics on only a handful of potential agents, even though the former Soviet Union is known to have developed at least thirty biological agents for use as bioweapons. Alarmingly, it takes only two to three years to develop a biological weapon but, in the best-case scenario, eight to ten years to develop a new vaccine.

It has been suggested that live vaccines are too reactogenic for general use. But, for the purpose of boosting our biodefense arsenal, perhaps this issue requires reëvaluation. In Russia, for example, all major vaccines—including anthrax, plague, and tularemia—are live vaccines. The United States had a good live plague vaccine and has a very strong live tularemia vaccine. The latter may not be approved for human use, but its protective efficiency is very high. Bioengineered vaccines are another possibility.

The use of alternate methods of vaccine administration must also be addressed. Biodefense vaccine administration techniques should not only be safe but must also provide for the vaccination of large numbers of people in a very short amount of time. Currently the U.S. focuses on injection vaccines, but there have been many studies on aerosol, inhalational, and oral vaccines. An aerosol plague vaccine, for example, can be used to immunize more than 1,200 people per hour, while a single operator can administer injection vaccines to only 20 to 30 people per hour. Inhalable plague, anthrax, and tularemia vaccines have all been extensively studied in Russia and have not shown any significant side effects.

This type of vaccine could work both systemically and locally, for example to induce mucosal immunity in the respiratory tract. However, though vaccines have proven extremely effective against infectious diseases in general, they are of limited utility in the defense against infections caused by biological weapons. Vaccination is a successful defense only when the target population is well-defined and can be identified well in advance of an attack; when the biological threat agents in the enemy's biological weapons arsenal are known; when vaccines for those agents have already been developed; and when the biological agents used are not genetically altered strains capable of circumventing a vaccine. Most military and nearly all terrorist scenarios will not meet all of these criteria. Therefore, vaccination of the general population against biological weapon agents is neither feasible nor advisable. In the context of biological weapons, the best use of vaccination is for troop protection, where both the target population and potential threat are more defined. Other, non-vaccine biodefense products need to be more seriously considered. In particular, over the past twenty years there has been extensive research on immunomodulators and their role in protecting against viral and bacterial pathogens. Although several such products have been developed that could potentially resolve many of our biodefense issues, none of them have been introduced yet into the field of biological weapons defense. In a biological attack, the target population would likely be large and poorly defined, the scale or even the fact of the attack may not be immediately apparent, and the biological agent used in the attack may not be immediately identified. For either military or terrorist use of biological weapons, creation of an aerosol cloud—usually accomplished by explosion or spraying—is by far the most effective mode for deploying biological weapons. This method can be used against large target areas and with practically any biological threat agent. Therefore, effective medical defense against biological weapons must incorporate protection against aerosol deployment. The nature of a biological weapons attack also dictates that the most successful medical defenses will be prophylactic, rapid-acting, long-lasting, effective against a broad spectrum of threat agents, and relatively easy to deliver to a large population.

Finally, we need to re-examine our knowledge about the pathogenesis of bacterial and viral infections. For example, we still refer to the three major virulence factors in any discussion of anthrax. However, many other virulence factors may exist. My laboratory has conducted hundreds of experiments on anthrax lethal toxin, and thus far we have found no evidence whatsoever that it is capable of inducing normal healthy donor immune cells to produce any cytokines involved in the development of septic shock. Human endothelial cells are, however, relatively susceptible to the effect and the action of lethal toxin. It is becoming apparent that current theories on the role of anthrax toxin must be reexamined and revised. Our experiments have indicated that other overlooked anthrax virulence factors exist, including cell wall components and (possibly) hemolysins. Our work has indicated that the only factor of the anthrax bacterium capable of consistently inducing the mediators of septic shock seen in late-stage anthrax infection is a component of the cell wall skeleton, not lethal toxin, and that there exist many other overlooked exogenous and endogenous mediators which contribute in the development of anthrax sepsis and septic shock. Although these are preliminary data with which we are not able to make any final conclusions, they do highlight the need to re-examine the pathogenesis of anthrax. They may also explain why people die when antibiotics are administered in the late stages of infection: these cell wall skeleton components are very powerful inducers of septic shock mediators, and their concentration remains very high in the bloodstream after bacterial death. The preliminary work we have conducted to this point has led us to the belief that the most successful strategy for anthrax treatment would be dependant on the stage of infection (postexposure, lymphatic, systemic, or late-stage). It is our recommendation that a task force be established to more carefully analyze the events that occur during anthrax infection. It is very important that we re-evaluate our knowledge of pathogenesis and identify what we have missed in the field of protection and treatment of infectious diseases caused by biological weapons.

AEROSOL TECHNOLOGY AND BIOLOGICAL WEAPONS

The threat of international terrorism to this country and others has never been as serious as it is today. The U.S. abandoned its program for offensive biological warfare in 1968, but the successful effort to weaponized infectious organisms and toxins should have educated the U.S. government to their dangers. The revelations that the Soviet state had a more extensive and similarly successful undertaking (Alibek, 1999) only increases the likelihood that the development of weapons of mass destruction lies within the reach of others. The extensive programs used by these two states are often cited as hurdles too high for other countries to surmount, but it must be remembered that they worked with multiple agents and manufactured literally tons of product in a time before many of today's advances in biology and fermentation technology. The Gulf war brought the potential of other states to produce biological weapons home, but the weapons were not used in spite of the argument that they are intensely destabilizing (Haselkorn, 1999). The spate of anthrax laced letters in 2001 has led to a re-awakening of concern.

Numerous commissions have reviewed the threat of bioterrorism (Countering the Changing …, 2000; Second Annual

Report, 2000) in recent years and uniformly concluded that the US was vulnerable and that the likelihood of such an event was high. Nations suspected of having offensive biological warfare programs have been named by the Office of Technology Assessment (1993) and these same states are often also identified as terrorist sponsors. In light of these agreed-upon threats, why has there been so little concern about this possibility in many quarters and why has so much surprise been expressed over the outcome of a handful of letters containing anthrax spores dispatched through the mail? One important component is the lack of familiarity with the concepts which were the pillar of the old US biowarfare program and also the Soviet program, particularly as refers to the danger of aerosols. Another reason may be that no one expected that the manufacturer of such a deadly powder as was placed in Congressional letters in autumn of 2001 would employ an envelope as a delivery route rather than using a more stealthy and lethal dissemination system. This complacency was reinforced by the large number of "anthrax" powder hoaxes that have occurred over the last few years, a social phenomenon worthy of study in itself. This short essay attempts to outline why we should be concerned about use of biological weapons in terrorism, why some scenarios are more dangerous than others, and some general observations concerning what we could do to combat bioterrorism.

Nature of the Threat

When one considers the ways in which BT might be carried out, the first rule should be that we do not know who the possible terrorist will be, his or her motivation, or the wherewithal that may be available for the attack. Thus, attacks to incapacitate selected persons to gain attention, or to cause serious illness for revenge might have a very different approach than attacks designed to cause mass casualties. An effort by a disgruntled clinical laboratory worker could have a very different scope than one by a well-funded non-state organization or a state-sponsored group. Parenthetically, the failure of the Japanese Aum Shinriko cult to succeed with biological terrorism should not provide much comfort concerning the need for state sponsorship given the manifest ineptitude of the perpetrators (Smithson, 2001).

The second issue is the dissemination of factual information concerning the real dangers of such an attack. Some would argue that the less said the better. Unfortunately for this approach, US society does not respond without facts and public opinion supporting programs. This means that the actual dangers must be explained to the public and responsible political leaders without inflammatory rhetoric or divulging detailed methods for the assaults, and we must take the chance that plain-speaking might motivate some to undertake the very actions we are trying to prevent. Furthermore, discussion of the facts may help the public, media, and health authorities respond in a calmer and more rational fashion than was observed with the aerosol anthrax attacks of 2001.

If we consider the methods by which microbes might be delivered to a target population there are multiple routes. Direct inoculation, infection of natural vectors or reservoirs and loosing them on the target population, or infection of a few persons and counting on their spreading the infection even further are some possibilities. If we focus on terrorist strategies that can inflict mass casualties none of these possibilities is highly feasible today with the exception of the use of smallpox, a virus that is well-known to spread from human to human after a long and successful career in that evolutionary niche. If we conclude that other organisms must be delivered directly to the target host, we should also consider water, food, and aerosols as potential vehicles of infection. Contaminated water from wells and storage containers has been associated with outbreaks of disease, but the odds are against this approach for causing mass casualties because of the dilution factor, chlorination, and the usual treatment of water before consumption in this country. Food-borne pathogens have caused many outbreaks in the US and are a major cause of morbidity and mortality. Even though our distribution system is highly centralized, food items are usually not consumed synchronously except at special events. Improved surveillance of food-borne disease and newer methods of molecular typing of offending organisms should provide a counterweight to the wide dissemination of contaminated food. If a few cases are recognized and traced to a food source, warnings and recalls may well serve to protect us.

The over-all societal impact of any one of these dissemination methods could be considerable, regardless of the actual health damage. We have case studies already, including non-lethal *Salmonella* infection of a few hundred citizens (Torok et al., 1999), Sarin gas attacks with only 20 deaths (Smithson, 2001), food tampering, and most recently anthrax delivered by letter or even anthrax hoaxes. Aerosols, however, are an important route of attack because of their ability to cause really large numbers of casualties. The deficiencies of aerosols such as dependence on metrological conditions, the unsuitability of most organisms for air-borne spread, and the technical demands may be counterbalanced in the hands of skillful perpetrators by the advantages of stand-off attack, silent spread of incapacitating or lethal disease, and wide-area coverage.

Aerosol Infections

Aerosol infection has long been recognized as a route of microbial transmission. Measles, influenza, smallpox, and tuberculosis are all known to be transmissible between patients by aerosols and additionally in the laboratory tularemia, rickettsiae, viral hemorrhagic fevers, and many other agents are threats to the microbiologist (DHHS, 1999). Decreases in human tuberculosis and virtual elimination of diseases such as measles and smallpox from common medical experience as well as development of enhanced methods of protecting laboratory workers (ironically using technology developed during the US biowarfare program) have resulted in a loss of appreciation for this route of infection, but the US and Soviet BW programs were largely based on the properties of selected agents for causing large scale infection of human populations under the proper metrological conditions and with carefully developed methods of dissemination. Moreover, the terrorist could attack enclosed environments such as stadiums or large buildings in order to eliminate the meteorological factors that degrade a small particle aerosol.

Biological agents have not seen widespread use in warfare so it is not surprising that there is skepticism as to their efficacy. It is not appreciated that the US program in offensive biological warfare (terminated on November 28, 1969) rigorously tested each step in the link between a microorganism selected by several criteria and the delivery of a credible biological attack. Tularemia would be an excellent example because extensive information is available in the published literature, congressional hearings, and popular press. From the initial isolation of the organism by Francis and coworkers, it was notorious for causing infections in the laboratory, a frequent hallmark of aerosol infectivity. The aerosol properties were intensively studied and methods were found to enhance its stability in storage and in aerosols. Animals and later humans were challenged with graded doses of the bacterium delivered in different particle sizes to establish the quantitative properties of these aerosols. Open air dissemination was mimicked using a surrogate organism, *Serratia marscens*, and this confirmed that an organism with the aerosol stability and infectivity of *Francisella tularensis* could cause mass casualties over large geographic areas provided attention was given to metrological conditions. The areas affected could reach thousands of square kilometers. The resulting environmental transmission from the large number of different nonhuman mammalian and arthropod species that would be infected in a tularemia attack cannot be evaluated. Thus, there is little doubt that large numbers of human casualties could be caused by efficiently weaponized organisms readily available from nature.

A relatively small number of agents are suitable for causing literally thousands or hundreds of thousands of casualties, and this may provide a basis for prioritization of medical and other measures to deny the intent of terrorists. Biological toxins, even the highly potent botulinum toxin, and chemical agents are absent because of their relatively low potential to cause casualties whether evaluated on the basis of purified agent or the basis of the likely highest concentration practically achievable. It is impossible to list every possible agent and there are always discussions among experts as to whether some should be added or omitted. Toxins are inherently of lesser efficiency because they cannot match the killing or incapacitating power of the highly infectious organisms; the toxins have to produce their effects as delivered, but the infectious agents grow and produce toxins or other effects in the recipient's body. According to a WHO scenario several infectious agents would be expected to produce 35,000 to >100,000 casualties if 50 kg were delivered in a line source and carried down-wind over a populated area. In the case of some of the more stable agents, down-wind reach would exceed 20 km. The Office of Technology Assessment (1993) has published similar figures. It must be borne in mind that the US and Soviet programs prepared literally metric tons, not kilograms, of agent and that appropriate devices for delivering line sources or multiple overlapping point sources were available (Alibek, 2001; Sidell et al., 1997). Impact on the infected members of the population would depend on the agent used and the nature of the response (for example, alacrity of recognition of initial patients, public health and medical infrastructure, vaccine and antibiotic stockpiles). The additional impact that might be possible through modification of naturally occurring organisms by methods well within the reach of simple biotechnology including induction of antimicrobial resistance, enhancement of virulence by addition of toxin genes, or selection of more stable or virulent organisms is formidable. Issues surrounding the more extensive engineering of threat agents are beyond the scope of this discussion, however, it is important to note that the potential exists, but that there would probably be a need for human testing of any resulting candidate.

Properties of Small Particle Aerosols

The basic properties of aerosols must be understood to appreciate the way in which such weapons could be used. The optimum aerosol particle size is thought to be 1–5 microns. This size provides two critical properties: the particles do not settle out over a several hour time period but rather are truly airborne and are carried on wind currents or through heating, ventilation, and air conditioning systems (HVAC) and they are of an optimum size to reach the terminal respiratory bronchiole or alveolus of humans and deposit in those critical areas to set up infection. Generation of small particle aerosols requires energy as evidenced by classical examples such as laryngeal tuberculosis, the wide dissemination of rubella by a disco singer (Marks et al., 1981), or the persistent cough of the index case of a nosocomial Lassa fever outbreak (Carey et al., 1972). Such particle sizes can be achieved intentionally by generating a liquid aerosol with a spray device or by using an appropriately manufactured powder. The dissemination system for a liquid must have the correct relationship between viscosity and solids content of the liquid, air pressure, orifice diameter, and other variables to attain the critical particle size, as well as have the proper stabilizers in the solution to assure that infectivity is not lost. The dry powders are difficult to manufacture, but they are extremely dangerous because they can be prepared so as to aerosolize with minimal energy input and can be manufactured in very fine particle sizes. If the skills to prepare these particles are available, it may also be possible to formulate encapsulated weapons of greater biological stability.

It is obvious that the preparation and testing of such weapons requires microbiological skills to attain the high concentrations of organisms needed. Equally as important is the expertise for dissemination of liquid or powder aerosols in a stable form in the correct particle size. Such capabilities may be available from many people in different walks of life. Nonetheless, assembling the needed skill sets implies an organization with some resources, particularly as one moves into the powders and into greater quantities of agent. Practice or trials would be important to assure success, although, as the saying goes, "the proof of the pudding ...". Persons with previous experience in offensive biowarfare programs could be extremely valuable resources to such an endeavor.

When these aerosol clouds are generated, there is a period of instability and larger particles or agglomerates fall out near the dissemination device with considerable surface contamination possible. Once the small particle aerosols are formed, they will move with wind currents and traverse the landscape, being gradually diluted by mixing and decay. Because of their dependence on wind currents, aerosols may be diverted from their planned target; warming of the earth's surface after sunrise will result in their being carried to higher levels of the atmosphere unless inversion conditions are present. Loss of infectivity by biological decay will also occur, depending on stabilizers in the suspension medium, ultraviolet intensity, humidity, and temperature. They will enter buildings through HVAC systems, but the urban landscape profile may result in extensive disturbances of air flow. The ultraviolet light sensitivity of most of the organisms, combined with the meteorological needs, will favor the use of an evening, night time, or early morning, attack if done outdoors. Terrorist attacks may also be directed toward buildings or enclosed stadiums, making the air conditioning systems the obvious route of the delivery of the aerosol.

The extreme "fluffiness" or ease of aerosolization of the most dangerous powders is difficult to imagine. The material in the Hart Senate office building seems to offer an excellent example: all present in the room when the offending letter was simply opened had spores in their noses when tested 4 hours later; anthrax spores traveled to adjacent rooms through the HVAC; extensive surface contamination was present. Subsequent examination of the powder showed it to have a very high concentration of anthrax spores (reportedly 1012/g), finely dispersed particles, and it was readily aerosolized with the slightest disturbance. Undoubtedly, without antibiotic prophylaxis most of those in the room would have suffered inhalation anthrax. Had this material been introduced clandestinely into the air conditioning intake, there would have been no warning until the first cases were recognized, perhaps too late for therapy. The magnitude of the exposure can be seen from studies done by the Canadian Defense Forces (Kournikakis et al., 2001) in a simulation using only 1/10th the number of spores and 1/20th the estimated quantity of a readily aerosolized powder containing *Bacillus globigius* as a surrogate for *Bacillus anthracis*. In less than one minute, spores spread throughout the room in similar concentrations as observed at the site of the envelope opening. Testing of the filter from the respirator worn by the subject opening the letter yielded 80,000 infectious units, equivalent to an estimated 15-320 human LD50 for anthrax spores.

These principles governing airborne particles in the 1–5 micron range are essential in our response to the possibility of an aerosol attack. First of all, buildings with their HVAC may provide little protection against small-particle aerosols if currents of air bring a widely disseminated agent into the zone of their air intake. Indeed, the HVAC systems may provide a particular vulnerability to bioterrorism. Secondly, environmental sampling of surfaces or clothing in areas exposed to such aerosols or nasal swabs of potentially exposed persons will not predict if a person was infected with any certainty; finding agent in these situations demonstrates that an attack has taken place. Thirdly, surgical masks and similar defenses are not effective against such small particles and only give a false sense of protection; highly efficient masks that can protect against small particles (e.g., N100 masks designed for medical staff working with tuberculosis patients) and which are properly fitted on trained personnel are needed (Lowe et al., 1999). Obviously, protective gear must be worn during the risk period, but these small-particle aerosols are odorless and invisible to the eye so the general utility of personal protective gear is limited.

Secondary Aerosols

The issue of secondary aerosols is an important one. Infectious agents on solid surfaces such as soil, counter tops, machinery are thought not to be subject to aerosolization unless considerable energy is applied. Studies of *Bacillus* spores have shown aerosols intentionally deposited on the ground are very difficult to re-suspend with ordinary traffic or even intentional beating of the surface (Patrick, 2001). Soil subjected to high air flow yields few particles in the dangerous 1–5 micron range (Chinn et al., 1990). These field evaluations show that even when the contamination of a surface reaches 107/meter2 the concentration above the surface, even with considerable disturbance, will be extremely low. Thus, in a field biowarfare situation there is little danger from secondary aerosolization. There is little experience with transfer of infectious powders from one solid surface to another or with the deposit of larger clumps of highly aerosolizable particles on hard solid surfaces. Surrogate infectious agents, fluorescent tracers or radioactive particles predict that highly concentrated biological agents (titers >109/g and perhaps as much as 1012/g) will extensively contaminate surfaces they impact and, if viable, pose a contact risk. Large quantities of organisms from dangerous powders can result in short-term presence of organisms in the external nares of exposed persons and the fall-out of larger particles can lead to environmental contamination near the site of dissemination.

The possibility of secondary aerosols in this situation is thought to be small, but application of high energy sources or the presence of physical clumps of particles could be problematic. The risk of aerosol infection to an exposed human would depend on the amount of material aerosolized and the infectious dose for humans.

The actual amount of tularemia or Q fever required to infect 50% of exposed humans is known and is on the order of 1–10 organisms. For other organisms such as anthrax it is necessary to extrapolate from cynomolgus monkeys or other experimental animals.

In this case the lethal dose for 50% of animals is 8,000 spores by aerosol. The LD50 is determined by exposing animals to graded doses of the infectious agent and calculating the linear relationship between the logarithm of the dose increment and the increase in response of the target animals (Finney, 1964).

This is usually done between 20–80% lethality and the LD50 calculated. In fact the linearity can probably be extrapolated further to furnish at least an approximation of the risk from lower doses; in the case of anthrax, published values for the slope (Glassman et al., 1965; Chinn et al., 1990) suggest that inhaling a dozen spores could be risky in a small percentage of the population. These concepts are important to the practical management of situations in which a suspicious powder is involved. The physical properties of a readily aerosolized powder will be recognized by an experienced observer or by laboratory analysis. An ordinary dried culture of, for example, anthrax will not pose a great hazard beyond the readily recognized and treated cutaneous anthrax. Decontamination of a building needs to address the dangerous states of the contaminating organism. Safety is the goal, not "sterility". In the case of anthrax spores, significant quantities of aerosolizable particles is the criterion. Sterility is less important than being certain that any residual infectivity is earth bound.

Relative Importance of Different Agents

Consideration of the different bioterrorism agents and some of their properties is the first step to prioritize defenses against them. Each has different properties as we see them today and thus each presents different threats and different opportunities for control. This discussion has been cast in terms of the worst case scenarios (effective broad-scale aerosol dissemination) but we must recognize that, although protection against this situation is important, the most likely eventuality is a less extensive or less successful attack. Fortunately, attention to the worst case is a step toward the more general solution, although the lesser eventuality should also be in the mind of planners. It is also important to note that biodefense efforts meld with the general struggle against infectious diseases. For example, strengthening the public health system will provide benefits regardless of whether a bioterrorist attack occurs. Money spent on communications within the public health system is long overdue. Planning will help in disaster response, regardless of the nature of the event. Perhaps much of the money spent on increasing smallpox vaccine stocks will eventually be "sunk costs" but we should not regard research and vaccine development on other agents as anything other than an benefit for human-kind. Smallpox provides a threat whose consequences are simply unacceptable, regardless of the probability of its use. Therefore we must develop clinician awareness, diagnostic systems, and stockpiles of existing vaccine that give us a validated countermeasure to deploy in case of attack. Whether additional antiviral drug and vaccine development is justified is a matter of prioritization against other threats.

Anthrax also is a special case. It is widely distributed in nature and thus readily available to terrorists in virulent form. The spores are extraordinarily stable on storage and in aerosols obviating many of the terrorist's research needs to develop an effective weapon. Inhalation anthrax is a fearsome disease if not treated early with effective antibiotics, and production of antibiotic-resistant anthrax is readily achieved. Plague and tularemia are both severe diseases but they require another level of sophistication in weaponization. Their cultivation in virulent form and their dissemination in stable aerosols is more difficult than for anthrax. The viral hemorrhagic fevers are essentially without therapy, have severe psychological impact, and carry a high mortality. Their production is still more difficult, but the technology is readily accessible to an experienced microbiologist (Peters, 2000). When considering the impact of limited or massive dissemination of the agents in tables 2-4 and 2-5, one must factor in the disruption of the health care system, the role of antibiotic resistance, the fear-factor in the population and medical staff, as well as the state of defensive preparations. One element that is often neglected is the influence of a communicable disease on travel and commerce. Any of these diseases could lead to severe disruptions in the free travel of U.S. citizens and others within the US and in international air transport systems. If the agent is also an agricultural pathogen, then internal movement of animals would be frozen and exports would be stopped, resulting in even more severe economic consequences.

Strategies to Confront the Problem

Any attempt to deal with BT should consider the entire spectrum of responses, including state and local organization supported by a comprehensive federal plan. The public health system will be the back-bone, but there will have to be participation of the entire society. Recognition by the clinician, laboratory diagnosis, and mobilization of countermeasures will all play a part. As noted above, the strategy should be tailored to each agent or group of agents. It must be emphasized that environmental detection and patient diagnosis of the specific agent employed are keystones of an improved response to the threat. Detection suffers from the need to be active at the time and site of an attack, so economics will probably limit its future usefulness to selected high risk venues.

Diagnostics are, in principle, more focused and also require the suspicions of informed clinicians; widely deployed they are a very significant expense. An additional demand on detection and diagnostics is the recognition of subversion of our defenses by inducing resistance to anti-infectives or other protective modalities. Vaccine approaches are suitable for selected at-risk groups, particularly for specific high-priority BT agents. However, specific vaccines are not general remedies for the threat to the civilian population.

The expense and difficulty of administration and the inevitable side effects will limit their widespread use. They remain important elements of our response in selected populations and specific circumstances.

Anti-infective drugs could be a very effective response if problems of drug development, drug-resistance, safety and efficacy testing, stockpiling, and distribution can be solved.

Other supportive measures directed to bacterial toxins or the over-exuberant inflammatory responses induced by some viruses could be useful, as well. Further definition of the Toll-like receptor family could open the way to broadly protective remedies that could be used in the event of BT attacks.

Some agents pose sufficient problems to demand immediate and thorough attention. Smallpox, because of its track record of interhuman transmissibility and high case fatality, is clearly a first-echelon target.

Anthrax, because of its ease of weaponization, deserves attention to the development of more effective therapy beyond antibiotics. Antitoxic strategies at the level of the toxin molecules as well as their down-stream effects should be developed in a very short time frame.

Furthermore, the terrorist use of antibiotic-resistant strains should be anticipated. Plague and tularemia might seem to be resolved in principle because of the existence of effective antibiotics, but their relatively short incubation periods place high demands on availability of effective antimicrobials and the facility with which antibiotic resistance can be induced has important implications for defensive strategies.

This is complicated because the log-normal distribution of incubation periods is "front-loaded" (Sartwell, 1950) and because late treatment can fail even though the bacteria are eradicated. The viral hemorrhagic fever agents would induce widespread fear and even panic among the both general population and health-care providers. The arenavirus drug ribavirin should be stockpiled in modest amounts in the mean while, but more general strategies against the arenaviruses and other viral threat pathogens should be pursued.

Of course intelligence information and any dissuasion afforded by international agreements would be most welcome. We clearly cannot depend on these modalities to protect us completely. Many of the agents are widely available and so measures designed to limit their access are illusory in their effectiveness; anthrax is a case in point.

However, limiting access to certain agents such as Ebola, Marburg, and smallpox viruses should be pursued. The equipment needed to produce limited amounts of biological agents is readily available and we cannot control or monitor access, but perhaps we can develop measures to track high output equipment and the movement of particularly sensitive expertise and genetic material.

A strong research program and the industrial base to develop promising research leads into practical human countermeasures will be the best defense. One of the impediments, in addition to the perennial need for funding, is the lack of suitable containment laboratories.

Furthermore, the diminution of expertise and suitable laboratories to study infectious aerosols is alarming. Another variable in play is the concern for limiting dissemination of research results; we have to be very careful not to suffocate our defensive effort with excessive secrecy unless the controls can be shown to add to our safety.

ENSURING THE AVAILABILITY OF COUNTERMEASURES FOR BIOTERRORISM

Recent events have brought the subject of vaccines as a defense against bioterrorism into very sharp focus. We have been forced to take action in an area that, for the civilian sector, had previously been largely an academic debate and planning exercise with inadequate definitive action. We have changed from a nation of skeptics concerning the threat of bioterrorism to a nation of believers. Several government agencies are working at unprecedented speed to acquire the needed vaccines and put the correct policies into place for utilization.

However, the use of vaccines for defense against bioterrorism presents multiple challenges that are quite different from the traditional public health use of vaccines for protection against endemic or epidemic diseases.

The issues are also quite different from those faced by the armed forces. The appropriate use of vaccines as a defense against bioterrorism presents major challenges in public policy development as well as public education. The ongoing public debates in the media highlight the complexity of the issues and reveal the widespread lack of understanding of the limitations of the current vaccines, especially vaccinia vaccine. For example, there is a call for widespread vaccination against smallpox but, in contrast, there is much misinformation and inappropriate fear about the effects of anthrax vaccine.

Some of the challenges involved with developing vaccine policies for defense against bioterrorism lie in the uncertainty of the threats.

In contrast, policies for the use of vaccines against naturally-occurring disease threats are based on a wealth of historical and current epidemiologic information about disease burden and potential.

Additionally, there is extensive data available on the safety of widely used vaccines that can be used to confidently assess risk benefit and cost effectiveness. In the case of agents of bioterrorism, however, risk assessment is much more difficult. The great difficulty in obtaining timely and reliable intelligence on the threat of biologic terrorism is a major part of the problem. Critical policy decisions—such as which vaccines will be needed, how large the stockpiles should be, and how the vaccine should be used—are greatly influenced by perceptions of threat. The very nature of terrorism produces a high level of uncertainty about what to expect and prepare for, and there is a wide and varying spectrum of perceived threats.

Obtaining the vaccines that are needed to protect our military and civilian populations depends entirely on effective government action. The potential market has been too small, at least up to the present time, to encourage the vaccine industry to make the large investments needed in research, development and manufacturing facilities.

This has changed dramatically in the past two months. Nevertheless, the current situation is a result of past misjudgments, which resulted in insufficient government investment in vaccine research and development, and manufacturing capacity.

There is an urgent need for rapid progress in R&D, manufacturing, and licensing processes, all of which are painfully slow processes when done by the usual methodologies. Vaccines have varying usefulness in defense against bioterrorism.

At the top of the list is the need for smallpox vaccine to prevent an outbreak from becoming a catastrophic global pandemic. Both smallpox and anthrax vaccines would be very useful in the medical management of exposed individuals, if the vaccines were readily available and placed in geographic proximity to multiple centers for distribution.

Less important to the civilian populations are vaccines against bacterial agents that can be managed with antibiotics and viral agents which, at least for the present, seem to be lesser threats. These include plague, tularemia, hemorrhagic fever viruses, alphavirus encephalidities, Rift Valley fever, and others. However, several of these vaccines should be available for both civilian and military use. A government-owned production facility may be the best means for meeting the needs of these lower priority vaccines which will probably, at least initially, be made in much smaller quantities than smallpox and anthrax vaccines.

Smallpox Vaccine

The acquisition of a smallpox vaccine stockpile for civilian use started in 1999, with an Acambis contract for 40 million doses which now has been increased to 54 million doses. The seed virus was developed by cloning a New York City Board of Health strain derived from Wyeth Dry Vax. Animal model studies indicate that this strain appears to be somewhat less neurovirulent than the parent virus. The clinical development plan is aggressive; the phase I clinical trial should occur, as planned, in the latter part of January 2002. A very rapid procurement action has been in progress over the past weeks. The goal is to stockpile enough smallpox vaccine to protect the entire nation within the year. The response from the vaccine industry has been very heartening and has provided excellent options for utilizing existing manufacturing capacity to meet current requirements. Every effort will be made by CDC, FDA and NIH to assure that these contractors succeed to meet goals, time lines, and regulatory requirements. This will require truly unprecedented coordination and responsiveness by both the manufacturers and the various agencies.

Although the first step in building the smallpox vaccine stockpile is to ensure that vaccine manufacturing is underway, there are several other immediate issues that need to be addressed:

- Vaccination policy issues continue to be controversial. The CDC recently sent out a draft smallpox response plan to the states for comment. The plan calls for primary reliance on ring vaccination—the traditional method—to control an outbreak. The CDC has vaccinated 140 staff members who are most likely to be involved in investigating an outbreak, but no further vaccination with potential responders or health care providers is planned at this time. Laboratory personnel working with pox viruses will, of course, continue to be vaccinated.
- There is a need for more vaccine immune globulin (VIG) or VIG substitute to deal with the consequences of vaccination in immunosuppressed or other high risk subsets of the population. An interagency working group is currently exploring options for expanding the VIG supply.
- There is a need to develop a safer vaccine for use in immunosuppressed individuals, pregnant women, and other individuals for which the current vaccine is contraindicated. This will not only be a challenging research and development problem but also a challenging regulatory problem due to the difficulties in proving efficacy.

Anthrax Vaccine

The current licensed U.S. anthrax vaccine is a filtrate of culture media that contains a high level of PA (protective antigen) absorbed to alum; it probably contains small amounts of the other factors as well. An ongoing study at CDC is testing immunization schedules that involve fewer than the currently recommended six doses for this vaccine. Conventional wisdom has it that the live attenuated vaccines used in Russia and China are too reactogenic to be licensed in the United States. Israeli scientists have published reports on animal studies of experimental vaccines engineered to over-express recombinant protective antigen, but no clinical data are available. The problems that the manufacturer has had with meeting regulatory criteria have limited the U.S. supply. A small amount of anthrax vaccine has been made available to DHHS by DoD, but that amount is far below what will be needed. There is an urgent need for a sufficient supply of anthrax vaccine for vaccinating high risk populations and for use as post-exposure vaccination in conjunction with antibiotics.

There are several immediate issues that need to be addressed. The production method for current licensed vaccine must be scaled up. Several commercial firms have made informal proposals to do this. However, this is a high risk option because of the inherent variability of the manufacturing process and the high risk of failure when scaling up so rapidly to such a high volume. There needs to be more serious consideration of the applications of the various platform technologies—such as plasmid DNA, viral vectors, and a variety of other delivery technologies—that are being developed within the biotech industry. Finally, we need to accelerate development of a second generation vaccine. The time to availability could be shortened by overlapping large scale production with clinical trials. It has been suggested that we might have a stockpile of IND recombinant protective antigen (PA) vaccine within 18 months. This may be an achievable goal if all involved interests work in an effective, coordinated manner. A recombinant PA vaccine produced in *E. coli* will likely be the first to enter a phase I trial.

In order to address this issue of a second generation vaccine, the National Institute of Allergy and Infectious Diseases has put together a team with contractor help. Efforts are underway to gather all available information on ongoing or planned development efforts for a second generation anthrax vaccine, and compile the information in a systematic fashion and convene several advisors to review the resulting data, findings, and policy options. This may involve a major research and development contract program similar to what exists for smallpox vaccine and which will hopefully build on the work that has been done by DoD and DoD-DHHS collaboration. It will hopefully involve some new players as well, including the large vaccine manufacturers. Although it is difficult to predict which particular options will receive aggressive support, there is nonetheless a system now in place that will hopefully pave the way for pursuing an effective strategy in a reasonable period of time. The speed at which a second generation anthrax vaccine is developed will depend on both the underlying science and the responsiveness of the vaccine industry to national needs.

8

Terrorism and Chemical Warfare

RISK OF EXPOSURE

Injury from chemical weapon agents, known as CWAs, may result from industrial accidents, military stockpiling, war, or a terrorist attack. Industrial accidents are a significant potential source of exposure to chemical agents. Chemicals such as phosgene, cyanide, anhydrous ammonia, and chlorine are used widely. These chemicals are frequently transported by industry. The accidental release of a methylisocyanate cloud (composed of phosgene and isocyanate) was implicated in the Bhopal, India, disaster in 1984.

Chemical weapons first were used in 1915, when the German military released 168 tons of chlorine gas at Ypres, Belgium, killing an estimated 5,000 Allied troops.

Two years later, the same battlefields saw the first deployment of sulfur mustard. Sulfur mustard was the major cause of chemical casualties in World War I.

CWAs have been used in at least 12 conflicts since, including the first Persian Gulf War (Iraq-Iran War). The Iraqi military also used chemical weapons against the Iraqi Kurds during the second Persian Gulf War.

Civilians also have been exposed inadvertently to chemical weapons many years after weapon deployment during war. Some 50,000 tons of mustard shells were disposed of in the Baltic Sea following World War I. Since then, numerous fishermen have been burned accidentally while hauling leaking shells aboard boats. Leaking mustard shells also have injured collectors of military memorabilia and children playing on old battlefields.

Although a number of international treaties have banned the development, production, and stockpiling of chemical weapons, these agents reportedly are still being produced or stockpiled in several countries.

Within the last decade, terrorists deployed chemical weapons against civilian populations for the first time in history. The release of sarin in Matsumoto, Japan, in June 1994 by the extremist Aum Shinrikyo cult left 7 dead and 280 injured.

The following year, the Aum Shinrikyo cult released sarin vapor in the Tokyo subway system during morning rush hour, leaving 12 dead and sending more than 5,000 casualties to local hospitals. Several characteristics of chemical weapon agents lend themselves to terrorist use.

Chemicals used in CWAs are widely available, and recipes for CWA production may be found on the Internet. CWAs are transported easily and may be delivered by a variety of routes. Chemical agents often are difficult to protect against and quickly incapacitate the intended targets. Most civilian medical communities are inadequately prepared to deal with a chemical terrorist attack.

TYPES OF CHEMICAL WEAPON AGENTS

Chemical weapon agents are hazardous substances. Major categories of CWAs include the following:

Nerve agents (such as sarin, soman, cyclohexylsarin, tabun, VX)

Vesicating or blistering agents (such as mustards, lewisite)

Choking agents or lung toxicants (such as chlorine, phosgene, diphosgene)

Cyanides

Incapacitating agents (such as anticholinergic compounds)

Lacrimating or riot control agents (such as pepper gas, chloroacetophenone, CS)

Vomiting agents (such as adamsite)

Physical Properties: CWAs generally are stored and transported as liquids and deployed as either liquid aerosols or vapors. Victims usually are exposed to agents via 1 or more of 3 routes: skin (liquid and high vapor concentrations), eyes (liquid or vapor), and respiratory tract (vapor inhalation). In general, some liquids may be harmful whether inhaled into the lungs or absorbed into the skin. Vapors can be affected by winds. Even a slight breeze can blow a nerve agent vapor away from its intended target. The effects of vapor are enhanced when used within an enclosed space.

Clinical Effects: Depending on the agent and the type and amount (concentration) of exposure, CWA effects may be immediate or delayed. Large inhalation exposures to nerve agents or mustards are likely to kill people immediately. Small exposures on the skin to nerve agents and mustards are more dangerous than they seem at first. People exposed to such agents need to be carefully observed for slowly developing or delayed effects. A chart of signs and symptoms is available from the North Carolina Statewide Program for Infection Control and Epidemiology.

Medical Management: Ideally, emergency personnel will wear personal protective equipment, decontaminate the victims immediately, provide medical support to the victims and provide specific antidotes to counteract the harmful effects.

Personal Protective Equipment: First responders to a chemical attack are at serious risk themselves from the chemically contaminated environment (known as the hot zone). They can come in direct contact with the CWA or inhale the vapor. They are also at risk if they handle skin and clothing of victims if a liquid chemical agent was used. Vapors pose little added risk for anyone outside the hot zone.

Decontamination: Decontamination is the physical process of removing the remaining chemicals from people, equipment, and the environment. Residual hazardous chemicals on those who have been exposed directly are a source of ongoing exposure to others and pose a risk of secondary exposure to first responders and emergency care personnel. Immediate decontamination is a major treatment priority for those with CWA exposure. Initial decontamination involves removing all contaminated clothes and jewelry from the affected person and then washing the body thoroughly with warm water and soap.

Hot water and vigorous scrubbing may actually worsen the effects by increasing chemical absorption into the skin.

Vapor exposure alone may not require decontamination. But if it is not known whether the exposure was to a vapor or liquid, or if exposed people have symptoms, they should undergo decontamination.

Ideally, decontamination will take place as close as possible to the site of exposure to minimize duration of exposure and prevent further spread. Hospitals receiving contaminated people may establish an area outside the Emergency Department in which to perform initial decontamination before people and equipment are allowed entry. Portable decontamination equipment with showers and run-off water collection systems are commercially available. All hospitals should have the capacity to safely decontaminate at least 1 person.

Supportive and specific therapy: Doctors will first make sure exposed victims are able to breathe. For many chemical warfare agents, doctors can only treat the symptoms they produce. But specific, well-established antidotes are available for nerve agent and cyanide exposures. Lab tests are not widely available in hospitals to rapidly confirm exposure to chemical agents.

Nerve Agents

The 5 nerve agents, tabun (GA), sarin (GB), soman (GD), cyclohexylsarin (GF), and VX, have chemical structures similar to the common organophosphate pesticide Malathion. These agents initially stimulate and then paralyze certain nerve transmissions throughout the body and cause other toxic effects such as seizures.

Physical properties: Under temperate conditions, all nerve agents are volatile liquids, which means they can evaporate quickly. The most volatile agent, sarin, evaporates at about the same rate as water. The least volatile agent, VX, has the consistency of motor oil, which makes it 100-150 times more toxic than sarin when victims are exposed on their skin. A 10 mg dose applied to the skin may cause death in up to half of unprotected people. All nerve agents rapidly penetrate skin and clothing. Nerve agent vapors are heavier than air and tend to sink into low places (for example, trenches or basements).

Signs and symptoms: Nerve agents produce various signs and symptoms depending on the agent someone might be exposed to, its concentration, and length of exposure.

Liquid exposure: Liquid agents easily penetrate skin and clothing. Symptoms may begin anywhere from 30 minutes to 18 hours after skin exposure. A small droplet on the skin, for example, may cause local sweating and muscle twitching, followed by nausea, vomiting, diarrhea, and generalized weakness. Even with decontamination, signs and symptoms may last for hours. In contrast, people with severe liquid exposures may show no symptoms (for 1-30 minutes) but rapidly may suffer abrupt loss of consciousness, convulsions, generalized muscular twitching, paralysis, secretions (from the nose, mouth, lungs), difficulty breathing, and death.

Vapor exposure: Vapor inhalation produces poisonous symptoms within seconds to several minutes. Effects may be local or throughout the body. Exposure to even a small amount of vapor usually results in at least one of the following categories of symptoms:

(1) in the eyes, blurred vision, eye pain, red eyes;

(2) runny nose; or

(3) difficulty breathing, shortness of breath, excessive productive coughing.

Respiratory tract: Nerve agents act on the upper respiratory tract to produce runny nose, drooling, and weakness of the tongue and throat muscles. High-pitched, distressed breathing can occur. A great deal of phlegm production and narrowing of the airways can occur. If untreated, the combination of symptoms rapidly progresses to respiratory failure and death.

Cardiovascular system: Nerve agents also act on the heart and may produce abnormal heartbeats, more likely to be too fast rather than slow.

Central nervous system: Nerve agents produce a variety of signs and symptoms throughout the central nervous system. People may lose consciousness (sometimes within seconds of exposure) and have seizures. Symptoms such as headache, dizziness, numbness or tingling, anxiety, insomnia, depression, and emotional instability also have been reported.

Musculoskeletal system: Nerve agents initially stimulate and then paralyze muscles. With minimal exposure, exposed people may complain of vague weakness or difficulty walking.

Eyes: Nerve agent liquid or vapor readily penetrates the eye tissues and may cause the pupils to contract, blurred and dim vision, headache, redness, tears, pain, nausea, and vomiting. Although contraction of the pupils is the most consistent clinical finding after vapor exposure to nerve agents (this occurred in 99% of people exposed in the Tokyo sarin attack), it may not occur or occur later if the exposure is on the skin. In severe cases, the pupils of the eye may remain narrowed up to 45 days.

Diagnosis: Routine testing is not reliable in identifying nerve agents in blood or urine. So doctors will make their treatment decisions based on the signs and symptoms a person shows and on information about the type of chemical exposure, if known.

Treatment: Treatment of victims exposed to nerve gas is similar to the treatment of those poisoned by organophosphate insecticides.

Atropine sulfate: Victims with symptoms require immediate treatment with atropine. Atropine helps people breathe by drying secretions and opening their airways to allow them to breathe more freely. Atropine also blocks other effects of poisoning, such as nausea, vomiting, abdominal cramping, low heart rate, and sweating. Atropine, however, does not prevent or reverse paralysis. Adults and children will be given appropriate doses of atropine by IV or injection. Another medication, pralidoxime chloride, may also be given. With adequate decontamination and appropriate initial therapy, serious signs and symptoms of nerve agent toxicity rarely last more than a couple of hours.

Mark I kit: The Mark I kit was designed for military self-administration in the field. It consists of 2 spring-loaded devices to inject yourself, containing atropine and pralidoxime, respectively. These antidote kits are not yet available for civilian use.

Prognosis: Peak toxic effects occur within minutes to hours and go away within 1 day. People who were exposed but show no symptoms are usually observed for at least 18 hours because some signs and symptoms can show up later.

Mustards

Sulfur mustard has been used as a chemical weapon since World War I. Nitrogen mustard, a derivative of sulfur mustard, was one of the first chemotherapy agents but never has been used in warfare. These agents cause blistering of exposed surfaces. Both mustard agents rapidly penetrate cells and generate a highly toxic reaction that disrupts cell function and causes cell death. The chemical reaction is both temperature dependent and aided by the presence of water, which explains why warm, moist tissues are affected more severely. Actively reproducing cells, such as skin and blood cells, are most at risk.

Physical properties: Mustards are oily liquids with odors of mustard, onion, garlic, or horseradish. Highly soluble in oils, fats, and organic solvents, mustards quickly penetrate skin and most materials, including rubber and most textiles. Sulfur mustard is considered a persistent agent with low volatility at cool temperatures but becomes a major vapor hazard at high temperatures. Exposure to mustard vapor, not mustard liquid, is the primary medical concern. More than 80% of mustard casualties in World War I were caused by exposure to mustard vapor. Mustard vapor is 3 times more toxic than a similar concentration of cyanide gas; however, mustard liquid is also quite toxic. Skin exposure to as little as 1-1.5 teaspoons of liquid (7 g) is lethal to half of those exposed.

Signs and symptoms: Mustards injure the skin, eyes, respiratory tract, GI tissues, and blood system. The pattern of toxicity depends partly on whether the person is exposed to liquid or vapor. Liquid exposure primarily damages the skin, producing an initial rash followed by blistering similar to a partial-thickness burn. Vapor exposure damages the upper respiratory tract (skin usually is not affected). Mustards penetrate cells in less than 2 minutes, yet signs and symptoms usually are delayed 4-6 hours (the range can be from 1-24 hours). The time it takes to show symptoms is shorter with high-concentration exposures, such as those occurring at increased room temperature and humidity.

Skin: Chemical burns caused by mustard often appear deceptively superficial at first. Earliest symptoms are itching, burning, and stinging pain over exposed areas. Moist, thinner skin is affected more severely. Affected areas appear red and swollen. If contamination is more extensive, superficial blisters occur within 24 hours of exposure. Most burns are partial thickness, but full-thickness burns with deep blisters may result from exposure to higher concentrations. Blister fluid does not contain active mustard and is not toxic.

Eyes: Eyes are especially sensitive to the effects of mustard. Symptoms begin 4-8 hours after exposure. Earliest symptoms include burning pain, a feeling that something is in the eye, sensitivity to light, tearing, and blurred vision. Permanent corneal scarring and blindness may occur with severe exposures, but is rare.

Respiratory tract: Mustards primarily damage tissues in the upper airway through a direct inflammatory effect. Following a period of 2-24 hours after exposure, symptoms may appear. Early symptoms include sinus congestion, a sore throat, and hoarseness. Later, cough, shortness of breath, and trouble breathing may develop. People with severe and extensive contact with mustard gas may develop respiratory complications up to several days after exposure.

Gastrointestinal tract: Rarely, mustard damages rapidly growing cells of the intestinal tract. GI involvement results in abdominal pain, nausea, vomiting, diarrhea, and weight loss.

Blood system: Rarely, mustards cause unpredictable loss in the production of bone narrow. Certain specialized cells begin dying 3-5 days after exposure reaching its worst point in 3-14 days, depending on the severity of exposure.

Diagnosis: Diagnosis of mustard exposure is based on what the doctor observes from the person's signs and symptoms. No laboratory tests are useful.

Personal protective equipment: Liquid mustard contamination poses a risk for emergency care personnel. Ideally, they will be wearing appropriate personal protective gear.

Decontamination: Immediate decontamination within 2 minutes of exposure is the most important intervention for people who have skin exposure to mustard, because it rapidly becomes fixed to tissues, and its effects are irreversible. Even if an exposure takes place and a person shows no obvious sign and symptoms, decontamination is still urgent. Remove clothing immediately and wash the skin with soap and water. Eye exposure requires immediate washing out with a large amount of saline or water.

Decontamination after the first few minutes of exposure does not prevent further damage later but at least prevents spread of the chemical to other parts of the body and protects emergency care personnel from further contact exposure.

Treatment: Treatment of mustard exposure is based on symptoms. Because the effects of mustards typically are delayed, people with complaints immediately after exposure may have an additional injury.

For those with signs of upper airway obstruction, doctors may treat by using a tube in the person's throat or perform surgery to open the airway.

Mustard-induced burns are especially painful. Doctors will use strong pain relievers. Adequate burn care is essential, because skin lesions heal slowly and are prone to infection. Severe burns may require removal of dead tissue, irrigation, and placement of antibiotics, such as silver sulfadiazine, directly on the burned area. The victim may need a tetanus shot.

Severe eye burns may be treated with daily irrigation, topical antibiotic solutions, topical corticosteroids, and drugs that dilate the pupil. Petroleum jelly may be applied to prevent eyelids from sticking together. More severe corneal injuries may take as long as 2-3 months to heal. Permanent visual problems are rare.

Although no antidotes currently are available to treat mustard toxicity, several agents are under investigation.

Victims with bone marrow suppression following mustard exposure may be treated with medication to stimulate the bone marrow, such as granulocyte colony-stimulating factor.

Prognosis: Victims with significant respiratory tract burns usually require admission to the hospital's intensive care unit. Also, victims with several skin burns will be admitted to the burn unit for burn care, pain relief, and supportive care. Blood cell counts will be monitored for 2 weeks following significant exposures. Most people recover completely. Only a small fraction have long-term eye or lung damage. About 2% of those exposed to sulfur mustard in World War I died, mostly due to burns, respiratory tract damage, and bone marrow suppression. Sulfur mustard is known to cause cancer, yet a single exposure causes only a small risk.

TYPES OF NUCLEAR WARFARE

The possibility of using nuclear weapons in war is usually divided into two subgroups, each with different effects and potentially fought with different types of nuclear armaments.

The first, a *limited nuclear war* (sometimes *attack* or *exchange*), refers to a small-scale use of nuclear weapons by two (or more) belligerents. A "limited nuclear war" could include targeting military facilities - either as an attempt to pre-emptively cripple the enemy's ability to attack as a defensive measure, or as a prelude to an invasion by conventional forces, as an offensive measure. This term could apply to *any* small-scale use of nuclear weapons that may involve military or civilian targets (or both).

The second, a *full-scale nuclear war*, could consist of large numbers of nuclear weapons used in an attack aimed at an entire country, including military, economic, and civilian targets. Such an attack would almost certainly destroy the entire economic, social, and military infrastructure of the target nation, and would probably have a devastating effect on Earth's biosphere.

Some Cold War strategists such as Henry Kissinger argued that a limited nuclear war *could* be possible between two heavily armed superpowers (such as the United States and the Soviet Union). Some predict, however, that a limited war could potentially "escalate" into a full-scale nuclear war. Others have called limited nuclear war "global nuclear holocaust in slow motion" - arguing that once such a war took place, others would be sure to follow over a period of decades, effectively rendering the planet uninhabitable in the same way that a "full-scale nuclear war" between superpowers would, only taking a much longer (and arguably more agonizing) path to the same result.

Even the most optimistic predictions of the effects of a major nuclear exchange foresee the death of many millions of victims within a very short period of time. More pessimistic predictions argue that a full-scale nuclear war could potentially bring about the extinction of the human race, or at least its *near* extinction, with only a relatively small number of survivors (mainly in remote areas) and a reduced quality of life and life expectancy for centuries afterward.

However such exaggerated pessimistic predictions, assuming total war with nuclear arsenals atCold war highs, have not been without considerable criticism. Such a horrific catastrophe as global nuclear warfare would almost certainly cause permanent damage to most complex life on the planet, its ecosystems, and the global climate - particularly if predictions about the production of a nuclear winter are accurate, it would also change the balance of global power, with countries such as Australia, New Zealand, China, Argentina and Brazil predicted to become world superpowers if the Cold war ever turned hot.

A study presented at the annual meeting of the American Geophysical Union in December 2006 asserted that even a small-scale regional nuclear war could produce as many direct fatalities as all of World War II and disrupt the global climate for a decade or more.

In a regional nuclear conflict scenario in which two opposing nations in the subtropics each used 50 Hiroshima-sized nuclear weapons (c. 15 kiloton each) on major population centres, the researchers predicted fatalities ranging from 2.6 million to 16.7 million per country. Also, they estimated that as much as five million tons of soot could be released, producing a cooling of several degrees over large areas of North America and Eurasia (including most of the grain-growing regions). The cooling would last for years and could be "catastrophic", according to the researchers.

Either a limited or full-scale nuclear exchange could occur during an *accidental nuclear war,* in which the use of nuclear weapons is triggered unintentionally.

Postulated triggers for this scenario have included malfunctioning early warning devices and/or targeting computers, deliberate malfeasance by rogue military commanders, consequences of an accidental straying of warplanes into enemy airspace, reactions to unannounced missile tests during tense diplomatic periods, reactions to military exercises, mistranslated or misscommunicated messages, and others.

A number of these scenarios actually occurred during the Cold War, though none resulted in the use of nuclear weapons. Many such scenarios have been depicted in popular culture, such as in the 1962 novel *Fail-Safe (released* as a film in 1964), and the film *Dr. Strangelove or: How I Learned to Stop Worrying and Love the Bomb,* also released in 1964.

HISTORY

Atomic Bombings of Hiroshima and Nagasaki

During the final stages of World War II in 1945, the United States conducted two atomic bombings against the Japanese cities of Hiroshima and Nagasaki, the first on August 6, 1945, and the second on August 9, 1945. These two events are the only use of nuclear weapons in war to date.

For six months before the atomic bombings, the United States intensely firebombed 67 Japanese cities. Together with the United

Kingdom and the Republic of China, the United States called for the unconditional surrender of Japan in the Potsdam Declaration issued July 26, 1945. The Japanese government ignored this ultimatum. By executive order of President Harry S. Truman, the U.S. employed the uranium-type nuclear weapon code named "Little Boy" on the city of Hiroshima on Monday, August 6, 1945, followed three days later by the detonation of the plutonium-type weapon code named "Fat Man" over the city of Nagasaki on August 9.

Within the first two to four months after the bombings, acute effects killed 90,000–166,000 people in Hiroshima and 60,000–80,000 in Nagasaki, with roughly half of the deaths in each city occurring in the first 24 hours. The Hiroshima prefectural health department estimates that - of the people who died on the day of the detonation - 60% died from flash or flame burns, 30% from falling or flying debris, and 10% from other causes. During the following months, large numbers died from the chronic effects of burns, radiation sickness, and other injuries, compounded by illnesses. In a U.S. estimate of the total immediate and short-term causes of death, 15–20% died from radiation sickness, 20–30% from flash burns, and 50–60% from other injuries, compounded by illnesses. In both cities, most of the dead were civilians.

Six days after the detonation over Nagasaki, on August 15, 1945, Japan announced its surrender to the Allied Powers, signing the Instrument of Surrender on September 2, 1945, officially ending the Pacific War and, therefore, World War II, as Germany had already signed its Instrument of Surrender on May 7, 1945, ending the war in Europe. The two atomic bombings led, in part, to post-war Japan's adopting of the Three Non-Nuclear Principles, which forbade the nation from developing nuclear armaments. The role of the bombings in the surrender of Japan, the ethical justification of the US for using them, as well as their strategic importance, is still hotly debated.

Immediately after the Japan Bombings

Immediately after the atomic bombings of Japan, the status of atomic weapons in international and military relations was unclear.

Presumably, the United States hoped atomic weapons could offset the Soviet Union's larger conventional ground forces in Eastern Europe, and possibly be used to pressure Soviet leader Joseph Stalin into making concessions. Under Stalin, the Soviet Union pursued its own atomic capabilities through a combination of scientific research and espionage directed against the American program. The Soviets believed that the Americans, with their limited nuclear arsenal, were unlikely to engage in any new world wars, while the Americans were not confident they could prevent a Soviet takeover of Europe, despite their atomic advantage.

Within the United States the authority to produce and develop nuclear weapons was removed from military control and put instead under the civilian control of the United States Atomic Energy Commission. This decision reflected an understanding that nuclear weapons had unique risks and benefits that were separate from other military technology known at the time.

For several years after World War II, the United States developed and maintained a strategic force based on the Convair B-36 bomber that would be able to attack any potential enemy from bomber bases in the United States. It deployed atomic bombs around the world for potential use in conflicts. Over a period of a few years, many in the American defence community became increasingly convinced of the invincibility of the United States to a nuclear attack. Indeed, it became generally believed that the threat of nuclear war would deter any strike against the United States.

Many proposals were suggested to put all American nuclear weapons under international control (by the newly formed United Nations, for example) as an effort to deter both their usage and an arms race. However, no terms could be arrived at that would be agreed upon by both the United States and the Soviet Union.

On August 29, 1949, the Soviet Union tested its first nuclear weapon at Semipalatinsk inKazakhstan. Scientists in the United States from the Manhattan Project had warned that, in time, the Soviet Union would certainly develop nuclear capabilities of its own. Nevertheless, the effect upon military thinking and planning in the United States was dramatic, primarily because American military strategists had not anticipated the Soviets would "catch up" so soon. However, at this time, they had not discovered that the Soviets had conducted significant nuclear espionage of the project from spies at Los Alamos, the most significant of which was done by the theoretical physicist Klaus Fuchs. The first Soviet bomb was more or less a deliberate copy of the Fat Manplutonium device.

With the monopoly over nuclear technology broken, worldwide nuclear proliferation accelerated. The United Kingdom tested its first independent atomic bomb in 1952, followed by France in 1960 and then China in 1964. While much smaller than the arsenals of the United States and the Soviet Union, Western Europe's nuclear reserves were nevertheless a significant factor in strategic planning during the Cold War. A top-secret White Paper, compiled by the Royal Air Force and produced for the British Government in 1959, estimated that British atomic bombers were capable of destroying key cities and military targets in the Soviet Union, with an estimated 16 million deaths in the Soviet Union (half of whom were estimated to be killed on impact and the rest fatally injured) *before* bomber aircraft from the U.S. Strategic Air Command reached their targets.

After the successful Trinity (test) July 16, 1945, which was the very first nuclear detonation, the manhattan project lead manager J. Robert Oppenheimer recalled:

We knew the world would not be the same. A few people laughed, a few people cried, most people were silent. I remembered the line from the Hindu scripture the *Bhagavad Gita*. Vishnu is trying to persuade the prince that he should do his duty and to impress him takes on his multiarmed form and says, "Now, I am become Death, the destroyer of worlds." I suppose we all thought that one way or another." —J. Robert Oppenheimer, The Decision To Drop The Bomb

The 1950s

Although the Soviet Union had nuclear weapon capabilities in the beginning of the Cold War, the United States still had an advantage in terms of bombers and weapons. In any exchange of hostilities, the United States would have been capable of bombing the Soviet Union, whereas the Soviet Union would have more difficulty carrying out the reverse mission.

The widespread introduction of jet-powered interceptor aircraft upset this imbalance somewhat by reducing the effectiveness of the American bomber fleet. In 1949 Curtis LeMay was placed in command of the Strategic Air Command and instituted a program to update the bomber fleet to one that was all-jet. During the early 1950s the B-47 and B-52 were introduced, providing the ability to bomb the Soviet Union more easily. Before the development of a capable strategic missile force in the Soviet Union, much of the war-fighting doctrine held by western nations revolved around using a large number of smaller nuclear weapons used in a tactical role. It is debatable whether such use could be considered "limited" however, because it was believed that the United States would use their own strategic weapons (mainly bombers at the time) should the Soviet Union deploy any kind of nuclear weapon against civilian targets. Douglas MacArthur, an American general, was fired by President Harry Truman, partially because he persistently requested permission to use his own discretion in deciding whether to use atomic weapons on the People's Republic of China in 1951 during the Korean War.Mao Zedong, China's communist leader, gave the impression that he would welcome a nuclear war with the capitalists because it would annihilate what he viewed as their "imperialist" system.

Let us imagine how many people would die if war breaks out. There are 2.7 billion people in the world, and a third could be lost. If it is a little higher it could be half... I say that if the worst came to the worst and one-half dies, there will still be one-half left, but imperialism would be razed to the ground and the whole world would become socialist. After a few years there would be 2.7 billion people again. — Mao Zedong, 1957

Several scares about the increasing ability of the Soviet Union's strategic bomber forces surfaced during the 1950s. The defensive response by the United States was to deploy a fairly strong "layered defence" consisting of interceptor aircraft and anti-aircraft missiles, like the Nike, and guns, like the Skysweeper, near larger cities.

However, this was a small response compared to the construction of a huge fleet of nuclear bombers. The principalnuclear strategy was to massively penetrate the Soviet Union. Because such a large area could not be defended against this overwhelming attack in any credible way, the Soviet Union would lose any exchange.

This logic became ingrained in American nuclear doctrine and persisted for much of the duration of the Cold War. As long as the strategic American nuclear forces could overwhelm their Soviet counterparts, a Soviet preemptive strike could be averted. Moreover, the Soviet Union could not afford to build any reasonable counterforce, as the economic output of the United States was far larger than that of the Soviets, and they would be unable to achieve "nuclear parity".

Soviet nuclear doctrine, however, did not match American nuclear doctrine. Soviet military planners assumed they can win the nuclear war. Therefore, they *expected* a large-scale nuclear exchange, followed by a "conventional war" which itself would involve heavy use of tactical nuclear weapons. American doctrine rather assumed that Soviet doctrine was similar, with the *mutual* in Mutually Assured Destruction necessarily requiring that the other side see things in much the same way, rather than believing - as the Soviets did - that they could fight a large-scale, "combined nuclear and conventional" war.

In accordance with their doctrine, the Soviet Union conducted large-scale military exercises to explore the possibility of defensive and offensive warfare during a nuclear war. The exercise, under the code name of "Snowball", involved the detonation of a nuclear bomb about twice as powerful as that which fell on Nagasaki and an army of approximately 45,000 soldiers on maneuvers through the hypocenter immediately after the blast. The exercise was conducted on September 14, 1954, under command of Marshal Georgy Zhukov to the north of Totskoye village in Orenburg Oblast, Russia.

A revolution in nuclear strategic thought occurred with the introduction of the intercontinental ballistic missile (ICBM), which the Soviet Union first successfully tested in August 1957. In order to deliver a warhead to a target, a missile was much faster and more cost-effective than a bomber, and enjoyed a higher survivability due to the enormous difficulty of interception of the ICBMs (due to their high altitude and extreme speed). The Soviet Union could now afford to achieve nuclear parity with the United States in terms of raw numbers, although for a time, they appeared to have chosen not to.

Photos of Soviet missile sites set off a wave of panic in the U.S. military, something the launch of Sputnik would do for the American public a few months later. Politicians, notably then-U.S. Senator John F. Kennedy suggested that a "missile gap" existed between the Soviet Union and the United States. The US military gave missile development programs the highest national priority, and several spy aircraft and reconnaissance satellites were designed and deployed to observe Soviet progress.

Early ICBMs and bombers were relatively inaccurate, which led to the concept of countervalue strikes — attacks directly on the enemy population, which would theoretically lead to a collapse of the enemy's will to fight. During the Cold War, the Soviet Union invested in extensive protected civilian infrastructure, such as large "nuclear-proof" bunkers and non-perishable food stores. By comparison, smaller scale civil defence programs were instituted in the United States starting in the 1950s, where schools and other public buildings had basements stocked with non-perishable food supplies, canned water, first aid, and dosimeter and Geiger counter radiation-measuring devices. Many of the locations were given "Fallout Shelter" designation signs. Also, CONELRAD Radio information systems were adopted, whereby the commercial radio sector would broadcast on two AM frequencies in the event of a Civil Defence (CD) emergency. These two frequencies-640 and 1240 marked with small CD triangles on the tuning dial can still be seen on 1950s-vintage radios on online auction sites and museums. Also, the occasional backyard fallout shelter was built by private individuals.

1960s

An extensive, complicated, and worrisome situation developed in 1962, in what is called the Cuban Missile Crisis. The Soviet

Union placed medium-range ballistic missiles 90 miles (140 km) from the United States - a move considered by many as a direct response to American Jupiter missiles placed in Turkey. After intense negotiations, the Soviets ended up removing the missiles from Cuba and decided to institute a massive weapons-building program of their own. In exchange, the United States dismantled its launch sites in Turkey, although this was done secretly and not publicly revealed for over two decades. Khrushchevdid not even reveal this part of the agreement when he came under fire by political opponents for mishandling the crisis.

By the late 1960s, the number of ICBMs and warheads was so high on both sides that it was believed that both the United States and the Soviet Union were capable of completely destroying the infrastructure and a large proportion of the population of the other country.

Thus, by some western game theorists, a balance of power system known as mutually assured destruction (or *MAD*) came into being. It was thought that any full-scale exchange between the powers would not result in an outright winner, with at best one side emerging the pyrrhic victor, and thus both sides were deterred from risking the initiation of a direct confrontation, instead being forced to engage in lower intensity proxy wars.

During this decade the Peoples Republic of China began to build subterranean infrastructure such as the Underground Project 131following the Sino-Soviet split.

One drawback of the MAD doctrine was the possibility of a nuclear war occurring without either side intentionally striking first. Warning system\Early Warning Systems (EWS) were notoriously error-prone. For example, on 78 occasions in 1979 alone, a "missile display conference" was called to evaluate detections that were "potentially threatening to the North American continent". Some of these were trivial errors and were spotted quickly, but several went to more serious levels. On September 26, 1983, Stanislav Petrov received convincing indications of an American first strike launch against the Soviet Union, but positively identified the warning as a false alarm. Though it is unclear what role Petrov's actions played in preventing a nuclear war during this incident, he has been honoured by the United Nations for his actions.

Similar incidents happened many times in the United States, due to failed computer chips, misidentifications of large flights of geese, test programs, and bureaucratic failures to notify early warning military personnel of legitimate launches of test or weather missiles. For many years, the U.S. Air Force's strategic bombers were kept airborne on a daily rotating basis "around the clock", until the number and severity of accidents, the 1968 Thule Air Base B-52 crash in particular, persuaded policymakers it was not worthwhile.

1970s

By the late 1970s, people in both the United States and the Soviet Union, along with the rest of the world, had been living with the concept of mutual assured destruction (MAD) for about a decade, and it became deeply ingrained into the psyche and popular culture of those countries. Such an exchange would have killed many millions of individuals directly, and possibly induced a nuclear winter if enough soot from firestorms reached the stratosphere, which was believed to have the potential to decrease post war agriculture yields, and with that lead to the death of a large portion of humanity and - potentially - the collapse of global civilization. On May 18, 1974, India conducted its first nuclear test in the Pokhran test range. The name of the operation was Smiling Buddha, and India termed the test as a "peaceful nuclear explosion".

According to the 1980 United Nations report *General and Complete Disarmament: Comprehensive Study on Nuclear Weapons: Report of the Secretary-General*, it was estimated that there were a total of about 40,000 nuclear warheads in existence at that time, with a potential combined explosive yield of approximately 13,000 megatons.

By comparison, when the volcano Mount Tambora erupted in 1815 - turning 1816 into the Year Without A Summer due to the levels of global dimming sulfate aerosols and ash expelled - it exploded with a force of roughly 1,000 megatons, however it must be noted that comparisons with supervolcanos are more misleading than helpful due to the different aerosols released, the likely air burst fuzing height of nuclear weapons and the globally scattered location of these potential nuclear detonations all being in contrast to the singular and subterranean nature of a supervolcanic eruption. Nonetheless, many people believe that a full-scale nuclear war would result in the extinction of the human species, though not all analysts agree on the assumptions required for these models.

The idea that any nuclear conflict would eventually escalate was a challenge for military strategists. This challenge was particularly severe for the United States and its NATO allies because it was believed (until the 1970s) that a Soviet tank invasion of Western Europewould quickly overwhelm NATO conventional forces, leading to the necessity of the West escalating to the use of tactical nuclear weapons, one of which was the W-70.

This strategy had one major (and possibly critical) flaw, which was soon realised by military analysts but highly underplayed by the U.S. military: conventional NATO forces in the European theatre of war were far outnumbered by similar Soviet and Warsaw Pact forces, and it was assumed that in case of a major Soviet attack (commonly envisioned as the "Red tanks rolling towards the North Sea" scenario) that NATO - in the face of quick conventional defeat - would soon have no other choice but to resort to tactical nuclear strikes against these forces. Most analysts agreed that once the first nuclear exchange had occurred, escalation to global nuclear war would likely become inevitable.

The 1980s

In the late 1970s and, particularly, during the early 1980s under U.S. President Ronald Reagan, the United States renewed its commitment to a more powerful military, which required a large increase in spending on U.S. military programs. These programs, which were originally part of the defence budget of U.S. President Jimmy Carter, included spending on conventional and nuclear weapons systems. Under Reagan, defensive systems like the Strategic Defence Initiative became emphasized as well.

Another major shift in nuclear doctrine was the development and the improvement of the submarine-launched, nuclear-armed, ballistic missile, or SLBM. It was hailed by many military theorists as a weapon that would make nuclear war less likely. SLBMs - which can move with "stealth" (greatly lessened detectibility) virtually anywhere in the world - give a nation a "second strike" capability (i.e. after absorbing a "first strike"). Before the advent of the SLBM, thinkers feared that a nation might be tempted to initiate a first strike if it felt confident that such a strike would incapacitate the nuclear arsenal of its enemy, making retaliation impossible. With the advent of SLBMs, no nation could be certain that a first strike would incapacitate its enemy's entire nuclear arsenal. To the contrary, it would have to fear a (near certain) retaliatory second strike from SLBMs. Thus, a first strike was a much less of feasible (or desirable) option, and a (deliberately initiated) nuclear war was thought to be less likely to start.

However, it was soon realized that submarines could "sneak up" close to enemy coastlines and decrease the "warning time" (the time between detection of the missile launch and the impact of the missile) from as much as half an hour to possibly under three minutes. This effect was especially significant to the United States, Britain and China, whose capitals all lay within 100 miles (160 km) of their coasts. Moscow was much more secure from this type of threat, due to its considerable distance from the sea. This greatly increased the credibility of a "surprise first strike" by one faction and (theoretically) made it possible to knock out or disrupt the chain of command of a target nation before any counterstrike could be ordered (known as a "decapitation strike"). It strengthened the notion that a nuclear war could possibly be "won" - resulting not only in greatly increased tensions and increasing calls for fail-deadly control systems, but also in a dramatic increase in military spending. The submarines and their missile systems were very expensive, and one fully equipped nuclear-powered and nuclear-armed missile submarine could cost more than the entire GNP of a developing country. It was also calculated, however, that the greatest cost came in the development of *both* sea- and land-based anti-submarine defenses and in improving and strengthening the "chain of command", and as a result, military spending skyrocketed.

South Africa developed a nuclear weapon capability during the 1970s and early 1980s. It was operational for a brief period before being dismantled in the early 1990s.

On Sept. 1, 1983, Korean Air Lines Flight 007 was shot down by Soviet jet fighters. On the 26th, a Soviet early warning station under the command of Stanislav Petrov falsely detected 5 inbound intercontinental ballistic missiles from the US. Petrov correctly assessed the situation as a false alarm, and hence did not report his finding to his superiors. It is quite possible that his actions prevented "World War III", as the Soviet policy at that time was immediate nuclear response upon discovering inbound ballistic missiles.

The world came unusually close to nuclear war - although perhaps not as close as during the Cuban Missile Crisis - when the Soviet Union thought that the NATO military exercise Able Archer 83 was a ruse or "cover up" to begin a nuclear first strike. The Soviets responded by raising readiness and preparing their nuclear arsenal for immediate use. Soviet fears of an attack ceased once the exercise concluded without incident.

Post–Cold War

Although the dissolution of the Soviet Union ended the Cold War and greatly reduced tensions between the United States and the Russian Federation, the Soviet Union's formal successor state, both countries remained in a "nuclear stand-off" due to the continuing presence of a very large number of deliverable nuclear warheads on both sides. Additionally, the end of the Cold War led the United States to become increasingly concerned with the development of nuclear technology by other nations outside of the former Soviet Union. In 1995, a branch of the U.S. Strategic Command produced an outline of forward-thinking strategies in the document "Essentials of Post–Cold War Deterrence".

As an effect of the 9/11 attacks on the USA, American forces immediately increased their readiness to the highest level in 28 years, closing the blast doors of the NORAD's Cheyenne Mountain Operations Center for the first time due to a non-exercise event. But unlike similar increases during the Cold War, Russia immediately decided to stand down a large military exercise in the Arctic region, in order to minimize the risk of incidents, rather than following suit.

The former chair of the United Nations disarmament committee stated that there are more than 16,000 strategic and tactical nuclear weapons ready for deployment and another 14,000 in storage, with the U.S. having nearly 7,000 ready for use and 3,000 in storage, and Russia having about 8,500 ready for use and 11,000 in storage. In addition, China is thought to possess about 400 nuclear weapons, Britain about 200, France about 350, India about 80-100, and Pakistan 100-110. North Korea is confirmed as having nuclear weapons, though it is not known how many, with most estimates between 1 and 10. Israel is also widely believed to possess usable nuclear weapons. NATO has stationed about 480 American nuclear weapons in Belgium, the Netherlands, Italy, Germany, and Turkey, and several other nations are thought to be in pursuit of an arsenal of their own.

Bibliography

Alexander, Yonah, and Paul A. Leventhal: *Preventing Nuclear Terrorism: The Report and Papers of the International Task Force on Prevention of Nuclear Terrorism,* Lanham, MD: Rowman & Littlefield, 1987.

Allison, Graham: *Nuclear Terrorism: The Ultimate Preventable Catastrophe,* New York: Times Books, 2004.

Ben Wisner : *At Risk, Natural Hazards, People's Vulnerability, and Disasters,* London, Routledge, 1994.

Cronon, William :*Uncommon Ground: Toward Reinventing Nature,* New York, WW Norton and Co., 1995.

Drewes, Jeanne : *Computers: Planning for Disaster,* Law Library Journal, Winter, 1989.

Heimanson, Rudolph: *Dictionary of Political Science and Law,* N.Y.: Oceana Publications, 1967.

Hoffman, Bruce, *Inside Terrorism,* New York: Columbia University Press, 1998.

Norton, Augustus R., and Martin H. *Greenberg, Studies in Nuclear Terrorism,* Boston: G.K. Hall & Co., 1979.

Qureshi, A. Iqbal : *Islam and the Theory of Interest,* Kitab Bhavan, New Delhi, 1994.

Rhodes, Richard, *The Making of the Atomic Bomb,* New York: Simon and Schuster, 1988.

Sidney Fox: *Klaus Dose, Molecular Evolution and The Origin of Life,* New York: Marcel Dekker, 1977.

Spindlove, J. R.: *Terrorism Today: The Past, the Players, the Future,* Upper Saddle Creek, NJ: Prentice Hall, 2000.

Thomas Arnold: *The Spread of Islam in the World, A History of Peaceful Preaching,* Goodword Books, 2001.

White, J. R.: *Terrorism: An introduction: 2002 update,* Belmont, CA: Wadsworth, 2002.

Index

P

T

W

❑❑❑